STOP THE
COMING
CIVIL WAR

STOP THE COMING CIVIL WAR

MY SAVAGE TRUTH

MICHAEL SAVAGE

CENTER STREET

NEW YORK • BOSTON • NASHVILLE

Center Street
Hachette Book Group
1290 Avenue of the Americas
New York, NY 10104

CenterStreet.com

Printed in the United States of America

RRD-C

Originally published in hardcover by Hachette Book Group.
First trade edition: September 2015

10 9 8 7 6 5 4 3 2 1

Center Street is a division of Hachette Book Group, Inc.
The Center Street name and logo are trademarks of Hachette Book Group, Inc.

The Hachette Speakers Bureau provides a wide range of authors for speaking events. To find out more, go to www.hachettespeakersbureau.com or call (866) 376-6591.

The publisher is not responsible for websites (or their content) that are not owned by the publisher.

Library of Congress Cataloging-in-Publication Data

Savage, Michael, 1942–
     Stop the coming civil war : my savage truth / Michael Savage. — First edition.
        pages cm
     Summary: "CAN AMERICA SURVIVE ANOTHER CIVIL WAR? According to Michael Savage, OUR NATION IS IN REAL TROUBLE and the seeds of a second conflagration have been sown. Not between the states - but between true patriots who believe in our nation's founding principles and those he believes are working every day to undermine them and change the very nature of the country. Not a war of bullets and blood - but one of commitment to freedom and courage of conviction. Michael Savage is convinced that we face more than just political differences now. He believes the split between right and left is possibly irreparable - unless we understand what's really happening and how we must act to stop it. Savage has been raising his voice for over 20 years as America's most outspoken and incisive talk radio host, and bestselling author. He argues that the situation is urgent and he is raising his voice even louder telling his Savage Truth in STOP THE COMING CIVIL WAR. — Provided by publisher.
     Includes bibliographical references and index.
     ISBN 978-1-4555-8243-3 (hardback) — ISBN 978-1-4789-8271-5 (audio book) — ISBN 978-1-4555-8242-6 (ebook)   1. Liberalism—United States.   2. Political culture—United States.   3. Right and left (Political science)—United States. 4. United States—Politics and government—2009-   I. Title.
     JC574.2.U6S284 2014
     320.520973—dc23

                                                                    2014027967

ISBN 978-1-4555-8241-9 (pbk.)

Contents

CHAPTER 1

Graduating to Treason?

I cannot comprehend the madness of the times....
Treason is in the air around us everywhere. It goes
by the name of patriotism.

—*Thomas Corwin to*
Abraham Lincoln, 1861

People can justify a government's controversial policies and
actions for only so long until they see a pattern of abuse of
power. Then, even the most devout supporters of any regime
must decide if they support these extreme policies and actions
or oppose them.

With the current government, this point of no return was
reached for some when they slowly realized the extent of the
vast National Security Agency spying scandal.

For others it was the release of known Islamist terrorists from the Guantanamo Bay prison without congressional
knowledge.

For most Americans, the flood of tens of thousands of illegal immigrants from Central America purposely created by

the administration to overwhelm our southern borders was the final straw.

Still other supporters kept justifying one extremist act after another, justifying the president's policies and actions with rationalizations that included saying that those who opposed them were "right-wing conspirators," "racists," "Obama haters," and the like.

Yet for those of us who study governments that have taken nations from freedom to fascism, the handwriting has been on the wall for many years.

My question is this: Will the Obama inner circle of extremist left-wing radicals trigger an event that will provoke an American insurrection, even a civil war?

Is this concern to be dismissed as a "right-wing conspiracy"?

Let me explain to you what is happening.

The desperate Democrats are all pursuing policies of race and class warfare. As their failures and many deceits become clearer to the people, as the war they're fighting against the freedoms promised in the U.S. Constitution materializes, they are counting on minority voters to turn out for them at the ballot box. Look at these excerpts from some of their speeches to high school and college graduates.

Here's Michelle Obama, the First Lady. Is she trying to agitate these children? Stir them up to do what?

The fact is that your experience here in Topeka would have been unimaginable back in 1954, when Brown v. Board of Education *first went to the Supreme Court. This would not be possible.... Back then, Topeka, like so many cities, was segregated, so black folks and white folks had separate restaurants, separate hotels, separate movie theaters, swimming pools, and, of course, the elementary schools were segregated, too.*

How do you feel about the First Lady stirring up such racial enmity in this speech? How would you feel if I told you that I believe it's not an isolated incident?

Here's what Attorney General Eric Holder said in his graduation speech:

Codified segregation of public schools has been barred since Brown [v. Board of Education]. *But in too many of our school districts, significant divisions persist and segregation has reoccurred—including zero-tolerance school discipline practices that, while well-intentioned and aimed at promoting school safety, affect black males at a rate three times higher than their white peers.*[1]

Do you hear what Eric Holder said? He told his audience that black males are targeted, not because they cause more disruption and violence in the classroom, but because they are black. It's *Animal Farm.* It's upside down. It's doublespeak. It's everything we were warned about since the dawn of social engineering in this country.

Tim Geithner, a spoiled, rich white boy from Queens who had everything handed to him as he grew up, has the nerve to "get down" with the other administration doublespeakers to push a biased and untruthful racial message:

We have tremendously high numbers of people living in poverty. We've had a long period where the median income has not grown, [and a] big rise in inequality. And, to an extent,

*this should not be acceptable to Americans. How well you
do in life today, how good your education is, how good your
health care is, depends too much on the color of your skin or
how rich your parent is.*

Finally, here is none other than Nancy Pelosi, a very wealthy
woman, acting as if she's a member of the Occupy Wall Street
movement. When you read this, you'll understand that these
four graduation speakers are trying to exacerbate class and
racial division in this country:

*Our founders were successful disruptors of the then status
quo. Being called a disruptor, in my view, is a very high
compliment. You here in Berkeley are already disruptors in
many ways. In 1964, Mario Savio and company were disruptors of the status quo, too. When he and his fellow activists occupied Sproul [Hall], their exercise of free speech could
only travel as fast as television, radio, and newspapers. Think
of your possibilities. Now it's all about you.*

Do you understand what Pelosi is doing?

She's inciting the graduating seniors from the University of
California, Berkeley, an institution that once was a hotbed of
free speech but where students and faculty now fear speaking
their minds to express an opinion that doesn't agree with the
opinion of those in power. In my view, Pelosi is inciting them
to become "disruptors."

Why would these four people put forth what I see as a message of class and racial division to graduating college seniors
on the same weekend, with Pelosi further telling her audience
to go out and become disruptors?

Why would they spread the message of racial inequality?

Not to be outdone by the race-baiting, Democrat Jay Rockefeller espoused his view that "skin color" was behind the rejection of our Euro-African president's failed policies.[2]

How do you feel about this government's stoking racial divisions?

Why do they do it?

I'm telling you, they're setting the stage for more confrontations between citizens of the United States and their government.

From the arguably traitorous foreign policy decisions to the bloated, biased, incompetent bureaucracy, the current administration is aiding and abetting our terrorist enemies while refusing to provide medical support to the soldiers who have fought against the very enemies this administration seems to be supporting.

Three events in the early summer of 2014 make very clear what this government's positions are:

• The release of five radical Islamist leaders from Guantanamo Bay prison in exchange for the return of an American soldier who deserted his post and may have aided and abetted the enemy in Afghanistan

• Inviting hundreds of thousands of Central American children and young adults—some of them known gang members with distinguishing gang tattoos—to enter the United States illegally and then providing food and shelter for them before sending them off to "friends and relatives" in other U.S. cities

• What I see as the intentional refusal to provide critical medical treatment for injured and ill American servicemen through the Veterans Affairs medical system

Let me take you through the Gitmo detainees exchange first.

According to Secretary of Defense Chuck Hagel, the president of the United States approved the transfer of five of the most dangerous long-term Gitmo inmates to the country of Qatar in exchange for Bowe Bergdahl, an American soldier who is described by some of his fellow soldiers—as many as six of them were killed attempting to find and rescue Bergdahl after he left his post—as a "deserter."[3]

The White House, of course, quickly denied that the president had made the call on the prisoner exchange and fingered Hagel as the one who had made the decision.[4]

The result of the prisoner deal was not that five terrorists were freed while one American soldier was released. In fact, I argue that the reason the Obama administration released Bergdahl might well have been that he was an Islamist sympathizer as well. The ultimate result may prove to be that six terrorist sympathizers were released in this swap.

All five of the Gitmo detainees were involved with the Taliban in Afghanistan when we invaded that country after the 9/11 attacks. One was a commander of the main force fighting against Americans, another was a Taliban governmental interior minister. Yet another was a Taliban provincial governor who also served as a coordinator of Taliban fighting forces. Two others were Taliban intelligence and communications officers.

These released detainees are not going to grab a rifle and head to the battlefield. They are hard-core terrorist leaders—commanders, intelligence and communications officers, Taliban government officials—who are most likely to return to positions of leadership. All of them had been held at Gitmo for more than a decade.

When the American people and Congress finally got the word that the exchange had been made, they were outraged. As Hillary Clinton was referring to them as "these five guys" and claiming that they "are not a threat to the United States,"[5] even Dianne Feinstein, the Democratic chair of the Senate Intelligence Committee, couldn't contain her disapproval of the swap.

The *Washington Post* explained that the president likely broke the law that required him to provide notification to Congress at least thirty days before executing such an exchange, and the leftist rag went so far as to acknowledge that other American soldiers would now be much more likely to be kidnapped and held for further prisoner exchanges because of Obama's action.[6]

In the wake of this action, we really have to ask the question: What kind of an administration would make a swap of this type unless they were utterly incompetent or they wanted to put these five terrorists back on the battlefield?

Obama's foreign policy mistakes continue to threaten our national security.

Because the president refused to conclude a status of forces agreement with Iraq and subsequently withdrew all American troops from that country, our former ally has become so politically divided and its central government so weakened that the most vicious of all terrorist groups, known as the Islamic State of Iran and Syria (ISIS), has used captured American weapons and vehicles along with military force to take over significant swaths of territory in Iraq and Syria. The group went so far as to declare the formation of a new Islamic caliphate in the territory it has captured.[7]

Do you want to know how distorted and perverse America's foreign policy has become under this president?

The U.S. troops our president has sent to Iraq to "advise" Iraqis and coordinate a defense against ISIS are fighting alongside Iranian troops sent to Iraq for the same purpose![8]

Making Iran an ally seems to be coordinated by the Oval Office.

Is it possible that our president will need to be removed from office by his own Democratic Party in the same way Neville Chamberlain was removed by his own Labor Party in England for giving in to Hitler's demands as World War II was beginning?

Are you starting to see why I titled this chapter "Graduating to Treason?"

Do you understand how this administration's policies are dividing the American people and threatening our freedom?

Because of the administration's immigration policies and its refusal to uphold existing immigration law, tens of thousands of illegal immigrants from Central America were housed on U.S. Army bases. Many were saying that the administration not only allowed these immigrant children to cross into our country, but that they actually encouraged the illegal immigrants.

The evidence of this surfaced just before this book went into production.

In mid-June, several websites posted notices that the federal government had publicly advertised on the government website Federal Business Opportunities (FedBizOpps.gov) for a vendor to escort tens of thousands of illegal alien children to locations around the United States. Here's the text of that ad:

> *The Contractor shall provide unarmed escort staff, including management, supervision, manpower, training, certifications, licenses, drug testing, equipment, and supplies necessary to provide on-demand escort services for non-criminal/non-delinquent unaccompanied alien children ages infant to 17 years of age, seven (7) days a week, 365 days a year. Transport will be required for either category of UAC or individual juveniles, to include both male and female juveniles. There will be approximately 65,000 UAC in total: 25% local ground transport, 25% via ICE charter and 50% via commercial air. Escort services include, but are not limited to, assisting with: transferring physical custody of UAC from DHS to Health and Human Services (HHS) care via ground or air methods of transportation (charter or commercial carrier), property inventory, providing juveniles with meals, drafting reports, generating transport documents, maintaining/stocking daily supplies, providing and issuing clothing as needed, coordinating with DHS and HHS staff, travel coordination, limited stationary guard services to accommodate for trip disruptions due to inclement weather, faulty equipment, or other exigent circumstances.[9]*

To me, that ad, on a federal government website, is evidence that this administration may well have initiated and encouraged bringing tens of thousands of illegal immigrant children into the United States and that they've once again misled us, this time at the expense of minor children from

Central American countries, in order to exacerbate the crisis that has been unfolding on our southern border for years.

The National Association of Former Border Patrol Officers put out a statement with these almost unprecedented words: "Certainly we are not gullible enough to believe that thousands of unaccompanied minor Central American children came to America without the encouragement, aid and assistance of the United States government."[10]

What you haven't heard from most of the national news media is that among the "children" who have entered our country in this unprecedented wave are many hardened criminals, gang members who are using our unwillingness to stop this flood of illegal immigrants to enter America with no threat of deportation. The vice president of the National Border Patrol Council Local 3307 said, "Until we start mandatory detentions, mandatory removals, I don't think anything is going to change. As a matter of fact, I think it's going to get worse."[11]

Beyond that, many of the children are teenagers, and the improvised shelters where they are crowded together have become a place where diseases are becoming rampant and where they are free to engage in sex,[12] even as military personnel are forced through necessity to change diapers and warm up baby formula to feed the infants who are also among this group of illegal aliens.[13]

But perhaps the most disturbing aspect of the surge of illegals across our southern border is the specter of disease epidemics.

I earned my doctorate in the field of epidemiology and human nutrition at the University of California at Berkeley. I know more about the subject than anyone else in broadcasting, and I have been trying to warn Americans about the dangers of illegal immigration into the United States and the risk of epidemics since the early 1980s. Only now are Americans finally waking up to the fact that the tens of thousands of illegal immigrants flooding our borders are bringing with them very dangerous infectious diseases, including tuberculosis, hand-foot-and-mouth disease, H1N1 swine flu, chicken pox, and Chagas disease, a potentially life-threatening condition caused by a parasite found in the feces of another parasite. It's most common in Central American countries, and it had been eradicated in Southern California.[14]

These diseases are being brought back in to this country by the horde of illegals now being "processed" as they cross the border and are transferred by buses and planes to cities around the United States. Members of the medical staffs that are trying to take care of the illegals in San Antonio were threatened with arrest if they revealed information about the diseases being brought into the country, but they spoke to reporters on condition of anonymity because they felt that Americans needed to know about the risks to their health posed by this surge of illegal aliens.[15]

Arizona governor Jan Brewer summed up what must be done:

> *The administration's refusal to properly verify that violent criminals are not among those entering the United States shows an alarming lack of concern for our homeland's security. As a nation, we cannot sit back and allow this policy to continue.*[16]

The one good thing that may have come about because of this event is that Eric Cantor, the House majority leader, was defeated in the Virginia Republican primary by one Dave Brat, an unknown who beat the highly favored Cantor in an upset for the ages.

The attempted cover-up of what's happening at Veterans Affairs hospitals as the VA tries to hide its refusal to treat our soldiers is another of the disturbing scandals that has emerged during this administration.

An audit of the Veterans Affairs hospitals and clinics has found that more than a hundred thousand military veterans face very long waits just to get in to see a doctor. For more than half of them, the wait has been longer than three months. For more than sixty thousand veterans, the wait is still going on: For the past ten years, that's how many veterans have been unable to get an appointment at all.

But the problem doesn't end there. The inspector general for the VA, Richard Griffin, reported that it is common practice for administrators to create two sets of books, one for the public and a second that reflected the fact that appointments were delayed, often indefinitely, and was never intended to see the light of day. Estimates are that hundreds of thousands of veterans wait longer than two weeks, the wait time within which the VA is committed to seeing patients.

Staff members at twenty-four of the VA hospitals reported that "they felt threatened or coerced" into entering false data to protect their facilities' fraudulent practices from being discovered.[17]

Oklahoma senator Tom Coburn had earlier called attention to the problems with our health-care system for veterans, but his attempts to bring the issue to the Senate floor for debate were blocked by Democrats. Coburn said Democrats share the responsibility for the VA scandal because they have refused to confront the issue.[18]

It's clear to me that what is happening with the VA health-care situation is a smaller version of what we face with Obamacare. While the number of cases unattended to is in the hundreds of thousands in the VA, where Obamacare is concerned the number of people who face this type of treatment will run into the millions. I can only imagine how horrifying the results of a bureaucracy charged with helping that many patients will be.

The federal bureaucracy is committed to one thing: making sure they keep their own jobs, even though they don't do them. The larger the bureaucracy, the more corrupt and incompetent it becomes. The losers are those poor people who must turn to the federal government for what they need.

Finally, I want to deal briefly with the incident at Cliven Bundy's ranch in Nevada. I felt that had it resulted in weapons being fired, it might well have been the first battle of the coming civil war.

What did Nancy Pelosi say about the Bundy standoff?

Do you think she supported him as a disruptor?

What does Eric Holder say about free assembly?

Has the civil war already begun?

On Saturday, April 12, 2014, millions of Americans monitored live newscasts of a confrontation between armed troops representing the federal Bureau of Land Management (BLM) and several hundred civilian supporters of Nevada rancher Bundy. Millions more followed the event on internet websites and through social media.

A federal force consisting of armored police SWAT team

trucks, hundreds of armed BLM rangers and special agents, and dozens of armored SUVs out of which the BLM militia emerged carrying automatic weapons moved into the area where Cliven Bundy's family had been grazing their cattle for 140 years. Helicopters monitoring the scene hovered overhead.

As BLM troops used helicopters to herd Cliven Bundy's cattle from the land on which they were grazing into makeshift pens, more than two hundred angry Americans arrived at the scene, some on horseback, some on foot, many carrying American flags and signs in support of Cliven Bundy. They, too, were armed, and they were bent on stopping the federal storm troopers trying to take away the Bundy family's livelihood. We were seeing images of federal troops with their rifles aimed at everyday Americans. We were seeing images that made what the federal government is doing to us concrete for Americans in a way that most of the scandals of this administration haven't done.

Here are a federal judge's words regarding Elwood Wayne Hage, another case in which a Nevada rancher was deprived of his right to graze cattle on federal land:

> *The government and the agents of the government in that locale, sometime in the '70s and '80s, entered into a conspiracy, a literal, intentional conspiracy, to deprive [ranchers] of not only their permit grazing rights, ... but also to deprive them of their vested property rights under the takings clause, and I find that that's a sufficient basis to hold that there is irreparable harm if I don't ... restrain the government from continuing in that conduct.*[19]

Still don't think that the Obama administration is leading this country into a civil war? I hope you are right. As a trained PhD scientist I can only study the evidence and give you my conclusions. Right now the prognosis is not good. We have an incompetent zealot taking the nation down the road of weakness and centralized governmental control of every aspect of our daily lives. Desiring to control us from inception to death, from womb to tomb. Monitoring our every word, controlling what we eat, drink, think, and speak. All in the name of "fairness." Just as individuals snap when the pressure becomes too great, so, too, does a nation.

CHAPTER 2

The Long March

As I see it, the state of our union is in the most perilous position it's been in since the 1860s. We are under assault from both inside and out as our government moves to consolidate its domestic power while at the same time weakening our defenses against the growing power of our global enemies. And all the while, the liberal government media complex watches the storm clouds gather with few keystrokes of reportage, outrage, or resistance.

I fear the worst.

Right now Americans are angrier and more divided than I've seen them since the 1960s. What fires this rage is that we've become a post-Constitutional society.

As you'll read in the coming pages, the system has been turned upside down. What's right is wrong. What's good is bad. What's subversive is patriotic. We now exist at the whim of lobbyists who control a government that is liable to do anything it wants to satisfy its lust for power.

Right now the nation is a tinderbox that can easily go up in flames, because we're increasingly under the thumb of an administration that is destroying our two-hundred-year-old tradition of defending our borders, language, and culture and replacing it with a culture of statelessness and corruption.

Yes, there are Americans who stand up against this tyranny; good, god-fearing people who have had enough of seeing their civil rights trampled, their jobs vanish, and their incomes seized through taxation. I hope it's not too late for recourse through democratic means.

But right now we're in a place that mirrors the darkest days of our country's history.

On February 10, 2007, some 146 years after Fort Sumter surrendered and the American Civil War began, Barack Obama announced his first presidential campaign in Abraham Lincoln's hometown of Springfield, Illinois. In that speech, Obama declared that, like Lincoln, he was out to "free a people" and "transform a nation." Without question, we're living in a nation more divided than any since Lincoln's presidency, and we've entered a time and place that may be as dangerous as it was during the Lincoln years. I worry, though, that as happened in Lincoln's time, we're moving not toward expanded freedom but toward civil war.

I fear the worst.

Let me be clear that while Barack Obama is the executive head of the current administration, I'm speaking in broader terms than simply about the president alone. I'm speaking of both Democratic and Republican senators and congressmen who are doing nothing to hold back a government that has, in my opinion, overreached its legal and Constitutional powers and brought us under its control. It is coming more and more to resemble a government based not on the rule of law but on the greed and hunger for power of a crony oligarchy. A civil war would enable this crony government to consolidate the power it has already granted itself through the broad use of executive orders, the power granted to Cabinet secretaries and other political appointees, and the unwillingness of our lawmakers to step in and put a halt to this takeover.

With our nation divided, the government could marshal all of those on its side—the Transportation Security Administration (TSA), street gangs, the National Guard, a military now purged of patriotic generals and without a command structure loyal to the Constitution—against those who would stand up to the oppression.

Something much like what we face today happened during Lincoln's presidency. Lincoln wasn't a saint. As great as he was, he committed crimes against the Constitution and against ordinary citizens.

In an 1862 proclamation, Lincoln declared that "Rebels and Insurgents" in the Southern states had created an "insurrection," they were "subject to martial law," and their right to a writ of habeas corpus was suspended.

Lincoln is estimated to have arrested and imprisoned some 20,000 civilians and detained them without trials. During the Civil War, Southern prisoners were held in internment camps under deplorable conditions. At Fort Delaware, more than 2,000 confederate soldiers died of scurvy and dysentery. Confederate prisoners in the Union camp at Rock Island were tortured by being hung by their thumbs.

Let us pray that Obama does not literally follow Abraham Lincoln's example. Given his record of ignoring the Constitution and rewriting the law, anything is possible with our rogue president. Don't think it can't happen here. As we have seen with Lincoln, it already has.

I fear the worst, and you should, too.

Can the situation in our country actually turn into a civil war?

Of course it can. We're seeing the signs of it everywhere.

It is no secret that Democrats are looking to take advantage of a divided Republican base to maintain their majority in the Senate. The most important thing we as a people must do in order to stop the ongoing assault against our freedoms by this administration is to unite behind Republican candidates. While for many conservatives this is a difficult thing to do, we must nonetheless oust Democrats from control over the U.S. Senate and hold on to our majority in the House. This means that we must turn out in large numbers for the coming elections, and we must elect Republicans.

If the status quo is allowed to remain, Democrats may keep their stranglehold on the Senate. As I see it, a Democrat-controlled Senate, as evidenced by recent history, guarantees a continued assault on the Constitution, congressional convention, and free speech.

Let me give you an example. In the wake of another maneuver by U.S. Senate Majority Leader Harry Reid—his suspension of the filibuster rule—Senate Democrats pushed through the appointment of four left-wing judges to the D.C. Circuit Court of Appeals. With these appointments, Democrats paved the way for the court—the second most powerful judicial body in the United States—to approve curtailing the political speech of nonprofit groups that support conservative values and to dismiss legal challenges to the Affordable Care Act. They were able to consolidate the court against Obamacare despite the fact that millions of people may have already lost their health insurance coverage and millions more will likely be notified that they are due to lose theirs in the coming year. I'll explain to you what Obamacare is really about in an upcoming chapter. For now, let me tell you that in the wake of the Harry Reid–led Senate Democrats' majority ruling, Obamacare supporters are rubbing their hands.

Do you remember the economic crash of 2008? One of the key causes of that crash was the collapse of the housing bubble in the United States.

It's happening again. Let me explain.

By mid-2013, a majority of the homes sold in the United States were being sold not to individuals but to large investors.[1] Often, these investors buy hundred of houses, then rent them out while they wait for prices to increase. This causes a housing bubble based on rising home prices. The bubble will burst when large investors sell their holdings and take their profits. This, in turn, will plunge us back into recession.

Let me ask you this: When was Barack Obama elected? In case you've forgotten, it was immediately after the last housing bubble burst. In tough times people are compliant. Those seeking to expand their power take advantage of crises like the one we experienced in 2008. When the time is right, they grab power when those that need leadership are at their most vulnerable.

The same thing is happening with health-care insurance. To put it bluntly, Obamacare is unsustainable. Once the health-care bubble bursts, and it will very soon, it's not out of the question that an executive order will be issued that puts a majority of physicians and hospitals under the direct control of the federal government.

Within the next few years, health care will very likely become a haves-versus-the-have-nots industry. Those who can afford it will bypass insurance and pay for their medical treatment directly to physicians who maintain private practices and to the best hospitals, which are excluded from Obamacare. The best medical research and treatment hospitals in the United States—hospitals like the Cleveland Clinic, the Mayo Clinic, Cedars-Sinai Medical Center—will very likely become oases for the überrich, the only people who will be able to afford the best medical care.

The remaining 90 percent of Americans may be consigned to wait in interminable lines to receive their health-care services from the rapidly diminishing number of physicians and hospitals still available to provide medical treatment for them.

Do you think Americans will stand still for that?

Meanwhile, the fragile economy—don't be fooled, it's not improving—will be driven to the brink of collapse by the bursting of the housing bubble, skyrocketing health-care costs, and several other factors.

Other nations will likely refuse to buy the U.S. Treasury bonds on which we've been financing our soaring debt. The U.S. dollar has long been the currency on which the world's economy is built. It is becoming increasingly unstable, and the consequences will not be good for us. The dollar, which has been the global reserve currency, will likely continue to lose value.

Prior to 2014, virtually all international sales of oil were settled in U.S. petrodollars. Now China, one of the largest importers of oil, has begun settling its foreign oil purchases in yuan, its own currency.[2] At the same time, the other so-called BRICS nations—Brazil, Russia, India, and South Africa—are also moving away from the petrodollar, settling oil trades in their own currencies.[3]

For the United States, which imports more foreign goods

than anyone else in the world, an unstable dollar means that Americans spend more to import less. We will be effectively importing inflation with every purchase of foreign goods. The government tries to hide this deficiency with three-card-monte statistics. Government inflation charts no longer include such items as food and gasoline and wage stagnation in their calculations. While they report inflation at less than 2 percent, the real number is near 10 percent and rising.[4] But the proof is in the dwindling bank accounts of regular Americans.

As the economy is challenged, so are our freedoms.

The National Security Agency (NSA) will almost certainly continue what I see as its hostile takeover of Americans' formerly private information. The technology and storage capacity of the NSA is nearly limitless. A massive amount of information about Americans' everyday activities is captured and stored in the million-square-foot federal data center in Bluffdale, Utah, in the form of "metadata."[5]

What worries me most, though, is not that the NSA is monitoring the communications of suspected terrorists in order to prevent them from staging another attack on this country. I'm much more worried about the fact that, as the *Washington Post* reported, based on information about more than 150,000 intercepted communications, nearly half of these exchanges contained *only* private information, including personal photographs, about the American citizens who shared them. Despite the fact that they were deemed to be "useless" by intelligence analysts, they were retained and stored by the NSA.[6]

In addition to collecting, storing, and distributing our medical and financial records as part of the Affordable Care

Act, the Internal Revenue Service has become the arbiter of political speech in the United States. Tax-exempt groups like the Tea Party, whose activities the IRS has been curtailing for years, are particularly vulnerable to the practices by this federal agency.[7] If what has already begun is allowed to continue, political speech that goes against the ruling powers may be censored completely.

Will Americans go quietly as they see their freedoms being lost on every front?

Our position as a world power has become greatly diminished. Our military culture has been strongly influenced, even corrupted, by changing values adopted by those who determine the rules under which our military operates. These changes are eviscerating our military power and readiness. Left unchecked, they threaten to destroy our armed forces.

High-ranking officers who run afoul of this increasingly subversive military culture are often dismissed summarily on the weakest of charges. Our military left growing chaos behind it following its exit from the Middle East. Russian despot Vladimir Putin takes advantage of the current administration's growing retreat from the world stage to expand his power into Eastern Europe. While he does that, our own military budget cuts are made at the expense of the technology our soldiers need in order to do their job effectively.

Our influence in the increasingly dangerous Middle East has all but vanished. In the wake of this, Middle East peace becomes more and more unrealistic. The weakness of our military influence in the Middle and Far East puts us in the most vulnerable position since Pearl Harbor was attacked.

But as bad as it is for us abroad, the economic conditions

and division at home are even more perilous. With the U.S. job market remaining soft and our money continuing to lose purchasing power, can it be long before Americans begin public demonstrations like the ones we see in European cities?

The United States may well be in the midst of a military, economic, and cultural collapse that is turning us into a country in danger of catastrophic failure and leading to the nightmarish scenario of a civil war.

With our international power and influence weakened dramatically, Republican and Democratic plutocrats may seize control of the political process while the will of the people goes unheeded. Conservative voices are increasingly being drowned out.

Several months ago I watched the opening ceremony of an Olympics held in a country that has been the archenemy of the United States for most of the past seventy years. The Sochi games swelled with Russian nationalism and pride. The rich history of the former Soviet Union was put on dazzling display and drew the delight and envy of the rest of the world.

At the same time, it brought tears of sadness from Americans at the lack of patriotism and nationalism here. We were once a country that was proud to be the land of the free and the home of the brave. We were a shining example of right and power. It was we—America, not Russia—who were the envy of the world. This book is ultimately about how we resurrect ourselves as a nation.

While you'll find that I focus attention on Barack Obama, the book is about much more than simply the president. His election wouldn't have been possible without the help of both Democrats and Republicans, and he wouldn't be able to implement his agenda without the aid of a broad network of people and organizations around the world who support his attempts to undermine our country.

Civil war is the most dangerous and destructive event that can occur in any country. It invariably involves atrocities committed by both sides against their own fellow citizens, atrocities like those that could have ignited in Nevada.

In August 1863, Quantrill's Raiders, a band of rebel guerrilla soldiers, attacked the town of Lawrence, Kansas, massacring some two hundred men and boys and stealing hundreds of thousands of dollars from the townspeople. In an 1864 battle, the Fort Pillow Massacre, more than three hundred African-American soldiers were killed—many as they stood weaponless with their hands raised—after the garrison had surrendered.

Union soldiers were equally murderous. In early September 1864, the city of Atlanta surrendered to the Union's Maj. Gen. William Tecumseh Sherman. Some fourteen thousand residents, mostly older men, women, and children, watched helplessly as Sherman's troops burned the great Southern city to the ground. Only ten percent of Atlanta's buildings escaped the inferno.

In the ensuing weeks and months, Sherman's troops marched to Savannah, leaving a swath of destruction forty miles wide across Georgia. Buildings were burned, family farms pillaged, innocents murdered. In no small measure, Lincoln's reelection that November came on the wings of Sherman's so-called glorious victory. Sherman's March might have been the most unholy act perpetrated on the American people by one of its own. But when voices rose in outrage, even some from the North, Lincoln not only turned a deaf ear, he ordered the censoring of news stories, to which a compliant Associated Press acquiesced.[8]

Now, 150 years later, a situation very similar to the one we faced before the Civil War is taking shape in America. While we are still enjoying relative peace, there are subterranean rumblings that portend danger ahead. The outrageous acts to which many have become numb remind us of the months and years before the outbreak of the Civil War. In the words Thomas Corwin addressed to Abraham Lincoln on January 16, 1861, "I cannot comprehend the madness of the times.... Treason is in the air around us everywhere. It goes by the name of patriotism."

As I see it, the state of our union is in the most perilous position it's been in since the 1860s. We are under assault from both inside and out as our government moves to consolidate its domestic power while at the same time weakening our defenses against the growing power of our global enemies. And all the while, the liberal government media complex watches the storm clouds gather with few keystrokes of reportage, outrage, or resistance.

By now, many of you have realized that we've come to a situation that may threaten our very existence as a nation. This is what will inevitably ensue if we fail to stand up against the forces committed to making it happen.

Stop the Coming Civil War: My Savage Truth is the most important book you will read this year. These pages contain what stands between us and ruin. It is imperative that you understand and put into practice what I say in these pages.

You must spread the word among your friends, neighbors, and family.

You must display this book on buses, on trains, on your coffee tables.

You must engage others in discussions about what I write here.

It may represent the last best chance we have to take back our country.

It may be the last best chance we have to avoid a second civil war.

I would add one more warning here: None of us has any control over the course of events. There's a gap between the time this book was delivered to the publisher and its release to the public. This book is a preamble to those events. I hope that the coming civil war that I predict does not happen, but I fear that the events leading up to it will continue to play out as this book is prepared for release. I hope that it will reach the public before the start of a second civil war in this country, and I hope that it will be instrumental in enabling us to avoid that outcome.

Only here will you get the whole truth no one else is telling.

Only in these pages will you will find all the facts about the coming civil war that is currently developing.

Only here will you get the Savage Truth.

CHAPTER 3

The War on Our Borders, Language, and Culture

Do you know what this administration means when it talks about "humane" enforcement of immigration laws? It means that it's freeing tens of thousands of illegal aliens who have been convicted of serious crimes, including nearly 200 homicides, more than 400 sexual assaults, thousands of thefts and kidnappings, and more than 10,000 drug and drunk-driving convictions. The administration has allowed more than 36,000 convicted criminals who should have been deported to return to America's streets.

If you've listened to my show, *The Savage Nation*, you know the importance I place on the preservation of our borders, language, and culture. And you know that this administration has done more to further the left's war against America by attempting to destroy these three foundation blocks of our republic than any other administration in our history.

When I speak to you about protecting our borders, language, and culture, I speak to you as a first-generation American. My ancestors didn't come over on the *Mayflower*. They came over from Russia in third-class steerage. They worked hard and died young. They learned to speak English, and they learned America's ways. They were true immigrants.

But the immigrants of the past are not the same as the immigrants today. I understand that the situation is different now than it was nearly a hundred years ago, but the fundamentals of immigration are the same: You come as a guest and then muster up every ounce of compliance and determination you can until you earn your full-time status.

This is not the immigration formula under the current administration. Their idea of immigration is to grant amnesty to those who have crossed our borders illegally.

I oppose amnesty for many reasons. First, we need to guarantee national security. Not all terrorists fly into the United States in jets. Some of them make their way to Mexico and then walk into the country. This is one of the most important reasons I oppose amnesty.

We must close the borders down. This should be our highest priority.

But we also have high unemployment, and 13 million Americans are receiving disability benefits. By giving jobs to non-citizens, we're not only taking away the diminishing employment opportunities that exists in the United States, we're supplying more of an excuse to those too lazy to look for work.

And third, 47 percent of Americans pay no income tax—yes,

the same 47 percent made famous by a truthful Mitt Romney. Do we really need to add to their ranks?

After illegal aliens are taken into custody, they're held in detention centers until their cases can be resolved. That's resulted in overcrowding. Do you know how immigration officials are dealing with that? They're giving women and minors documentation that allows them to travel anywhere in the United States, then releasing them from custody while telling them they must appear for immigration hearings in the future.[1]

In addition to overcrowded detention centers, illegals are overwhelming many of our emergency rooms and schools. New immigrants are naturally aligned with liberals and socialism. That means more votes for Democrats.

I don't see these people as aliens, but as human beings. Many of them are wonderful, churchgoing people with strong families. And yet I tell you: Amnesty will destroy America. The biggest victims will be our poor citizens, white and black.

The situation came to a head for me during the 2014 Super Bowl.

Now, I have nothing against all the languages spoken on the Earth—I just prefer English spoken in America. But when I saw the Super Bowl multicultural, multilingual Coca-Cola ad, I wanted to smash my television in with a brick. Coca-Cola should fire whoever came up with the idea for the ad. Better yet, they should be deported.

The commercial opened with "America the Beautiful" sung by a beautiful female voice. There were images of a pickup truck, cowboys, and horses. It was very moving. Then, all of a sudden, the anthem was being sung in a different language, and then another language, and then another. It was in Hindi, Senegalese, and Arabic. As the language changed so did the images. Instead of cowboys, you had women in burkas and two "dads" roller-skating with their daughter. It was the first Super Bowl ad to feature a gay family, according to the Gay and Lesbian Alliance Against Defamation (GLAAD).

Let me explain why this ad was not patriotic. If you were to show a Coca-Cola ad in China and start to play the Chinese national anthem in Mandarin, and then suddenly broke into English and other languages, the Chinese would burn down the theater. If you're gay, and you have an adopted daughter and you want to roller-skate with her, be my guest. I don't think it's right, but I'm not going to fight you about it. But I do care when Coca-Cola makes you emblematic of the country that I love. You're not emblematic. I'm an American. And I'm sick and tired of having to make excuses for the USA. This has gone too far. Stop debasing our most cherished possession: our pride in our country.

The reason Coke can get away with a commercial like this is because we now live in a country whose moral fiber degenerates by the minute. This administration's relentless assault on our borders, language, and culture has expanded to include an assault on every one of our fundamental values and institutions. They are determined to destroy a once righteous and heroic America and replace it with a leftist government defined by immorality and greed.

Obama's Immigrant Surge Threatens to Destroy America

How far has it gone? Let me tell you a true story about an illegal alien suing the people who rescued him.

In September 2013, floodwaters submerged the car Roy Ortiz was driving outside the town of Lafayette, Colorado. Heroes from the North Metro Fire Department risked their lives by diving into what had become a raging river. How did Ortiz display his gratitude to those who rescued him from certain death? He filed a notice of intent to sue the town and those who saved his life for $500,000. He claims signs should have been posted warning drivers of the danger and that crews should have realized he was trapped in his car and pulled him out sooner than they did. The North Metro Fire Department responded this way to Ortiz's intent to sue: "I'm sure it was a traumatic experience for [Ortiz]," their spokesperson said. "Ultimately, we were just very grateful we were able to save his life that day."[2]

Shortly after the intent to sue was filed in March 2014, Ortiz's attorney admitted to Fox News that his client was in the country illegally.[3]

Ortiz is one of millions of illegal immigrants who are attempting to find ways to game the system in the U.S., taking advantage of a federal government that is bypassing the law to make it possible for illegals to stay in this country and receive food, welfare money, medical care, and education for their children at taxpayer expense.

A week after Ortiz announced his lawsuit, young Mexicans marched through the streets of Tijuana to the Otay Mesa crossing in San Diego, where they tried to cross into the United States even though they didn't have legal documentation to do so. They were protesting what they claimed to be a rising rate of deportations of illegal immigrants. The protesters blocked two traffic lanes at the crossing.[4] They called themselves "dreamers" after the DREAM Act, which would have given young illegals the right to stay in this country. When the DREAM Act didn't pass, the president issued an executive order that, for all intents and purposes, accomplished everything drafters of the faulty bill had hoped for.

There was one little problem with the protest at the Otay Mesa crossing. Under this administration, the deportation rate isn't increasing—it's going down. The administration is inflating the numbers to make it look like more people are being deported than the real numbers indicate. The administration claims it has deported more than two million illegal aliens during the past five years, making it tougher than George W. Bush on illegal immigration. What this administration doesn't tell you is that more than half of those who were supposedly deported were people who were caught trying to cross the border illegally. They had never really entered the United States. The Bush administration counted only illegals who were caught after they had already established themselves in the United States. This finagling of the numbers of illegals deported is just a smokescreen the Obama administration puts up to cover the immigration practices in which it engages. *Look at us*, they say. *We're abiding by the law for a change.*[5] But nothing could be further from the truth.

Here's the truth: In the state of Texas alone, four field offices of the U.S. Immigration and Customs Enforcement Agency (ICE) deported more than seven thousand illegal aliens in just four years. So that doesn't sound like such a big number, right? And it's not, except when you consider they were deported not only because they were illegal—which in my view is reason enough to expel them—they were deported because they were sex offenders. Seven thousand illegal alien sex offenders, more than a quarter of whom had committed *crimes against children.*[6]

If these rapists and pedophiles had not been allowed into the country in the first place, nearly two thousand children—not to mention five thousand other victims, mostly women—would have been spared the terrible consequences they suffered at the hands of these criminals.

Barack Obama's dreamers? More like a living nightmare.

Do you know how much gall these people possess? Even the ones who have already been deported show no respect for our country. In early March 2014, a group of some 250 deportees who had lived much of their lives in the United States illegally staged a protest march. They chanted "undocumented and unafraid" as they attempted to cross from Tijuana to San Diego. The demonstrators demanded entry and called the U.S.-Mexico border "arbitrary."[7]

That's how much respect they have for our borders.

They have even less respect for themselves.

There has been a dramatic increase in the number of children unaccompanied by adults who are crossing the Mexican border and entering the United States illegally. The reason this is happening? The White House gives de facto amnesty to foreign children in the country illegally through its DREAM Act–inspired executive order. The federal government provides what amounts to a babysitting service for unaccompanied children in the country illegally with no parent or adult to care for them. In 2013 that number reached nearly twenty-five thousand, almost double that of the previous year.

The fact remains that under Obama administration policies, immigrants are more likely to be allowed to stay here when they enter this country illegally than when they do it legally. Even though Obama's executive order supposedly applies only to children who have been here for at least five years, the White House and the Department of Homeland Security (DHS) are not going to refuse entry and/or support to any minors who enter the country without permission.[8]

Even though the administration has already softened its deportation policy and is not deporting as many illegals as it says it is, DHS officials are planning to make it even easier for illegals to stay here. The president says he is pushing for "more humane" enforcement of DHS policy.

Do you know what the president means when he talks about "humane" enforcement? He means that he's freeing tens of thousands of illegal aliens who have been convicted of serious crimes, including nearly 200 homicides, more than 400 sexual assaults, thousands of thefts and kidnappings, and more than 10,000 drug and drunk-driving convictions. The administration freed more than 36,000 convicted criminals who should have been deported and allowed them to return to America's streets.[9]

That's what the president calls "humane."

How about being more humane to Americans who can't find a job? How about being more humane to American citizens who suffer because emergency room services are overwhelmed by the onslaught of illegal aliens? How about being more humane to the people you were elected to be humane to?

Our president seems to care more about the health-care status of illegal aliens—whom he has repeatedly tried to recruit for Obamacare to inflate the numbers of his signature legislation—than he does about American citizens. In an interview on a Spanish-language sports radio station that should have sparked outrage among American citizens, he explained that Hispanics here illegally don't need to worry about being deported if they try to sign up for Obamacare:

Well, the main thing for people to know is that any information you get, you know, asked with respect to buying insurance, does not have anything to do with . . . the rules governing immigration. You know, if you have a family where some people are citizens or legally here, and others are not documented, the immigration people will never get that information.[10]

New DHS secretary Jeh Johnson isn't about to disagree and recently encouraged illegals "to come out from the shadows." Shortly after taking office, Johnson explained that illegals are "here, and they're not going away."[11] Of the estimated— I would say "underestimated"—11 million illegal aliens currently in the country, Johnson says they've "earned the right to be citizens." In Johnson's view, allowing illegals an unimpeded path to citizenship is "a matter of who we are as Americans."[12]

As I see it, the fact that they're costing us billions each year by sponging off the U.S. welfare system and overwhelming our medical care facilities doesn't seem to factor into his assessment of illegals in our country.

For the record, Johnson has expressed his pro-leftist political views frequently. He was an important fund-raiser for Obama's 2008 campaign, and he was in favor of repealing the military's "Don't Ask Don't Tell" policy. He's also spoken out in support of Eric Holder's position against upholding the Defense of Marriage Act.

Although no immigration reform legislation has been passed and a new immigration law won't be passed in Obama's second term, Johnson is making plans to enforce it anyway. He explained, "I have already directed the deputy director of Homeland Security to coordinate the process to ensure we are ready to implement the law."[13] Johnson didn't need to say that he's "making plans"; he's already doing everything in his power to enforce the nonlaw.

At the same time, as Obamacare threatens to undermine American businesses, the White House has unilaterally imposed a policy that encourages businesses to hire illegal aliens by cutting fines imposed on businesses that do so. The Justice Department inspector general overseeing the Department of Homeland Security recently revealed in a report that the DHS has reduced the penalties by an average of 40 percent for those hiring illegal aliens. This at a time when, as the report says, "the federal government was supposed to be putting more of an emphasis on going after [those] employers." The legislation imposing such penalties is written to allow a great deal of discretion: Fines can be reduced or suspended "if it seems the businesses' finances can't handle a large penalty." The inspector general explained that "the knowledge that fines can be significantly reduced may diminish the effectiveness of fines as a deterrent to hiring unauthorized workers."[14]

If you want to know where the values and principles of congressional Democrats lie today, you don't have to look any further than Harry Reid. He decided to allow his party's extension of unemployment insurance benefits to die in the Senate rather than even allow a vote on a Republican amendment that would restore benefits to veterans that had been cut. Right now, tax credit payments that should go to military veterans are instead being diverted to illegal immigrants. Reid, who has not bothered to consult Republicans about the unemployment insurance bill he wants to pass, wouldn't even consider an amendment that ensures that people applying for the Additional Tax Credit program show their Social Security number. This amendment alone would take $4.2 billion tax credit money that was obtained by illegal aliens in 2011 and distribute it to our military veterans.

Reid said no.[15]

Reid couldn't care less about our veterans. He has more important things to think about, like making sure illegal immigrants have enough money for strollers, bassinets, and the Baby Gap outfits they buy for their anchor babies born on American soil.

Are We Becoming Cultural Marxists?

As I see it, in addition to doing everything it can to eliminate our borders, the current administration is promoting the stealth takeover of our government, our education system, our popular culture, and the profession of journalism in this country. The advance of leftist values and policies that characterizes this takeover has weakened the moral and cultural foundation on which this country rose to become the most powerful nation on earth. Under this administration, the war on culture has expanded to include the left's war on Christians, on women, on men, on children, on minorities, and on the rule of law.

What most people don't understand is that this war has been going on under liberal leadership for well over a century, dating back to the Civil War.

And the result of this century and a half of moral erosion? Today you can't turn on a television set, sit down in a movie theater, or open a newspaper or magazine without being bombarded with filth that would have gotten its creators jailed little more than half a century ago. The leftist lack of principles behind the disappearance of moral and cultural decency has infiltrated our federal government and many of our most important institutions. From the Department of Justice to the IRS to the U.S. military, our institutions are rife with corruption that threatens U.S. politics and our national security. Chicago and New York are under the control of Rahm Emanuel and Bill de Blasio, leftists who are making Tammany Hall look like child's play. They'll stop at nothing until they've reduced their cities to rubble that rivals Detroit.

The history of the political convictions that have consistently formed the foundation of the left's agenda is a history of anger at, and hatred of, capitalism, religion, and individual initiative. Leftists hate the very foundations of Western culture. Every baseless critique launched by contemporary Democrats brands them as implicitly remorseless and unapologetic practitioners of a reductive and degenerate method of operation based on lies and unrelenting criticism of the opposition. The leftist commitment to destroying capitalism and democratic government in the United States has metastasized to the point where we no longer have an option: We've got to find ways to eliminate the influence they've accumulated as they infiltrate every aspect of American life.

What we're facing in the United States today is the rise of what can be called cultural Marxism. In the 1960s, the slogan "Make love, not war" became the rallying cry of a generation of hippies and leftist subversives who opposed the War in Vietnam. The words were credited to Herbert Marcuse, a communist professor who escaped Nazi Germany in the 1930s and set up shop in America. Marcuse and another popular Marxist author, Erich Fromm, became influential leaders of the movement toward Marxism in this country. Both Marcuse and

Fromm were proponents of what was called "polymorphous sexuality." That term for them represented the ultimate liberation of mankind from sexual repression and from the need to work for a living. They envisioned a society in which American citizens would give up individual freedom to the state and become pleasure-seeking functionaries whose only value consisted in pushing the envelope of hedonism.

The idea surfaced again in early 2014 when the Congressional Budget Office (CBO) released its estimate that Obamacare will eliminate 2.5 million jobs over the next decade. The left was quick to respond. The *New York Times* explained that reducing the work force by millions would be "liberating." The paper explained that it "will free people, young and old, to pursue careers or retirement without having to worry about health coverage." These people no longer need "to feel locked into a job they don't like because they need insurance for themselves or their families."[16]

Nancy Pelosi quickly added her voice in defense of the Affordable Care Act. In her response, Pelosi agreed with the *Times*, saying that the goal of the ACA is to "give people life, a healthy life, liberty to pursue their happiness."[17] Her words are merely a resurrection of Marcuse's 1960s slogan, only with this slight change: "Make love, not money."

To me, it has already become clear that federal subsidies of any kind destroy the work ethic that has made America the most powerful and economically successful nation on Earth. Since President Lyndon Johnson's Great Society legislation was passed in the 1960s, the federal government has spent $20 trillion to fund programs that dole out everything from cash to food stamps to housing to medical care to Americans who are unable or unwilling to provide for themselves and their families. We spent nearly a trillion dollars on subsidies in 2012 as Obama ramped up his administration's efforts to make sure that minorities and other low-income people would remain trapped in the inner-city public-housing prisons that were also part of Johnson's vision. Nearly a third of America's 315 million people received assistance from at least one of the eighty federal subsidy programs now in existence. The average cost was $9,000 per person.[18]

At the same time, as this spending was skyrocketing, Americans most in need of finding the employment that would truly raise their standard of living and provide them with the means to support their families remained hostage to a federal culture that insists on clinging to a 1960s leftist agenda. What the American left has done to its neediest citizens is criminal.

Before Lyndon Johnson intervened to make sure blacks would become dependent on the government for just about everything they needed to live, black participation in the labor market was equal to or greater than that of whites. Today the "official" African-American unemployment rate—which doesn't take into account the enormous number of blacks who aren't even trying to find jobs—is around 14 percent. In fact, when you count those who don't even try to find a job, it's nearly 50 percent. When the numbers are added up, under this administration more than 60 percent of young black people are no longer even part of the labor force. It's the lowest ever recorded in our history.[19]

While the president is ostensibly trying to improve minorities' educational outcomes by handing out $200 million through executive order so he can keep this important constituent base dependent on government subsidies, Attorney General Holder and New York City mayor Bill de Blasio are doing everything in their power to keep blacks from realizing their full potential by making sure they're deprived of exactly the opportunities Obama's money is supposed to provide.

As I've already mentioned, both Holder and de Blasio have done everything they can to make sure blacks and Hispanics don't have the educational opportunities they need. Finally a group of New York City parents has filed a federal lawsuit against de Blasio for violating their civil rights in denying the charter schools access to space in public schools without giving them time to find other space. In doing so, he was effectively closing down the charter schools that were providing their children with the quality education that's sorely missing in New York City's bureaucratic public school educational tangle.[20] The parents are also suing the Department of Education—run by another Chicago liberal, Arne Duncan—to challenge de Blasio's reversal of former mayor Michael Bloomberg's wholehearted support of charter schools.

The left is all for improving the educational outcomes of the underprivileged as long as it doesn't interfere with their efforts to keep the underprivileged trapped in what I see as the leftist hell Democratic policies have created for them.

The situation with blacks in America is similar to that with Jews: I cannot understand how African-Americans can vote for a president who is out to destroy their chances of ever rising out of the poverty and dependence in which so many of them still live, and I can't understand why Jewish voters in this country vote for a president who hates Israel and is doing everything he can to destroy our homeland.

But the cultural Marxism that is being imposed on the most vulnerable of Americans has crept far beyond merely spending money to keep them imprisoned. It's invaded everything from our military to the Christian churches and communities so reviled by the left.

As I've said many times on my show, I'm a sexual libertarian. What you want to do with a consenting partner is your business. I don't care. You can dress up like Tinker Bell and run around your bedroom in tights and a tutu. As long as I don't have to watch you, I don't care. I should say, I don't care as long as it's within the law, and you're not hurting another person, and it doesn't involve children.

And as long as you don't run the country.

Our president is a metrosexual.

And metrosexuality is a foundational component of leftist values.

Marxist culture is built on the inherent distrust of strong males. The cultural Marxists base their hatred of men and their suppression of maleness on the fact that they see patriarchal societies and culture as the enemies of the state. Male-dominated capitalism equals oppression to Marxists, or so they say. They beat this drum to rally those who feel oppressed. A virile, successful man is cast as the enemy. The left's agenda can succeed only if the male population is neutralized and disempowered.[21]

Part of this administration's war against American males is carried out through what I see as its decimation of the military, which I'll talk about in the next chapter. For now, let me talk about another aspect of this conflict.

This administration seems to be spending on defense only when that money goes to embarrass the military. The president signed off on an appropriation to change the dress hat marines have been proudly wearing since 1922. The new one, which some commanders are calling "a porter's hat" and "a girly hat," would cost the military $8 million. "We don't even have enough funding to buy bullets," one commander said, "and now the [Department of Defense] is pushing to spend $8 million on covers that look like women's hats!"[22]

I'm not stupid. I know what the political correctness police are going to say about this, especially about the "girly hat" remark above and other cultural observations I might make. But this isn't about political correctness. This is the administration injecting a deadly virus into a proud military organization to corrupt it from within. Retired Army major general Patrick Brady calls it "girly-men leadership" and says the president gives medals for not shooting and for operating a computer. "This president will never fight if there is any reason to avoid it," said the Medal of Honor recipient, "and with a helpless military he can just point to our weakness and shrug his shoulders."[23]

This administration's military policies include expanding the cultural Marxism that characterizes all his policies to include Christians in the military. One of the president's pet projects is the DoD's Defense Equal Opportunity Management Institute. The DEOMI was formed in 1971 to help address racial inequality in the military. From that admirable start, it has morphed into a leftist propaganda factory promoting radical feminist issues and spreading anti-Christian directives while shredding the iconic image of our armed forces.

Here's what the DEOMI manual states:

Simply put, a healthy, white, heterosexual, Christian male receives many unearned advantages of social privilege, whereas a black, homosexual, atheist female in poor health receives many unearned disadvantages of social privilege....

In spite of slave insurrections, civil war, the 13th, 14th, and 15th amendments, the women's suffrage movement leading to the 19th amendment, the civil rights movement, urban rebellions and the contemporary feminist movement, the [white male's] club persists.[24]

Think about those statements. Think about the garbage being fed to impressionable young men and women by this administration, and then recall the square-jawed soldiers that for decades on recruitment posters successfully encouraged men—and, yes, even women—to join the armed services. What do you think the recruitment posters of the near future will look like?

The Persecution of Christians Knows No Borders

In one of its presentations, a page dealing with "Religious Extremism," the DEOMI manual lists radical extremist religious groups including al Qaeda, the Nation of Islam, and the Ku Klux Klan. But it also lists "Evangelical Christianity (U.S./ Christian)" and "Catholicism (U.S./Christian)." The sourcing the Defense Department uses for this training material is the Southern Poverty Law Center (SPLC).[25] The SPLC is an anti-Christian, anti-conservative group that exists primarily to attack Christians and members of the Tea Party. In my opinion, they're one of the most biased leftist organizations you can find, and their influence now extends to contaminating our military's training material.

So how does the administration respond to criticism of this

group by Christians and conservatives? The DoD says that the SPLC will continue to be an important source for developing training material for the U.S. military. It doesn't matter that the SPLC's website features a "hate map" that identifies Christian organizations that defend traditional marriage.[26]

There is one piece of good news about the SPLC: The FBI no longer counts the group as a "resource" on which it depends. Fifteen family groups had petitioned Eric Holder and FBI head James Comey to stop endorsing the group, and they agreed.[27]

The administration's war on Christians also extends to their First Amendment rights in the military. In one of our military academies, Christians are no longer allowed to write Bible verses on the whiteboards in their dormitory rooms, although Air Force Academy officials have not yet required them to remove these expressions of faith. And they're not supposed to talk about their religious views, either, although they're specifically permitted to do so by law.[28]

The Military Religious Freedom Foundation, an organization that is precisely the opposite of what its name states, is a radical anti-Christian organization that maintains close ties with the Defense Department in order to eliminate religious expression from the military. The Pentagon under this administration seems committed to not allowing religious freedom of expression, despite the fact that the protection of religious expression was signed into law in late 2013. The president had threatened to veto the legislation but let it pass.

In other words, it became one more law the president would simply choose to ignore. It's one more way in which the cultural Marxism that characterizes Obama's regime is imposing its views on our military.

So in today's upside-down military world, patriotic soldiers are publicly humiliated and fired, while corrosive organizations like the DEOMI are liberally funded and thrive.

How can this go on, you ask?

I'm just getting started.

This administration's war against men goes way beyond the military, and its attack extends to everything that defines men, from their civil rights to the way they dress to their health care to male culture. I'll give the president this: He didn't start the left's war against the patriarchy; that's been going on forever. To the left, a strong man is the very emblem of democratic capitalism's evil power.

When a film such as *Lone Survivor*, which celebrates the heroism of America's Navy SEALs, is released, leftist critics pan it as a multi-million-dollar recruitment video, a tool "of military indoctrination geared toward the young and impressionable." The critics go on to complain that the Taliban commander featured in the film "is presented as a terrible guy," and that the film is unsympathetic to the Taliban terrorists attacking the SEALs.[29]

Thanks to the war on masculinity, there are no more men left to pair up with women. It's no wonder couples are putting off marriage and having children later and later these days. The administration had already decided not to enforce the Defense of Marriage Act, even before the U.S. Supreme Court struck much of the law down. Now Holder's Justice Department is advancing the cause further. The DoJ released a memo instructing federal government lawyers to give "full and equal recognition, to the greatest extent possible under the law" to same-sex marriages. Like heterosexual married couples, gay married people can file jointly for bankruptcy, are excused from testifying against their "spouses" in legal cases, and when their spouses are in prison, they have the same right to visit them as heterosexual couples have. Holder explained that same-sex marriage "stabilized families and expanded individual liberty."[30]

I want to see what Holder says when the gay divorces start piling up. I'm announcing right now, I have dibs on the reality television show.

Let me simplify things: If it's illegal, Democrats are for it. Period. They support prisoners' right to vote, and they're actively enrolling prisoners in Obamacare. They run guns across the border to Mexican drug lords and other criminals with impunity. They turn a blind eye as illegal aliens and drug dealers cross our southern border in droves, jeopardizing American citizens and defying U.S. laws and those who try to enforce them.

The cultural elite fawn over Miley Cyrus's disgusting "twerking" displays and watch as Justin Bieber receives no more than a slap on the wrist for racing his sports car through a residential neighborhood. We live in a society in which our civil rights are being eliminated, even as we must make our way through a leftist-dominated culture that has become even more hedonistic, amoral, and degenerate than that of Germany's Weimar Republic of the 1920s.

Planned Parenthood, which is responsible for killing millions of babies since legalized abortion was forced on Americans by the Supreme Court, has taken its immorality to an inconceivable level: It's now promoting bondage and sadomasochistic sex to teenagers. The agency received nearly $3 million in federal grant money that it used to promote these sexual practices while recommending that teenagers who engage in them follow the "rules" outlined in a video titled *Getting Kinky (BDSM 101)*. The video calls October "National Kink Month" and says that Halloween and kink are both about adventure and fun and exploring roles and dynamics that are maybe a little bit different from everyday life. Their justification for spreading this filth? Bondage and sadomasochism "relies upon and creates trust," according to video host Laci Green.[31]

And don't for a second think this filth isn't approved and sanctioned by the White House. The administration's grip on the media is so tight, their knuckles are white. Even though the mainstream press and television news corps turn a blind eye toward the excesses and corruption of this administration, they're not satisfied. They monitor and censor even their strongest supporters in the media. This even extends to the George Soros–funded Center for American Progress (CAP).

As I've said elsewhere, George Soros may be the most dangerous anti-American pro-socialist power monger in the world. Soros played an important part in manipulating the 2008 presidential election in order to put Barack Obama in office. How did the president thank him? He turned the tables on Soros, ordering his thugs to make sure CAP adhered to the Obama party line in the articles it published.

Zaid Jilani is a blogger who began working at Think-Progress, one of the adjuncts of CAP. When Jilani began writing in opposition to the continuation of the war in Afghanistan, the administration leapt on her. "Phone calls from the White House started pouring in," she said, "berating my bosses for being critical of Obama on this policy." The administration was acting more like the Kremlin than like the leaders of the world's freest nation. Jilani described the pressure she received from publishers and sponsors (i.e., the White House) as "suffocating."[32]

Reporters Without Borders, a group that monitors freedom of the press around the world, took notice of the Obama administration's stifling of the press. The self-described "most transparent" administration in American history has caused America's rank in the index of freedom of the press around the world to drop from 32nd to 46th among the 180 countries measured. Among the criteria used to measure freedom of the press were the things Jilani complained about: official abuse and lack of media independence.[33]

In maybe the most outrageous transgression against our freedom of the press, the administration planned to place government operatives in the nation's newsrooms through the Federal Communications Commission. The project was titled "Multi-Market Study of Critical Information Needs" (CIN), and these FCC "researchers," as they called themselves, would question everyone from reporters to editors to owners on how they decided which stories they would run.

Though the FCC said their motive for being in the newsrooms was research, it was apparent to nearly everyone that the real reason they were there was to police the newsrooms and eventually dictate which stories they could cover.

The people involved in assisting the FCC are the real indicator of how dangerous and subversive this project is. The FCC commissioner directly involved in trying to set up this incursion on the freedom of the press was Mignon Clyburn, the daughter of longtime representative James Clyburn, a former head of the Congressional Black Caucus and a man who has supported Obama's policies blindly. Mignon Clyburn is a committed leftist ideologue who described her mission with the FCC's proposed invasion of our news organizations as a way to "chart a course...to a more effective delivery of necessary information to all citizens...be they native born, immigrant, disabled, non-English speaking, low income, or other."[34]

As you can see, Clyburn named just about every interest group this administration caters to in its destruction of our borders, language, and culture. The "study" she was planning to conduct included topics such as emergencies and risks, health and welfare, the environment, education, transportation, economic opportunities, civic information, and political information. As I see it, they're all leftist code words for entitlements and dependency. My take is that Clyburn's intent was nothing less than to find out if America's newsrooms were meeting the criteria of the left. In other words, the FCC had an overtly political function.

Obama lieutenant John Podesta stomped on suggestions the project was a lightly veiled attempt at controlling the news, insisting that "any suggestion that the FCC intends to regulate the speech of news media or plans to put monitors in America's newsrooms is false." What Podesta failed to mention was that in 2007 he was running the Center for American Progress, and under his leadership the group produced a report that explained how the FCC could weaken conservative talk radio and replace it with progressive talk show hosts. Here's what he proposed:

> *Ownership diversity is perhaps the single most important variable contributing to the structural imbalance based on the data. Quantitative analysis conducted by Free Press of all 10,506 licensed commercial radio stations reveals that*

stations owned by women, minorities, or local owners are
statistically less likely to air conservative hosts or shows.[35]

Mignon Clyburn's FCC research project was the first step in bringing Podesta's vision of a shackled press into reality.

The Constitution specifically forbids anyone or any agency from "abridging the freedom of speech or of the press," but I see that was precisely what Clyburn and the FCC intended to do with this project. Was it all to be done in the interest of "fairness"?

Here's what "fairness" means to the administration when it comes to our religious beliefs: Just as he is intent on denying Christians and Christianity the freedom of their religious beliefs when they're serving in our country's armed forces, the president looks the other way as Islamist rebels in Syria kill Christians, wantonly torture women and children to death, and destroy Christian churches.

My question is this: Does this administration look the other way because it is jihadists who are committing these atrocities? In Syria, Bashar Assad—dictator that he may be—has always protected Christians; the "rebels"—who this administration appears to be supporting—are perpetrating the slaughter of Christians.[36]

The same thing happened in Egypt. When the military rose up to overthrow Egyptian president Mohammed Morsi, they were getting rid of a Muslim Brotherhood ruler who supported the murder of Christians.[37] The president sided with Morsi. In the events that led up to Morsi's election and subsequent removal, the administration had joined forces against a longtime American ally and defender of Christians' rights, Hosni Mubarak.

Political leftist leaders are waging war against Christians in places you wouldn't have suspected. New York governor Andrew Cuomo has declared that extreme conservatives "have no place in the state of New York."[38] At the same time, Pope Francis declared that liberation theology—the same doctrine espoused by Obama's pastor, the Rev. Jeremiah Wright—can no longer "remain in the shadows to which it has been relegated for some years." Of the principles and practices of capitalism, the Pope says, "A new tyranny is thus born."[39] The new tyranny, though, is not the tyranny of capitalism, under which Christianity has flourished; it's the tyranny of the leftists the Pope is aligning himself with, people for whom Christianity is anathema.

The Pope's words came as the Obama administration was persecuting the Little Sisters of the Poor for not being willing to give up their religious principles against birth control and abortion. Across the United States, the Little Sisters of the Poor run some thirty hospitals, which provide medical services for the elderly poor. The financial penalties this organization faces if they are forced to comply with Obamacare's mandates would put the nuns out of business in a matter of months.[40]

The United States is overwhelmingly a Christian nation. The editor in chief of the Gallup polling organization estimates that "about three-quarters—75, maybe up to 77 percent of Americans—identify with the Christian religion." Another 17 percent of Americans profess no religious affiliation, so the percentage of U.S. citizens with a religious practice other than Christianity is very small, likely as low as 5 or 6 percent.[41]

The president appears to be committed to the destruction of the majority religion of the country over which he presides.

Will English Become America's
Second Language?

I've mentioned Coca-Cola's Super Bowl commercial that featured "America the Beautiful" being sung in eight different languages. Ray Charles, who recorded the most moving version of that song I've ever heard, must be turning over in his grave. There was a day when immigrants took pride in learning the language of their adoptive home. Everyone knows that today you can't make a phone call to a government agency or business without being asked to press 1 if you want to speak English or 2 if you want Spanish. Somehow we managed to avoid "Press 3 for Ebonics." Healthcare.gov offers people who access the website a choice of forty-six different languages to buy their health care in. Forty-six!

Don't believe there's a war against the English language being waged in this country? In Texas, a grade-school principal was fired for requiring students to speak English in the classroom. More than half the students in the school district are Hispanic, and her critics said, "When you start banning aspects of ethnicity or cultural identity, it sends the message that the child is not wanted: 'We don't want your color. We don't want your kind.' They then tend to drop out early."[42]

In fact, it should send exactly the opposite message. Teaching Spanish-speaking kids the English language says to them that this country wants them to succeed, wants them to become American citizens and to be able to succeed in this country. Learning English is the one fundamental skill that guarantees they'll have a good chance to better themselves.

English is the standard language of international communications. Virtually every head of every Western nation speaks English. Every champion of every international athletic tournament I've ever watched—from soccer to tennis to the Olympics—has conducted his or her postgame interview in English, no matter what their native country is. But here in the United States, we're allowing the left to dictate which language we're required to speak, because politicians are too weak-kneed to make English the official language of the United States. It's the official language of the world, but we're not willing to acknowledge that here.

And that's by design.

It's possible that this administration's most remembered accomplishment will be the degeneration of our language and communication.

Nothing less than the very preservation of our borders, language, and culture is at stake right now. What makes us Americans is being taken from us. The survival of our beloved country has entered its most critical stage.

CHAPTER 4

The War on the U.S. Military

The insidiousness of Obama's military evisceration plan, one that has already seen hundreds of high-ranking officers dismissed, is that it not only removes our best and most dedicated soldiers, it destroys morale across our armed services. When capable young soldiers who once thought of making a career in the armed forces see what's happening to their superior officers, they decide to leave military service. Those who stay have to navigate a minefield of Obama's operatives just to do their job.

Let me start this chapter by giving you a quick history lesson. In early September 1901, then-vice president Theodore Roosevelt stood on a stage at the Minnesota State Fair and quoted an old proverb that would be from that moment on and forever his. Just two weeks later, he'd begin his tenure as one of our strongest presidents. And although an assassin's bullet—which ripped through President William McKinley's stomach—put Roosevelt in the Oval Office, the phrase he spoke to the Minnesota fairgoers is the foundation on which his presidential legend began: "Speak softly but carry a big stick."

I tell you this for one reason, so you can make a comparison with what we have in the White House right now. I don't think anybody since Teddy Roosevelt has put together a sentence that better captures how the president of the United States should act.

For this president, it's "Speak loudly and carry a limp stick."

What has been happening to veterans in our VA hospitals is a telltale sign of this administration's attitude toward the military.

Americans are beginning to wake up to the travesty that a federal government that controls our medical care has become. Everyone is finally realizing that what's happening in veterans' hospitals now will happen across our entire medical system under the Affordable Care Act. Many are now saying that what we see going on in our VA medical system—double sets of books, people dying because of delayed or unavailable treatment—is likely to be what's coming to the American medical industry.

The Veterans Affairs scandal finally surfaced in the spring of 2014, and we're all justifiably outraged as case after case comes to light in which our veterans are forced to wait, often for years, in order to even be seen by a VA doctor, let alone receive medical treatment.

Hundreds of veterans have died for lack of care, and thousands more have seen their health deteriorate to the point where they may not be able to recover. All this as the bureaucrats who fail to manage their care cover up their incompetence by creating phony wait lists and publishing outright lies in the form of reports.

Do you realize how bad the VA situation has become?

Do you realize that the current administration seems to care more about the health of illegal aliens in this country than it does about our veterans?

Let me give you a few examples.

The VA canceled some forty thousand tests and treatments that our veterans with cancer and other diseases and conditions needed. They did that so they could hide a backlog of treating our veterans that spanned more than a decade.[1]

At the same time, in one major city, upward of 40 percent of the patients receiving dialysis for kidney failure are illegal aliens. In Arizona alone, $700 million was spent providing medical treatment for illegal aliens, this while more than three dozen veterans died waiting for treatment in Phoenix VA facilities.[2]

More than two dozen VA facilities are now revealing that the veterans they're responsible for treating are backlogged, while the federal government that's responsible for treating them provides services for noncitizens in this country illegally.

The VA medical system is the same system that one commentator has said was a model for the entire U.S. health-care system to follow.[3]

The administration's military decisions are equally as questionable as their treatment of the soldiers who risk their lives in carrying out those decisions.

Think back to the president's making the case for a "targeted" military strike in Syria. We witnessed a mass of contradictory assertions and yet another "red line" drawn in the Middle Eastern sand that quickly disappeared as events there escalated.

Don't get me wrong. I'm not saying that the president

should have ordered a military strike on Syria. If you listen to my show at all, you know I'm an anti-war conservative in the best sense of that term. We're not the world's policeman. We should go to war *only* when our national interests are at stake. But that doesn't mean I'm against a strong military. The very definition of "anti-war conservatism" is having a "big stick." A nation with a muscular military is a nation whose borders are safe and whose ideals are intact.

The evidence indicates that our president is committed to the exact opposite. His goal appears to be to weaken our military until it can no longer defend our national interests. His military agenda, as you'll read in this chapter, is now becoming so obvious that even some of his once loyal following have begun to question it. He is sabotaging our proud military culture as he fires our most patriotic and competent commanders.

Let me start with what happened to one of our best military men.

Lt. Col. Matthew Dooley was an instructor at the Joint Forces Staff College at the National Defense University. The course he taught, Perspectives on Islam and Islamic Radicalism, was a very popular elective, mostly because of Dooley's teaching style. He was provocative and encouraged high-energy debate in his class. A West Point graduate and a highly decorated combat veteran, he brought his hard-earned, first-hand knowledge into his classroom. He received glowing reviews from his students and exemplary evaluations from school administrators.

Then, in September 2011, coinciding with the tenth anniversary of the worst terrorist attack ever to befall our country, *Wired* magazine published an unflattering and incendiary article about the treatment of Islam in antiterrorism courses taught by the FBI at Quantico. The fallout from the article prompted fifty-seven Islamic organizations to send a letter of outrage to the Department of Defense. The DoD ordered a review of the screening process of all antiterrorism instructors under its control, including Dooley. That April, *Wired* published a follow-up story that told of the suspension of Dooley's class.

It didn't stop there. Dooley was publicly criticized by the highest-ranking military officer in the U.S. Armed Forces, chairman of the Joint Chiefs of Staff General Martin Dempsey, who described the course material Dooley had developed as "totally objectionable." After Dempsey's criticism, Dooley received a career-ending Officer Evaluation Report.[4]

What had Dooley done to deserve all this? As I see it, he prepared our officers and civilian defense workers to confront the most dangerous aspects of radical Islamic jihad. His sin was that he tried to keep us safe.

Dooley's dismissal is one of many similar cases. They indicate that the military is engaging in what I find to be the dangerously subversive tactic of leveling serious charges at dozens of top military commanders. The targets of what I see as a wholesale purge are experienced, patriotic, high-ranking officers. They are being forced to resign or retire, or they are having their careers red-flagged.

Since 2009, more than two hundred U.S. military officers at the rank of colonel or higher have been removed from their commands. That's a rate of nearly one a week.[5]

One of those superior officers is Gen. James Mattis, the former head of the United States Central Command (CENT-COM). In January 2013, Mattis was dismissed for being too much of a hawk, especially when it came to the administration's lenient policy toward Iran. Unlike others in the administration, Mattis understood how dangerous a nuclear-armed Iran would be to our allies and to U.S. interests in the Middle East, and he wasn't afraid to speak out about it.[6]

Mattis—who once famously said, "There are some assholes in the world who just need to be shot"[7]—was known among his peers as someone who could defend the military in its ongoing dialogue with government functionaries. Both soldiers and civilians respected him, and he wasn't about to kowtow to anyone. He was exactly the type of commander our president both shrinks from and does all he can to remove.

The general received a note from one of his aides telling him he was being replaced as the head of Central Command. No one from the Pentagon or the White House was gracious enough to inform him about this.[8]

Two of our top nuclear commanders, Maj. Gen. Michael Carey and Vice Adm. Tim Giardina, left the armed forces within days of each other—both because of personal misconduct, according to reports and e-mails leaked to the press. The official report on Carey's dismissal says that while on temporary assignment in Moscow, Carey went on a vodka-drinking binge one night; he "needed assistance standing" at one point, and he had tried to get up onstage with a Beatles cover band in a Mexican restaurant…in Moscow![9]

At the time, he was commander of the Twentieth Air Force, responsible for all 450 of the Air Force's Minuteman 3 intercontinental ballistic missiles located in five U.S. states. Prior to that, General Carey served in both the Iraqi Freedom and Enduring Freedom operations. He is also the recipient of no fewer than thirteen major military awards and decorations.

Carey is an American hero, and yet he was "relieved of duty" for drinking vodka in Russia?

Was it not possible for the Air Force to provide an officer with Carey's credentials rehabilitation for the alleged alcohol problems instead of firing him?

Charges against Vice Admiral Giardina were no less fantastic. Giardina is graduate of the United States Naval Academy, a three-star admiral who is now the former deputy commander and chief of staff of the Pacific Fleet. You'd think that if you were going to relieve someone of this stature of his command and reassign him to a desk job, you'd come up with serious charges related to the performance of his duty. But, in a move that had to be approved by the president himself, Giardina was demoted for playing poker with counterfeit $100 chips in the Horseshoe Casino in Council Bluffs, Iowa.[10]

In other words, both of these commanders, who have outstanding military records and who have risen to the tops of their commands, were dismissed on charges that in my opinion would likely have gotten an enlisted man no more than a slap on the wrist.

One commentator described it this way:

The move is exceedingly rare and perhaps unprecedented in the history of US Strategic Command, which is responsible for all US nuclear warfighting forces, including nuclear-armed submarines, bombers and land-based missiles.[11]

It is no secret that our nuclear capability is rivaled only by Russia; actually, Russia is a pretty clear second in the nuclear arms race. Our nukes make us a superpower. We have the ability to win any war at any time. Period. It would stand to reason, then, that if the aim is to emasculate our military, one of the first targets would be our nuclear weapons capabilities.

Are you beginning to see a pattern here?

In January 2014, the Air Force suspended 93 of the 180 or so nuclear launch officers who are stationed at the Malmstrom Air Force Base in Montana. Malmstrom houses one-third of our ICBM force. The officers were suspended for allegedly cheating on their proficiency exams. News stories described the suspensions as the largest cheating scandal ever in the U.S. nuclear force. An investigation of allegations of illegal drug use led to the discovery of the possible cheating.

Those same stories, however, told of the low morale among the officers in Malmstrom. This particular command isn't the most exciting in our armed forces. Yet we're being told that nearly half of the officers there would risk their rank and military career to pass the proficiency test that certifies them for duty at Malmstrom. So we're supposed to believe that they hate being at Malmstrom but they'd cheat on a test to stay there?

Don't get me wrong: I don't condone cheating. But it seems to me that in this instance, the cheating may have more to do with the military culture at the base than with the character of the men accused.

After an investigation was initiated, the scandal grew to include widespread drug use among the officers. Before it was finished, nine mid-level nuclear commanders had been fired, and dozens of junior officers were disciplined. Air Force officials described the punishment as unprecedented in the history of our intercontinental missile program.

Rather than attempt to identify and correct the conditions that brought about the alleged cheating and drug use, our military chose to take punitive action. By the time our military operatives in the Air Force are through at Malmstrom, there'll be no one left manning the gates of hell.

The neutering of our missile defense didn't stop there.

The proposed military budget cuts $128 million from the Tomahawk missile program for fiscal year 2015, and money to support the Tomahawk program is eliminated altogether for fiscal year 2016. In other words, the world's most advanced cruise missile is being removed from our arsenal. The budget for another effective weapon, the Hellfire missile, has been eliminated entirely for 2015. We won't need the missile base at Malmstrom at all once the administration gets finished eliminating our most effective military weapons.[12]

The fact that these cuts of critical weapons came as a shock to legislators and military experts shows you that they don't understand that this administration is out to neuter our military and our capability of defending ourselves against attack.

I'm only getting started telling you about what I see as the incalculable damage this administration is doing to our military.

Firing generals in wartime is a very rare occurrence, but that hasn't prevented this administration from conducting a wholesale dismissal of our military commanders. The number of officers relieved of their command is extraordinary. During the eight years of the Bush administration, only once did the position of commander of the International Security Assistance Force (ISAF) in Afghanistan change. Under the current administration, there have already been five.[13]

In 2009, Gen. David McKiernan, the Afghanistan commander of the ISAF, resigned. One source explained the reason for McKiernan's resignation this way: "He [McKiernan] had demanded competency from an incompetent Democrat [Obama]."

Another source explained that he was "fired" because he was too "old school."

In other words, he was a patriot who might well have stood in the way of the ongoing dismantling of the U.S. military.[14]

The officer who replaced McKiernan as ISAF commander didn't last long in the job. Gen. Stanley McChrystal was not old school. He was young and had fresh ideas about how to conduct the war against a terrorist enemy. McChrystal's mistake was making his contemptuous opinion of Barack Obama known in a *Rolling Stone* magazine article, "The Runaway General."

McChrystal made the mistake of telling what he saw as the truth about Obama.

He explained that in their first face-to-face meeting the president didn't even know who McChrystal was, let alone anything about the general's war record.[15] In the article, McChrystal also correctly described the administration's chief national security advisor, James Jones, as "a clown."[16]

It's understandable that McChrystal had to be dismissed, but his dismissal raises a much deeper concern about the administration's relationships with the country's top military officers.

As the news about the president's inability, even his unwillingness, to deal fairly with military commanders began to reach the public, the White House felt the need to respond. White House chief of staff Denis McDonough told the *Washington Post* that the president appreciated candid military advice "above all else." In his public statement, McDonough explained that the president maintains "close, and in some instances warm, relationships with his military chiefs." One general recently returned to the States after serving in Afghanistan had a different view, saying that the White House would rather the military be seen and not heard.[17]

The Benghazi Murders

Perhaps the most obvious example of how what I see as the decimation of our military is making us a pawn to the world's leftist movement is the murders in Benghazi. I would be remiss if I didn't explain how that night fits into what's happening with our military.

Do you remember the general whom Obama appointed to replace McChrystal?

It was David Petraeus.

Petraeus lasted nearly two years before he resigned. By the time he left government service, Petraeus had graduated to the position of head of the CIA.

The alleged reason he resigned?

He had been involved in an extramarital affair.

The administration had known about Petraeus's dalliance with the woman who wrote his biography since he was vetted to assume the position of CIA director. The administration had known about his affair for months before he resigned.

Two of America's most experienced military commanders also lost their jobs in the wake of the Benghazi murders. Gen. Carter Ham and Rear Adm. Charles M. Gaouette were relieved of duty because they tried to intervene and prevent the loss of four Americans' lives.

The first eyewitness to the Benghazi attack, a security guard who worked at the compound helping to protect American personnel, has made it clear that the State Department had known for a long time that an attack on the consulate in Libya was inevitable, yet few steps were taken to fortify the compound or to otherwise secure it.[18]

Here's what former assistant secretary of defense Frank Gaffney believes happened on the night of September 11, 2012, based on the available evidence: The Obama administration appears to have been involved in a gunrunning operation that was being managed by Ambassador Christopher Stevens out of the Benghazi consulate. Stevens is alleged to have been coordinating the delivery of military weapons, including as many as twenty thousand Stinger missiles, to rebel fighters involved in the overthrow of Libyan dictator Moammar Gadhafi. After Gadhafi was ousted, Stevens was said to be further coordinating a massive transfer of weapons to rebels in several Middle Eastern areas, including Syria. Many, if not most, of the rebels were affiliated with al Qaeda.[19]

The Obama administration appears to have been supporting terrorism through providing weapons to the very Islamists the United States is supposedly fighting against in the war on terror. If this is true, the administration certainly feared that Stevens would make details of the gunrunning public.

Was that the reason why, when the attack on the Benghazi compound began, the decision was made not to send help?

Contrary to the Obama administration's official story, Gen. Carter Ham, then the commanding officer of the U.S. Africa Command, was receiving live communications from various intelligence assets that provided real-time details of what was happening on the ground. In addition, there were dozens of CIA operatives on the ground in Benghazi who could have been used to rescue those in danger.[20]

Ham began organizing a Special Forces team to intervene in Benghazi immediately after he received news of the assault on the Benghazi ambassador's compound.

Even though he received the order to stand down—likely from Defense Secretary Leon Panetta, who may have been receiving his orders from Valerie Jarrett[21]—Ham went ahead with his rapid response plan. In order to stop him, one source says that the administration had the commanding general apprehended. Ham was informed that he was relieved of his command, which stopped his attempt to save American lives.[22]

In making preparations to intervene, Ham had been communicating with Rear Admiral Gaouette, commander of Carrier Strike Group Three. Gaouette, who like Ham had received the desperate requests for help from Stevens and his team, was also preparing the assets under his command to intervene and save the lives of those under attack in Benghazi.[23]

I think that Gaouette was relieved of his command because he wouldn't stand down and watch Americans die, as he may have been ordered to do.

Ham, the general in charge of military assets in North Africa and one of the men who could have saved the four lives that were lost in the Benghazi massacre, told a Republican congressman that he had not received any requests for military intervention in Benghazi.[24]

After an official investigation, Gaouette, too, was disciplined, ostensibly because he had been accused of using profanity in a public setting and making at least two racially insensitive comments, officials familiar with the investigation said.[25]

No mention was made of Benghazi.

Is it possible that Obama may have recognized that these two decorated military officers were patriots who put duty to their country first? Might he have thought that their refusal to deny help to Americans in Benghazi would have denied the administration the ability to cover up the fact that it was supplying weapons to "rebels" who were often fighting on the side of al Qaeda? Might the president have been thinking that patriots like Gaouette and Ham would stand in the way of his power grab if it became necessary?

There were other casualties on the night of the Benghazi attack.

David Ubben, a diplomatic security agent, was in Benghazi on the night of the terrorist assault. Ubben acted heroically on that night.

Early in the evening he went back into the burning Benghazi consulate several times in an effort to rescue Sean Smith, one of the four killed. When he finally found him, Smith was already dead from smoke inhalation. Smith had also reentered the consulate several more times in an effort to locate Ambassador Stevens, but he was unsuccessful.

As the attack progressed, Ubben joined Tyrone Woods and Glen Doherty on the roof of the CIA annex as they tried to defend the building against dozens of terrorists who were attacking it.

The mortar that killed Woods and Doherty also shattered Ubben's leg.

Fox News reported the incident this way:

David Ubben waited for twenty hours after he was hit on that rooftop with Tyrone Woods and Glenn Doherty. His leg was shredded. We know that he had been recovering for ten months afterward at Walter Reed National Military Medical Center. He was defending the U.S. consulate, and yet no medical assets were sent to the scene to help him. How could this be?[26]

What wasn't reported at the time was what the commander in chief of the United States Armed Forces was doing.

First, the president was getting a good night's sleep as the attack raged on.

When he woke up on the morning of September 12, 2012, he flew to Las Vegas to make a campaign appearance—although the attack was still not resolved.[27]

In the wake of the Benghazi murders, Rep. Frank Wolf accused the administration of operating a gunrunning operation that sent weapons captured in Libya to Syrian rebels. In the wake of these accusations, the military has been ordered to conduct polygraph tests as often as once a month on dozens of people who have knowledge of what happened on the night of the Benghazi murders. The polygraph tests are almost certainly done to determine if those people have told others what really happened. It's very likely that this is the administration's way of intimidating anyone who's tempted to speak out against the decisions made at the top of the administration.[28]

A year and a half later, the House Subcommittee on Oversight and Investigations released a report that said, "White House officials failed to comprehend or ignored the dramatically deteriorating security situation in Libya." The White House statements to the contrary were exaggerations. Despite warnings from embassy and other personnel close to the situation, Hillary Clinton's State Department was recommending that security personnel be reduced leading up to the Benghazi murders.

When the attack occurred, U.S. forces that might have intervened were not ready, and there was no clear description of how a response might have been launched if needed.

In other words, neither the State Department nor the Department of Defense had taken the "deteriorating security environment in Libya" seriously.[29]

The report explains all this, but it leaves out the most important aspects of the Benghazi failure. My view is that even despite the lack of preparation and the underestimation of the chance of an attack, those who did try to mount a counter-offensive to save our personnel were forbidden to take action.

They were forced to stand down.

Americans died.

In January 2014, the U.S. Senate Select Committee on Intelligence released its bipartisan report on the Benghazi terrorist attacks. It contained information so shocking, I can't believe it hasn't been the focus of an investigation. The report said that "as many as fifteen individuals supporting the investigation or otherwise helpful to the United States have been killed in Benghazi since the [September 11, 2011] attacks."[30]

Fifteen people who helped us in Benghazi have been killed since then?

Are we supposed to believe that those deaths are not somehow connected to the fact that these people helped us on that night? Are we supposed to believe that their deaths are just a coincidence?

Or do you think that their identities might have somehow gotten into the hands of our jihadist enemies and that those who helped us are being systematically eliminated by terrorists?

The purging of our own seasoned military commanders may well go beyond what happened in Benghazi.

As I've said, it is likely that there is a contingent in the U.S. military that wants to see President Obama ousted. In addition, though, some of the most powerful men and organizations in the world are also in favor of ousting Obama. They would love to see the president marched out of office.

Is it possible that the president has for the past several years been appointing his own handpicked military officers to second-in-command positions in many areas of the military? Might they be put in place in order to monitor how the commanders are handling their jobs and to report any threats their commanding officers might present to what many see as an ongoing takeover of the U.S. military by the current administration?

Obama seems to be continuing his purge of the military in order to avoid the kind of refusal to obey his orders that occurred on the night of the Benghazi attack. But his purge has other implications.

Is Our Military Being Emasculated?

The president's weakened military faces new threats from around the world. I'll deal at great length in the next chapter with the threat that Russia poses for us as it annexes Crimea and advances its takeover of bordering countries. For now I want to explain to you the threat we face as Iran and China up the military ante in the Middle and Far East.

In late 2011, Iran threatened to station its warships off the U.S. coast. The threat came only a few months after Iran had sent warships through the Suez Canal, the first time that nation had ever deployed warships in the Mediterranean Sea.

In early 2014, Iran made good on the threat, announcing that its warships were on their way across the Atlantic Ocean with the intention of being stationed in international waters near the U.S. coast. This move is assumed to be a response to the U.S. stationing its warships near Iran.

One expert sees the Iranian move as a dry run in order to embarrass Barack Obama and at the same time make U.S. military commanders and advisors drop their guard when the ships take no hostile action. The most likely tactic the Iranians might use from military vessels would be an electromagnetic pulse attack, which could disable our electrical grid and disrupt communications.

It may be more than a dry run. After Iran had said it would station its warships in a threatening position, the Iranian Revolutionary Guard claimed that it was in possession of missiles capable of carrying multiple warheads. Iranian defense minister Hossein Dehghan formally announced the delivery of four different types of ballistic missiles, named Qiam, Qadr H1, Fateh-110, and Persian Gulf. He said, "These missiles are able to hit and destroy enemy targets with precision, and they meet a variety of the armed forces' needs. The weapons have strengthened Iran's deterrence power and military might."[31]

Now that might be nothing more than military bluster, but what it does point out is that Iran is mocking Obama and his unwillingness to oppose its terrorist intentions against our country. One Iranian general called Obama a "low-IQ president" whose threats to intervene in the Syrian crisis were "the joke of the year." He elaborated: Obama and John Kerry "speak of the effectiveness of 'the US options on the table' on Iran while this phrase is mocked at and has become a joke among the Iranian nation, especially the children."[32]

The threat that the Iranians were laughing at? Obama had said in an interview that he has "a high degree of confidence" that the Iranians will flinch "when they look at 35,000 US military personnel in the region that are engaged in constant training exercises under the direction of a president who already has shown himself willing to take military action in the past, that they should take my statements seriously."[33]

The reason he needs to *tell* Iran and our other enemies around the world that they should be afraid of us is that what he's doing to the military sends exactly the opposite message.

He's cutting back on the U.S. military drastically in the face of growing threats from Iran, China, and Russia. How serious are those cuts? The Pentagon plans to reduce the number of soldiers by 70,000 to 80,000, to as few as 440,000. That represents the elimination of more than an eighth of the total number of soldiers in our armed forces. Chuck Hagel explains it as a matter of cutting costs: "Congress has taken some important steps in recent years to control the growth in compensation spending, but we must do more."[34]

In a time of global military conflict, Obama wants to weaken our military even further than he has already. A president who has never met a domestic spending program he didn't want to triple in size has decided to cut spending where we most need it: from our defense of our country against foreign enemies who already understand he is the weakest president in U.S. history.

In the 1960s, about 7 percent of members of the U.S. armed forces were married. Today, nearly 50 percent of America's volunteer army, navy, and air force are married. So, of course, Obama decides to slash benefits, including health-care copays and deductibles. He would also reduce the subsidies military families receive for housing and other goods. So how does Obama propose to make some of these cuts? On the backs of our married military fighters. The proposed cuts would make it much more difficult for military families to make ends meet. A 1 percent ceiling on military pay increases, coupled with a likely 5 percent increase in housing costs, would mean that an army sergeant with a family of four would face a $1,400 annual salary cut, while an army captain would lose $2,100 in income.[35]

Obama cuts our military families' benefits while he's giving free food and medical care to illegal aliens. As former vice president Dick Cheney put it, Obama "would much rather spend the money on food stamps than he would on a strong military or support for our troops." Beyond that, Cheney said, "our allies around the world are absolutely convinced that they can no longer trust the United States to keep its commitments—that includes the Israelis, Saudis, a lot of others in that part of the world." In addition to decimating our military capability, the Obama administration has not taken steps to increase our grid security, and military advisors are recommending that the governments of states along our coastlines do that on their own.

So much for Obama's "threat" that Iran should be wary of U.S. military power in the Middle East. It's Iran's own threats that we need to be worried about. Those threats should be interpreted as a thumb in Obama's eye. Iran sees the president as having submitted to its will and will not stop it from gaining nuclear weapons.[36]

At the same time, a top Iranian commander has indicated that Iran has used Hezbollah troops to infiltrate the United States, saying, "America, with its strategic ignorance, does not have a full understanding of the power of the Islamic Republic. We have recognized America's military strategy, and have arranged our abilities, and have identified centers in America [for attack] that will create a shock."[37]

As the Geneva nuclear deal is being implemented, security officials in the Middle East have confirmed that Iran is proposing to participate with Russia in joint military exercises.[38] Iran is in Russia's backyard, and not in America's backyard. The United States has effectively given up its positions of strength in the Middle East because the Obama administration has sided with the wrong players in every foreign policy decision it has made.

In addition, China has developed a new supersonic missile capable of delivering both conventional and nuclear warheads. It's what's known as a hypersonic glide vehicle, which is launched into space, from where it is allowed to glide to its target at speeds of up to eight thousand miles per hour. It is very difficult to defend against, and the Chinese have indicated that it is intended for use against aircraft carriers at sea.[39]

As this threat was being revealed, Adm. Afshin Rezayee Haddad, the commander of Iran's Northern Navy Fleet, announced that "Iran's military fleet is approaching the United States' maritime borders, and this move has a message."

The message he's trying to send to Barack Obama is that

this is Iran's response to the presence of American warships in the Persian Gulf.[40]

Adding insult to injury, Iran media showed a "documentary" video that contained simulated footage depicting Iranian drone missiles bombing the Israeli cities of Tel Aviv and Haifa, as well as the Ben Gurion airport and the Dimona nuclear reactor. This was intended to show what would happen in the event of an Israeli or a combined U.S.-Israel attack on Iran. In the video, Iranian drone missiles were also shown engaging in attacks on the USS *Abraham Lincoln* and other targets in the Persian Gulf.

Iranian leader Ayatollah Ali Khamenei explained that he thought it was "amusing" that the United States thought Iran might diminish its military capabilities.[41]

Don't get me wrong: Iran is no military match for the United States.

The problem is that we have a commander in chief who is decimating our military.

He's allowing America to be bullied by forces that are not close to what our military is capable of.

I believe that he's signaling to the world that he's afraid. Beyond that, I'm convinced that he's intentionally attempting to gut our military with what amounts to a leftist, anti-American military cleansing.

The U.S. military is increasingly unready to respond to the forces amassing against it.

The Middle East is in chaos thanks in large part to Obama's mismanagement of the situation in Syria and his failure to negotiate a status of forces agreement with Iraq, which is descending into chaos at the hands of terrorists who are taking over more and more territory in that country. Afghanistan will soon follow.[42]

Obama's hostility toward making sure our military is prepared to fight in the event it is necessary, coupled with the steep decline of morale among our war-weary soldiers, make the threats of China and Iran more disturbing.

Retired army general Robert Scales says this: "The Army has 85% of its brigades not combat-ready. It does not have one single developmental program for a combat system at all. Zero."[43]

The question is, how far will Obama go in order to save his presidency?

The insidiousness of Obama's military evisceration plan, one that has already taken down Dooley, Mattis, McChrystal, and others of their superior level, is that it not only removes our best officers, it destroys morale across our armed services. When capable young soldiers who once thought of making a career in the armed forces see what's happening to their superior officers, they decide to leave military service. Those who stay have to navigate a minefield of Obama's operatives and political correctness just to do their job.

For instance, at a time when radical Islam is at our door, more attention is paid to so-called "sexual assaults" in the military than to how enemies are trying to attack us. In the past year, reports of sexual assaults on women have risen by 46 percent.[44] Forty-six percent! So, all of a sudden, just like that, our military is filled with sexual predators?

Listen. I don't think there is anything more despicable than a man forcing himself on a woman. There's no place for that type of crap in the military. But equally reprehensible, in my view, is the false accusation of sexual assault. And I don't think there's any question that false accusations, and Obama's feminist agenda, have driven the reports of sexual assaults to implausible heights.

Feminism's influence in the military is growing faster than Antarctic ice. Assault can mean something as simple as being told, "Honey, you're cute."

Feminists have long lobbied for women to be allowed in combat, and the military is planning on making that happen by 2016. And in keeping with the Obama army's attempts to feminize the military, the Marine Corps seems to want to "ensure that female Marines are provided with the best opportunity to succeed."[45]

Do you know how they're likely to help female Marines "succeed"?

By lowering the physical standards for them.

According to traditional army requirements, recruits have to be able to do a minimum of three pull-ups. Anecdotal evidence from boot camps indicates that nearly half the female recruits cannot accomplish the pull-up requirement.

In chapter 9, I'll explain to you how our school system has been reduced in quality by defining educational success as having equal outcomes for all students, regardless of their intelligence or capabilities.

The military is gradually doing the same thing. It has redefined itself, so it seems, to include women on the battlefield, despite the fact that in this case, unlike in education, soldiers' lives may well be put at risk by having to depend on other soldiers who are physically unable to meet the requirements necessary to do their jobs.

The military's transformation based on the principle of the equality of the sexes doesn't stop with attempting to put women in combat or redefining sexual assault in order to include behavior that has nothing to do with sexual assault. It is part of Obama's agenda, and it has only one goal: to weaken the military on every single level.

The government has spent more time on gerrymandering standards than on prosecuting Maj. Nidal Hasan, a Muslim who killed thirteen and wounded thirty-two at Fort Hood. Beyond that, because soldiers are not allowed to carry weapons at Fort Hood—this thanks to another Democratic president, Bill Clinton—three more were murdered and more than a dozen injured in a second shooting at the same base.

And no one is looking into the likely penetration by agents of radical Islam into the FBI, the CIA, the DHS, and the military itself.

I see these as the by-products of a radical regime.

I believe that the president's decimation of our military's command structure has roots in his fear of losing his authority over our armed forces. My view is that he is removing military commanders who he suspects of being patriotic and bound by oath to the Constitution and replacing them with officers he thinks will be loyal to him.

Thanks to this administration's handling of the military, I fear that our armed forces are weakened to the point at which the remaining Western democracies have no reliable ally against the threat of our enemies today. The world is a dangerous place. As Islamist terrorists expand into standing armies, and as the military threat of China and Russia grows, there is no place for vulnerable nations to turn.

After the president announced a military pivot to focus more on the Far East and the increasing military belligerence of China, Adm. Samuel J. Locklear III, chief of the Pacific

Command, had this to say about our military presence there: "Our historic dominance that most of us in this room have enjoyed is diminishing."[46]

In the wake of Obama's ongoing purge, the question is not "Who will our allies turn to for protection?" but "Who will *we* turn to when we can no longer defend ourselves?"

Are you starting to see a pattern?

Ask yourself these simple questions:

Why are top commanders being purged from our military?

Is the president responding to those in our military who might disagree with his policies?

Is the president fearful of a potential military *coup* against his presidency?

Let's go back to some not-so-distant history for the answers.

Former Egyptian president Mohammad Morsi abandoned the democratic principles he was elected to uphold and tried to make Egypt into an Islamic dictatorship under the Muslim Brotherhood. But, ultimately, Morsi failed, was overthrown, and placed in jail. By the Egyptian military.

As I see it, the president may be fearful of having his authority challenged by his own military commanders. It may go so far as his intentional purge of our military commanders in order to preemptively guard against the possibility of a coup such as the one that overthrew Morsi.

In my opinion, the reason why Obama initially suspended *some* U.S. financial aid to Egypt after Morsi's ouster was that he favors the Muslim Brotherhood and hates any movement toward democratic governance in the Middle East. But beyond that, I think he sees the overthrow of Morsi, who had assumed dictatorial powers, as a foreshadowing of what might happen to him as he moves in a similar direction.

I haven't lost hope. While the story I'm about to relate might seem insignificant, I find it very promising.

Some of you might be familiar with the Navy Jack "Don't Tread on Me" flag. Similar to the Gadsden flag, used by our Marines during the American Revolution, the Navy Jack, with its snake insignia, has struck fear in the hearts of our enemies on the seas. More recently, at the beginning of the war on terror, the U.S. Navy instructed its ships as a matter of code to fly the Navy Jack flag, and Navy SEALs were allowed to wear the flag as a shoulder patch, which they did in unison.

A former Navy SEAL by the name of Carl Higbie publicized an e-mail that a former SEAL teammate had intercepted on October 22, 2013. The e-mail came from a senior enlisted advisor stating that SEALs were no longer allowed to wear the Navy Jack "Don't Tread on Me" patch:

> *ALL:*
>
> *WARCOM and GROUP TWO/ONE have pushed out the uniform policy for NWU III and any patches worn on the sleeve.*
>
> *All personnel are only authorized to wear the matching "AOR" American Flag patch on the right shoulder. You are no longer authorized to wear the "Don't Tread On Me" patch.*
>
> *Again the only patch authorized for wear is the American flag on the right shoulder. Please pass the word to all*
>
> > *Thanks*
> > *Senior Enlisted Advisor*

Higbie responded with an op-ed piece in the *Daily Caller*. "The Obama administration and the yes-men top brass have decided to wage war on our Navy's heritage," he wrote. "Will the SEALs choose to defend that heritage and defy them, with all the impertinence the flag's slogan implies? Or will they be tread upon?"[47]

As it turns out, it was the former. I know of not one SEAL who removed the patch. And the administration not only blinked, it caved. Earlier this year, a spokesperson for the Navy released a statement saying that the flag patch, once authorized only for personnel who were deployed overseas, is now also authorized for wear in the continental United States.

Though this victory might have been small, the significance is huge. Our side has a heartbeat, and it pounds in the chests of the brave men in our fighting force. This is where we start to fight back. This is where we begin, by following our military's lead in standing up for the Constitutional principles on which this nation was built.

Ultimately, we must find a way to fight back that avoids a civil war. Like the military commanders whose stories I've told in this chapter, we must stand up and fight for what is right.

CHAPTER 5

The War on the Middle Class

The goals of this administration's economic policies are simple: funnel increasingly worthless billions of dollars into the hands of the economic vultures that have taken over the economy while increasing the number of Americans dependent on the federal government to support them at a subsistence level.

Historians will argue about the turning point of the American Civil War until they run out of breath. Some will say it was the Battle of Gettysburg, others the crossing of Burnside's Bridge in the Battle of Antietam. Still more insist it was the death of Stonewall Jackson that ended a Confederate hope for victory.

What I find remarkable is that there was a turning point at all. The Civil War was not a fair fight. The South was out-machined, out-manned, and out-moneyed—and by a considerable margin. The amount of resolve, guile, and guts the

Confederate Army showed was such a surprise to the North they almost lost the war before they knew what was happening to them.

But when the discussion turns to the economic factors that tipped the balance of the Civil War, there are few who dispute the importance of the Union Navy's capture of New Orleans.

To give you the junior high school summary: The North had an industrial-based economy. The South's was agricultural, mostly tobacco and cotton. It was primarily cotton exported to England that funded the war for the South. Now, from which port do you think the cotton from the South was shipped?

If you said New Orleans, you get an A.

Once the North was successful in its blockade of New Orleans and other Southern ports, the South was in big financial trouble. They had no money coming in; they couldn't trade cotton for guns or supplies; they couldn't even pay their troops.

So what did they do?

They printed money. They printed it until they nearly ran out of ink. Until they practically papered all of Dixie with worthless Confederate notes.

And how do you think that worked out for them?

At the beginning of the Civil War, the Confederate States dollar was worth ninety cents on the U.S. dollar. Toward the war's end, the Confederate buck had dropped to less than two cents on the dollar against its northern counterpart.

If the South's solution to its financial trouble sounds familiar, it should. I'll tell you why in a moment, but first let's put down some factual foundation to this chapter.

I've told you the ways this administration's policies are

designed to polarize every segment of the population, from gender to age. But the most serious wedge, the wedge that causes the most pain and does the most damage, is the wedge they drive between the economic classes.

The goals of this administration's economic policies are simple: *Funnel increasingly worthless billions of dollars into the hands of the economic vultures that have taken over the economy while increasing the number of Americans dependent on the federal government to support them at a subsistence level.*

The End of the Middle Class

Under the Obama administration, the number of have-nots continues to climb to levels not seen since the1930s.

How bad has it gotten? Let me give you an example. Outside of Baltimore, Maryland, in an area called "the woodlands," a makeshift community has sprung up. The houses are made of sheets of plastic or canvas and furnished with discarded mattresses, crates, and busted lawn chairs. The city's homeless, who feel safer living out on their own than in homeless shelters, occupy this shantytown.[1]

The same phenomenon occurred during the Great Depression. The shantytowns then were called Hoovervilles, after Herbert Hoover. Many held our thirty-first president responsible for the dire economic conditions that forced so many into poverty.

The tent community outside of Baltimore has been appropriately named after another president.

It's called "Obamaville."

And Obamavilles are now starting to appear like skin cancers across the country.

Their occupants are the most visible victims of our stagnant economy.

You don't have to be a Republican or a conservative to understand what kind of economic danger we're in right now. While the White House is inundated with scandals, the gang on Wall Street that broke the economy in 2008 is at it again.

They're speculating beyond comprehension.

They're trading on derivatives that don't even exist. They have created fiduciary instruments that aren't real.

They've run the stock market up to unsupportable levels.

Why?

Because federal power brokers have given them the green light.

The fat cats on Wall Street don't care that they're profiting off an agenda that has an ultimate goal of socialism and ruin. It doesn't bother them in the least that the money that fuels their private jets and pays for their personal chefs and exclusive country clubs comes right out of the pockets of a dying middle class.

As long as the greenbacks are flowing, the Wall Street gang will keep their mouths shut.

As long as they're making billions of dollars in trades on information you and I will never see, they're happy.

As long as Wall Street regulations do more harm than good to American taxpayers, they're perfectly content.

Rather than setting policies that put the poor back to work, those who steer our fortunes have built a kind of trapdoor economy through which more and more middle-class Americans have dropped into poverty.

Here's how they're getting away with it:

- Setting near-zero "stimulus" interest rates that wildly inflate the stock market while gutting middle-class savings.
- Creating an absurd number of new regulations that business owners, especially owners of small businesses who want to expand, have to abide by.
- Redefining full-time employment as thirty hours a week through Obamacare, which has all but eliminated the core jobs of many middle- and upper-middle-class employees, pushing them into part-time status or causing them to lose their jobs altogether and become dependent on the government for unemployment benefits, food stamps, and welfare in order to survive.

Our increasingly manipulated economy is destroying the middle class, robbing taxpaying Americans who have jobs and run small businesses of their hard-earned money by using their tax dollars to bail out the biggest and most corrupt banks in the world. At the same time, the administration turns a blind eye to the corruption of the megabanks that now control the economy.

So what does the South's economic policy during the Civil War have to do with the way things are now? I'll tell you. But I must warn you first, the results of this administration's agenda are at least as devastating as those that crippled the Confederate States and quite possibly could signal the end, not just of economic prosperity in this country, but of free-market capitalism itself.

The Fed

The Federal Reserve Bank, formerly under Ben Bernanke and now under Janet Yellen, has effectively become the lead player in what, as I see it, amounts to a banking conspiracy.

Our founding fathers were very clear when they drafted the Constitution. They said that it was Congress, and not a banking system, that had the authority to "coin Money [and] regulate the value thereof."[2] Now, I'm not saying that today's Congress would do a better job than the Fed of controlling the money supply, but at least we could vote them out of office if we felt they were driving us into financial ruin.

The Fed is "a unique public/private structure that operates within the government, but is still relatively independent of government."[3] It is effectively immune to the will of the people.

It's become the tool of crony capitalists around the world who have commandeered not only the U.S. financial industry but global finance as well. And as I noted earlier, one of the primary ways the Fed is manipulating our economy is through artificially keeping interest rates near zero percent.

It's done that through its policy of quantitative easing.

The Fed started the practice of quantitative easing, or QE as it's known, after the economic crash of 2008. Its purpose was to use taxpayer money to bail out the largest U.S. financial institutions. What started as a temporary and limited attempt to restore the liquidity of major U.S. banks became a perpetual nightmare. Since the bailout began, there have been three rounds of quantitative easing. We're now well into QE3.

In implementing quantitative easing (and here's where we're

replicating the fiscal policy of the Confederacy), the Fed prints tens of billions of dollars a month—up to a trillion dollars annually—for the purpose of buying U.S. Treasury bonds and worthless mortgage-backed securities in order to keep interest rates near zero percent.

When Ben Bernanke stepped down and Janet Yellen, another financial crony of the corrupt bankers, took over, Bernanke had printed $4,102,138,000,000.00—that's $4 trillion in what amounts to Confederate counterfeit money.

It shows up on the Fed's balance sheet as debt, and American taxpayers are on the hook for that debt. To give you an idea of how much counterfeit money $4 trillion is, it's more than the IRS collects in income taxes from American citizens in an entire year. The worthless debt on the Fed's balance sheet has increased almost 400 percent since Bernanke took over as Fed chairman in 2006.

That $4 trillion represents the administration's attempt to simulate the economy.[4]

When Bernanke tried to "taper" down the amount of QE debt he was creating each month from $85 billion to $75 billion, the stock market tanked.

Don't get me wrong. I'm all for business being profitable. What I object to is our government funneling money to financial crooks so they can continue to game the system.

When the Fed dropped monthly QE spending down to $65 billion a month, stocks plunged again.

Bernanke has handed the American taxpayers a four-*trillion*-dollar saddle, fiat currency that is backed only by the increasingly hollow "full faith and credit" of the U.S. federal government.

Come to think of it, what the South did during the Civil

War was more responsible than what is happening now. The South only printed money.

The Fed is printing debt.

As long as the interest rate remains near zero, we pay only a small amount—about 6 percent of federal government spending a year[5]—as interest on the federal debt. But each increase of 1 percent in the interest rate adds another $200 billion the feds have to shell out. At 5 percent, they'll be spending more than a trillion dollars a year on interest payments alone. This money comes out of taxpayers' pockets.

Let me put that into perspective for you: The total amount the federal government takes in annually through income and other federal taxes is less that $3 trillion.[6]

When the interest rate on the federal debt reaches 5 percent—not an outrageous number by any means—we'll be paying more than a third of federal revenues on federal debt interest alone.

The Fed's solution? Keep adding to the debt in order to keep interest payments low.

The problem is this: If interest rates rise, and they always do, then we're broke.

It's the most utterly irresponsible policy imaginable; the policy affects everything from quality of life to foreign policy to our ability to defend ourselves militarily.

Since QE and the Fed's money printing spree, do you know what has happened to Americans' savings?

They've disappeared.

Those artificially low interest rates have cost Americans $9 trillion in interest that they should have received on the money in their savings accounts. Instead of the interest going to Americans who responsibly saved their money, it was transferred to megabanks so they could gamble it away on risky investments.[7]

If you had put $100 in a savings account in 2008, by 2014 you would have made about ninety cents in interest. Less than one dollar—or nine-tenths of 1 percent—in six years. After you factor in cost-of-living increases, you actually lose money when you put it in the bank.

Retired people, unable to earn any interest on their savings because of the Fed's zero-interest-rate policy, are being forced to draw down their savings in order to pay their bills.[8]

Eliminating their ability to save money is one of the ways the left continues its ongoing attack on responsible middle-class Americans.

A former Ronald Reagan advisor sums up quantitative easing this way:

> QE [is] a scheme for pumping profits into the banks and boosting their balance sheets. The real purpose of QE is to drive up the prices of the debt-related derivatives on the banks' books, thus keeping the banks with solvent balance sheets.[9] The financial world is under Washington's thumb. And Washington is printing money for the sake of 4 or 5 mega-banks.[10]

I'd change one thing in the advisor's statement: It's clear to me that the financial world is not under Washington's thumb.

It's Washington that is under the financial world's thumb.

How good is quantitative easing for fat-cat bankers and hedge fund crooks? "It's the greatest Wall Street backdoor bailout of all time," says one former Federal Reserve official.

Andrew Huszar was in charge of the Fed's bond-buying spree after the 2008 financial collapse. In late 2013, Huszar finally came to his senses and realized that quantitative easing was implemented only to increase the price of the derivatives in order to keep the big banks solvent. Derivatives are nothing more than worthless securities manufactured out of thin air and given whatever value those trading them choose to assign. After he left the agency in disgust, he wrote an opinion piece for the *Wall Street Journal* in which he explained how he had had his eyes opened. He started with an apology: "I can only say: I'm sorry America." He went on to describe his role in creating the financial disaster we're currently in the middle of, saying that he "was responsible for executing the centerpiece program of the Fed's first plunge into the bond-buying experiment known as quantitative easing." He went on, "Because QE was relentlessly pumping money into the financial markets during the past five years, it killed the urgency for Washington to confront a *real* crisis: that of a structurally unsound U.S. economy."[11]

Quantitative easing is nothing short of robbery, but it's only the latest felony in big banking's sordid history, which dates back to the repeal of the Glass-Steagall Act during the Clinton administration; since the 1930s, this act had prevented banks from being brokerage houses and making risky investments with their clients' money. With a stroke of his pen, Clinton signed legislation that effectively made it no longer necessary for banks to manage their assets responsibly and honestly.

The result has been that banks are hiding tens of trillions of dollars in debt off their books because of failed investments. When they're no longer able to hide that debt, we face a devastating economic crash.[12]

The financial crash of 2008 was engineered by an elite group of financial professionals in order to help ensure the election of Barack Obama and guarantee the continued complicity of the U.S. government and its cadre of economic advisors, advisors who formerly worked with financial behemoth Goldman Sachs.

The government's response to the crash was the passage in 2010 of the Dodd-Frank financial reform act, a 2,300-page behemoth containing more than four hundred new regulations. When he signed the bill into law, the president promised that the American taxpayer "will never again be asked to foot the bill for Wall Street's mistakes." The president even added his favorite word for emphasis, as he does frequently when he's deceiving the American people: "There will be no more tax-funded bailouts—period."[13]

Nothing could have been further from the truth. Period.

We've done nothing *but* foot the bill for Wall Street's financial mismanagement.

The banks have continued to engage in extremely high-risk trading while at the same time manipulating everything from interest rates to the price of commodities such as gold and silver.

Let me give you a few examples:

LIBOR, the London Interbank Offered Rate, is the interest rate banks charge when they're borrowing money from each other. Big bankers decided to get together, write down what they think their borrowing costs should be, average those costs, and agree that that average interest rate would be what they charge when they trade interest-rate derivatives among themselves.

The thing is, the banks aren't borrowing *their* money from each other, they're borrowing *your* money from each other, and then fixing the interest rate however they see fit. It's a win-win, unless of course you're an average American taxpayer.

In the third quarter of 2013, the big banks in the United States collectively pocketed $2.8 billion on their interest rate derivatives alone.[14]

The riskiest markets for banks intent on keeping interest rates low are precious metals. Gold has been trading at artificially low levels between $1,200 and $1,350 an ounce for an extended time. Silver remains stuck in the $20-dollar-an-ounce range. There's a reason for this: If those prices ever do rise to the levels they should be trading at, it's likely that our economy will collapse.

Gold, for instance—if it were being traded freely and without manipulation—would be priced at around $7,000 an ounce, according to one knowledgeable investor.[15]

Why do banks want to keep the price of gold and silver artificially low?

As the Fed continues to print fiat money at the rate of nearly a trillion dollars a year, the market is flooded with new U.S. currency. That drives the value of the currency down relative to commodities such as silver and gold. If the banks, including the Fed, ever let the value of the gold rise to its normal level, the value of our currency—and of many currencies around the world—would plummet.

And interest rates would likely skyrocket.

The cost of servicing our federal debt would escalate beyond our ability to pay.

In order to prevent that from happening, U.S. banks, especially JPMorgan Chase, sell paper contracts for gold they do not own. It's called naked short selling, and it has the effect of damping the price of gold, keeping it down so that the U.S. dollar will manage to artificially maintain its value against gold and silver.[16]

It's market manipulation at its most subversive.

The Fed's activities are also at the root of what amounts to the indirect manipulation of the stock market.

Because the Fed is essentially giving money to the banks in exchange for taking fraudulent mortgage-backed securities and other derivatives off their hands, the banks are constantly on the lookout for places to "invest" their excess cash. With low interest rates, the ongoing housing market uncertainty, and the risks associated with lending to small and midsized businesses, banks have virtually stopped lending to the American people.

With interest rates close to zero, banks can't make much money lending to small businesses and for other purposes, including mortgages. And so the money gets shuttled into the stock market, which has been on a dramatic climb.

In other words, instead of lending money to the American people—who could use it to build small businesses, or buy houses, or pay for their kids to go to college—the banks are playing the stock market.

But they're not investing in the way you and I would invest.

They're letting robots do their trading for them.

It's called high-frequency trading.

High-frequency trading involves the use of powerful computers to analyze market data at unimaginably high speeds. Based on their analyses, the computers execute trades—often involving hundreds of thousands of shares—that generate enormous profits in microseconds, even though the value of the stocks they're trading may change by only hundredths of a cent as the trade is completed. A single one of these powerful robot traders can execute as many as twenty thousand transactions in a single second.

Robot trading has changed the way the stock market works. It's driven normal people interested in developing a stock portfolio out of the market. More than 70 percent of U.S. stock trades are now executed by robot traders, and that number is rising.[17]

While all this market manipulation and centralization of wealth has been going on, the Dodd-Frank bill has proven to be worthless in preventing corruption. The big banks' blatant, reckless manipulation of the value of fraudulent derivatives continues to rise to unheard-of levels.

Let me just point out a few of the many failures of this legislation.

First, as I've just explained to you, banks are still gambling with your money—money that the Federal Deposit Insurance Corporation guarantees will be safe in your bank account—by using it to make risky trades.

Even though banks, despite Dodd-Frank, have actually increased the number of illegal practices they engage in, not a single banker has been arrested and tried, let alone sent to jail. Let me put that in perspective. In the 2008 crash alone—and not taking into account the continuing Wall Street larceny since then—the average American household lost $108,000. Whether or not you had that much in the bank at the time, that's the figure the crash would eventually cost you.[18] Every single American family was robbed of over a hundred thousand dollars, first because the Fed has kept the interest rates at zero so that money in the bank earns nothing, and second because federal policies have led to no income growth, not to mention a dramatic decrease in the number of jobs available.

Not one person has been put on trial, let alone served time, for perpetrating what I see as an enormous crime.

The Rise of Poverty

As many opinions as there are about the turning point of the Civil War, there are that many and more over what caused it. State versus federal rights, economic differences, Abraham Lincoln's election, and other reasons are often mentioned as the impetus behind the war. In fact, it was money that caused the Civil War.

If you listen to today's liberals, however, you would think that slavery is the reason for the high unemployment rate among African-Americans today.

In the past fifty years, as Lyndon Johnson's War on Poverty grew exponentially, the U.S. has spent some $20 trillion in tax-payer money to fund such programs as Medicaid, Head Start and the Food Stamp Act.

The result?

The poverty level in the United States recently reached a five-year high.[19]

One of the key demographics that Democrats depend on to maintain their hold on American politics has been African-Americans. Over the years, the left has effectively consigned American blacks to life in inner-city ghettoes and bought their votes with government-subsidized programs that discourage 14 percent of the American population from seeking meaningful jobs and careers. By the beginning of the president's fifth year in office, African-Americans had the lowest participation rate in the labor force ever recorded.[20]

While the White House boasted that the unemployment rate among blacks had fallen by 5 percent, they failed to mention that the statistical drop occurred only because blacks had dropped out of the job market at an unprecedented rate: Only 60 percent of African-Americans were even bothering to look for jobs.

The picture for minority youths looking for jobs is not any better. Some 25 percent of African-American youths do not work.[21] And 18 percent of Hispanic people between the ages of sixteen and twenty-four—the future of the Democratic Party—are unemployed.[22]

I just don't understand how Mexican- and South American–Americans can vote for this president in such numbers. He might promise you the world, but he delivers on nothing. The unemployment rate among American minority youth is almost guaranteed to continue to worsen under this administration.

The consequences of the current U.S. economic policies have also been devastating for the middle class. While the administration continues to focus on what it characterizes as the decline in the unemployment rate, in fact what we're seeing is nothing more than a decline in the number of people who are searching for jobs.

More than 90 million Americans have given up looking for jobs.

That's the lowest the labor participation rate in thirty-five years.[23]

What is this administration's solution?

Increase the minimum wage.

One of the themes that Democrats are pushing is "income inequality."

How do they plan to address the fact that successful Americans make more money than those less successful?

Bump up the wages we pay to those working the lowest-paying jobs.

As if that will somehow make so much as a dent in the lives of the increasing number of Americans living at or near the poverty level.

Let me explain why this strategy won't work.

First, less than 3 percent of working Americans are employed in minimum-wage jobs. More than half of those are people who come from families whose average income is more than $50,000 a year. They may be students working as they attend school, or people starting out in the labor market. They are only temporarily working these jobs.[24] Or, as Joe Biden pointed out on *The View*, they may be single mothers "trapped in that job because if you leave, you lose your health insurance."[25]

The Congressional Budget Office, normally supportive of this administration's unworkable economic policies, didn't cooperate when Obama announced he wanted to raise the minimum wage. In fact, the CBO couldn't have been any clearer in its opposition to Obama. It said that raising the minimum wage would cause the loss of half a million jobs.[26]

That report came at about the same time the CBO told the American people that Obamacare is a disincentive for people to work, and that the Affordable Care Act would cause the loss of another 2.5 million jobs over the next several years.[27] That's because if you're an unemployed person getting a subsidy to help you pay your medical insurance premiums, you lose that subsidy if your income goes up. Not only do the Obama regime's policies cause the loss of jobs, they provide an incentive for people not to look for a job.

What most people on the left will not tell you is *that's exactly what the president wants to accomplish*.

As I see it, the president is after nothing more than to make

America into a permanent welfare state, where people who once worked for a living no longer have any incentive to do so. He's out to expand even further the permanent underclass that liberal policies have created over the past half century. He will not stop until the 99 percent have no means of support beyond what the federal government gives them.

Even though he couldn't push through legislation to increase the minimum wage, the president had a solution. In his weekly radio address, he said too many Americans haven't seen increases in their wages, while the wealthy "are doing better than ever."[28] Because of that, he decided to issue an executive order raising the minimum wage of federal employees to $10.10 an hour.

Raising the minimum wage will do absolutely nothing to help the tens of millions of people trapped in poverty by the policies of an administration that actually encourages them to become dependent on the government as they give up their jobs and career aspirations.

Let me ask you, what would you do if you were a young black man trapped in poverty with no hope of ever escaping your chains? Would you take a job for $10.10 an hour? At thirty hours a week, the workweek this administration now deems as full-time, you're making $300, taking home say $250, $240. Or you can make that much on unemployment, get $75 a week in food stamps, and free health insurance for doing nothing. What would you do?

Those now trapped in poverty are being discouraged from even looking for jobs by federal policy. If they do find a job, they'll lose government benefits that pay much more than they could earn in the increasingly poor job market.

The dramatic rise in federal benefit payments, including welfare, unemployment benefits, food stamps, and other federal government subsidies, is killing our economic freedom.

The food stamp program is the federal government's way of instituting food rationing in the United States, something every centralized government in history has done as their economies collapsed.

Nearly 50 million Americans—almost a sixth of our population—are receiving food stamps. For months, the administration flooded the radio market with advertisements in order to attract more and more people to sign up for what are now known as SNAP (Supplemental Nutrition Assistance Program) benefits. That number is up by more than 20 million people since 2009.[29] Many of those now getting food stamps are illegal aliens.[30]

But do you know who makes the real money that this administration steals from taxpayers to fund food stamps for illegal aliens?

JPMorgan Chase.

Yes, I mean the same JPMorgan Chase bank that has been running up huge hidden balance-sheet deficits through keeping worthless securities off its books, short sales of precious metals, and trading worthless securities.

Chase processes Electronic Benefits Transfer cards. In fact, the bank has made more than $560 million processing food stamp cards, charging the U.S. government between thirty-one cents and $2.30 for every person on food stamps, whether they're here legally or not.[31]

As the federal government executes its takeover of the medical industry in the United States—the same thing it did to the trillion-dollar-a-year college loan business—new regulations regarding what it means to be employed full-time have driven down Americans' hopes for securing employment even further.

Every person and family who drops through Obama's trap-door into poverty enters a life of hell on government subsidies. The same goes for those businesses that board their windows and lay off their employees as they're forced to fold.

Is it possible that with every life and business destroyed, this administration takes one step closer to its ultimate goal: a post-civil-war socialist society that is at the command of a global über elite?

More Economic Similarities to the American Civil War

I've explained to you that I believe the American Civil War was not primarily about freeing the slaves. It was about dislodging wealthy Southern farmers from their position of economic power. That power was based on their plantation economy, and that economy would have been impossible to create without slavery.

The elimination of slavery became the battle cry of the Northern elites who wanted a larger piece of the economic pie.

Their reasoning?

If slavery was abolished, the Southern economy would implode, and Northerners would assume economic control in the power vacuum that followed.

Here's some background.

Prior to the Civil War, wealthy Southerners dominated the U.S. government. But with the great majority of new factories being built in the North and employing 90 percent of the country's skilled industrial workers, much of the country's wealth had moved to the northeast.[32]

In the middle of the nineteenth century, you were wealthy if you had a net worth of more than $100,000, the equivalent of several million dollars today. Thanks to the industrial revolution, by 1860 there were more than five times as many wealthy men in the North as there had been only thirty years earlier.

At the same time, the presidency, the Senate, and the Supreme Court continued to be dominated by Southerners. There was no room in Washington for the North's nouveau riche.

Slavery may have been a rallying cry—and the abolition of slavery was the paramount achievement of the conflict—but economics and political power were at the heart of the Civil War.[33]

Today something similar is happening.

In 2009, there were fewer than one thousand billionaires in the world. Since then, the number has increased more than 60 percent, to over two thousand. The net worth of this group has more than doubled, from $3.1 trillion to $6.5 trillion, in that time.[34]

There's a critical difference between the wealth that was created in the years leading up to the American Civil War and the wealth that has been created in the lead-up to the coming twenty-first-century civil war. The nineteenth-century wealth was built on a real-world foundation of manufacturing and trade. Today's über-wealthy exist overwhelmingly because of the creation of money that amounts to nothing more than global theater.

The increase in the number of today's billionaires is, as I've explained, the result of the rise of an economic oligarchy that creates debt by printing money in order to give that money to banks so the banks can buy bonds that the government prints.

The whole reason for this corrupt process is to enable the government to keep interest rates near zero, therefore depriving Americans from receiving a return on their savings and making sure that small businesses can't get loans that would enable them to expand.

While the president complains that the 1 percent control too much of the wealth of this nation, his policies and those of the Fed are enabling the 1 percent to radically increase their wealth. They're doing this at the expense of the middle class.

Do you know what this administration's policies are doing to the middle class?

They're driving the businesses that depend on middle-class customers for their revenues out of business. In every area of the country, restaurants like Red Lobster and Olive Garden—which cater to the middle class—are having financial difficulties. At the same time, you can't get a table at upscale restaurants like The Capital Grille and the haunts of the Wall Street fat cats.

You fly coach today, and they stuff you in your seat with a shoehorn. You pay extra for your bags, a can of Coke, and even a skimpy pillow. Yet there are more private jets flying today than ever before.

General Electric reports that demand for high-end appliances dwarfs the sales of the appliance models middle-class customers choose. The fact is that businesses that appeal to middle-class customers are having an increasingly difficult time surviving as the Obama economy destroys the middle class, while businesses that cater to the upper class are thriving.[35]

The administration insists it's in favor of eliminating the

differences between the haves and the have-nots, but every one of its policies has exactly the opposite effect. They create outrage among the have-nots against the haves. The have-nots see real estate prices in many cities rising to the point where only the wealthy can afford them. While the president talks in platitudes about how much he supports the poor, at the same time he consorts with the Hollywood power brokers and financial behemoths who fund his campaign and to whom he sends billions in taxpayer money for projects that result in bankruptcies from which they walk away richer and unscathed. There are no more telling examples than in the fraudulent green energy companies like Solyndra, whose principals reaped millions through their failure.

It's a certain way to ensure the collapse the U.S. economy.

China has been the world's largest buyer of U.S. Treasury bonds and holder of U.S. dollar reserves. I've explained that China and several other nations are beginning to settle their foreign oil purchases in their own currencies, a trend which threatens the position of the U.S. dollar as both the world reserve currency and the petrodollar, the standard currency in which oil sales are settled.

Vladimir Putin is using the decline of the U.S. dollar as the currency used to settle oil sales as a weapon in his confrontation with Barack Obama over Ukraine. After his annexation of Crimea, he explained that Russia would move to settle oil deals in rubles and not in U.S. dollars in order to protect its interests. The decline in the value and power of the dollar that the Fed's QE has created is limiting and weakening our bargaining power in international relations.

China has for a long time tried to hold down the value of its currency, the yuan (also known as the renminbi), against other world currencies. If the value of the yuan remains low relative to the U.S. dollar and other world currencies, foreign exports from China remain less expensive and more attractive to nations, such as the U.S., that are importing them.

In order to do keep the value of its currency low, China has amassed some $3.5 trillion worth of other nations' currencies. Rather than let those currency reserves remain idle, it has used them to purchase foreign debt, including U.S. Treasury bonds and other securities. In doing this, China has amassed holdings of more than $1.3 trillion in U.S. Treasuries. China is the largest holder of our federal debt, with Japan close behind at nearly $1.2 trillion.[36]

The Fed's policy of quantitative easing devalues the U.S. dollar and upsets the favorable trade balance that China is bent on maintaining. In response, and because China sees itself as a challenger to the United States for world economic and military domination, China has said that it is "no longer in China's favor to accumulate foreign-exchange reserves."[37]

Which may also mean that China will look to decrease its purchases of U.S. Treasury bonds as the value of the yuan increases relative to the dollar. This may signal that China is in fact moving to enable the yuan to replace the dollar as the world reserve currency.

Both of those moves could result in the United States' moving further into recession and increasingly losing economic power and influence in the world.

That's not the only bad news on the horizon.

The decline of our economic status in the world is mirrored by our loss of economic freedom here at home. One of the most disturbing pieces of news is that, according to the 2014 Index of Economic Freedom, the United States has, for the first time, dropped out of the top ten in the list of the most economically free societies in the world. We're now only the twelfth-freest economy of all the countries in the world, behind Mauritius and Estonia, among others.[38]

The increase in regulations—more than thirteen thousand in Obama's first term[39]—and taxes on everything from energy production to tanning salons to medical devices has discouraged our citizens from starting new businesses.

The Affordable Care Act's reduction of the full-time workweek to thirty hours has caused a devastating loss of true full-time jobs in this country. Add to that the fact that the United States, at 40 percent, has the highest corporate tax rate in the world, and it begins to become clear what this administration's economic policies are really aimed at accomplishing: diminishing the power of capitalism as economic activity is increasingly taken over by an overreaching central government.

The president's economic philosophy—to the extent he has one at all—has always been characterized by the blind insistence that the only way to create economic "fairness" is to redistribute a static amount of money.

As economist Lawrence Kudlow puts it, "Obama comes from a long line of liberals whose guiding star is the equality of result, i.e., income leveling, rather than the equality of opportunity, which is the heart of free-market capitalism."[40]

I've told my radio audiences about the influences on our president's economic philosophy. He listened approvingly while Reverend Jeremiah Wright preached the tenets of liberation theology in his Chicago church.

And now even the Catholic Church is reinforcing that philosophy.

Recently, Pope Francis came out basically calling for income redistribution. He ripped trickle-down economics and an unfettered free market. The Pope said he was sympathetic to the tenets of liberation theology, which combines the teachings of Jesus Christ with those of Karl Marx.

I want to go into some detail here to show you what the implications of the Pope's politics are.

The association of the Catholic Church with socialism began and flourished in Latin America in the middle of the last century. Not coincidentally, Pope Francis is the first Pope from that region. The new Pope is spouting the Catholic Church's version of liberation theology, the same thing Reverend Wright preached to the president for twenty years.

Pope Francis has signaled several times that he is a believer in liberation theology. He has strongly indicated that he would like the Church to act as a spearhead for economic change in the world.

People who think like the Pope believe that unfettered global capitalism is unjust and leads to social, political, and economic oppression of the poor. And they want to punish the successful, which, by their logic, will create equal opportunity for those less fortunate. It amounts to nothing less than Christianized Marxism.

The Pope has made it clear that he wants to hold capitalism accountable for the problems of the world. He wants to punish the haves simply for having more than the have-nots. According to his way of thinking, this is a sin.

Here are his words:

While the earnings of a minority are growing exponentially, so too is the gap separating the majority from the prosperity enjoyed by the happy few. This imbalance is the result of ideologies that defend the absolute autonomy of the market-place and financial speculation.[41]

The Catholic Church had all but eradicated this ideology nearly a quarter century ago under Pope John Paul II. But although Pope Francis, who was originally from Argentina, had never practiced liberation theology, he was certainly shaped by it.

In early 2014, the Pope named nineteen new cardinals, sixteen of whom are under eighty years of age and considered cardinal electors. They'll be charged with electing the next Pope after Francis either retires or dies.

So why is this so significant to the resurgence of liberation theology in the Catholic Church?

These new cardinals are from predominately poor countries, including Nicaragua, Ivory Coast, Brazil, Argentina, South Korea, Chile, Burkina Faso, the Philippines, and Haiti. It signals yet another move by this Pope to reduce the influence of wealth and money on the Church.

But there is another, more long-term impact of this move: the ability of these cardinals to elect the next Pope should serve to ensure the continuation of this liberation theology, which is rapidly becoming official Church policy.

As the redistribution-of-wealth crowd has been mainly fractured and rudderless, the emergence of the Church as a leader in this kind of thinking is a new and dangerous trend. It represents nothing less than Papal-sponsored Marxism. The economic struggle has mass appeal, and it will soon be co-opted by those who seek to destroy the world, if that hasn't happened already.

Before the advent of liberation theology, though, Catholicism hated communism. Pope Leo XIII wrote an encyclical condemning it. Let me give you some quotes from his *Encyclical on Capital and Labor*, written more than a hundred years ago:

> *The socialists, working on the poor man's envy of the rich, are striving to do away with private property, and contend that individual possessions should become the common property of all, to be administered by the State or by municipal bodies. They hold that by thus transferring property from private individuals to the community, the present mischievous state of things [the gap between the rich and the poor] will be set to rights, inasmuch as each citizen will then get his fair share of whatever there is to enjoy. But... [were these plans] carried into effect the working man himself would be among the first to suffer. They are, moreover, emphatically unjust, for they would rob the lawful possessor, distort the functions of the State, and create utter confusion in the community.... Socialists, therefore, by endeavoring to transfer the possessions of individuals to the community at large, strike at the interests of every wage-earner, since they would deprive him of the liberty of disposing of his wages, and thereby of all hope and possibility of increasing his resources and of bettering his condition in life.*

Pope Leo then asks and answers an important question:

> *Is it just that the fruit of a man's own sweat and labor should be possessed and enjoyed by anyone else? As effects follow their cause, so is it just and right that the results of labor should belong to those who have bestowed their labor.... The authority of the divine law adds its sanction, forbidding us*

in severest terms even to covet that which is another's: "Thou shalt not covet thy neighbor's wife; nor his house, nor his field, nor his man-servant, nor his maid-servant, nor his ox, nor his ass, nor anything that is his."...And in addition to injustice, it is only too evident what an upset and disturbance there would be in all classes, and to how intolerable and hateful a slavery citizens would be subjected. The door would be thrown open to envy, to mutual invective, and to discord; the sources of wealth themselves would run dry, for no one would have any interest in exerting his talents or his industry; and that ideal equality about which they entertain pleasant dreams would be in reality the leveling down of all to a like condition of misery and degradation.

He finishes with this:

Neither justice nor the common good allows any individual to seize upon that which belongs to another...under the futile and shallow pretext of equality.[42]

In the face of what the Catholic Church has stood for for the past century, Pope Francis is now embracing the very socialistic principles Pope Leo XIII decried.

He believes our system of running a business should be discarded, while the right of states to control the economy for "the common good" is laudable.

Lenin could have written the words of Pope Francis.

The Pope has joined the current administration in declaring war on free markets and capitalism.

He's a popular man, and I have no reason to believe he isn't a good man. But his naïveté in world economics is very, very concerning.

Look at how another powerful person who claims to support income redistribution actually redistributes our money.

Our president spent nearly a trillion dollars of taxpayer money on a stimulus plan for the rich. He gave General Motors $50 billion so the labor contracts that had caused the automaker to face bankruptcy wouldn't destroy the company. He lost half a billion of your dollars on the Solyndra green-energy debacle, while his cronies who ran the company lined their pockets and walked away.

You've got to understand what happens when leftists are allowed to take over governments at any level and redistribute wealth that rightfully belongs to the people who earn it: Those economies collapse.

The bottom five states in terms of economic stability and performance are New Jersey, Connecticut, Illinois, Massachusetts, and California.[43] Notice what those states have in common? Every one of these Democrat-controlled state governments has allowed public pension plans and labor union activism to expand unchecked. They got that way because they engaged in the same corrupt crony statism that now infects the U.S. government.

The employment figures released by federal government agencies are fraudulent. Real unemployment in the United States is not under 7 percent; it's closer to 37 percent, despite what the White House, the Fed, and the U.S. Treasury try to tell you. The Misery Index, a measure of how Americans feel about the economy, is over 14 percent, not at the 8 percent level the government claims.[44]

Food and energy prices are rising dramatically, while wages remain stagnant. While the administration tries to push climate change as the most critical danger to the United States, Americans can't find jobs. It's getting harder and harder to disguise what's really going on. According to the Bureau of Labor Statistics, food prices are up 9 percent since June 2009. That's caused by increases in the price of pork (14 percent), poultry (12 percent), eggs (27 percent), and milk (20 percent). During the same time, energy prices have risen by 18 percent, and the gas you need to operate your car is up 27 percent, not to mention a 23 percent rise in what it costs you to send your kids to college.[45]

As I've said, you'd have to be an idiot to believe that most wars are started by anything other than economic factors. We're facing an economic crisis that not only holds the possibility of driving more and more American citizens into poverty, it may well mean the decline of U.S. economic power globally; and it is most certainly the main wedge with which Obama is driving us apart—and into civil war.

CHAPTER 6

The War on American Medicine

As incompetent as this administration appears to be, it may well be engaging in purposeful incompetence. Like the phrase *planned obsolescence*, used to explain the 1970s automobile industry in Detroit, years from now they'll be using the phrase *purposeful incompetence* to describe the Obama White House. The administration's missteps in rolling out Obamacare could actually be part of a devious but ingenious plan that would reduce the best, most advanced health-care system in the world to one that rivals Venezuela's.

When U.S. Supreme Court chief justice John Roberts folded and cast the swing vote that upheld most of the "Un-Affordable Care Act," he may have signed the death warrant of the best medical system in the world.

It didn't matter that the Obamacare website was nothing more than smoke and mirrors. It didn't matter that Henry Chao, the Health and Human Services official who was in charge of developing the Healthcare.gov software, set the project's bar so low that he once admitted he hoped it wouldn't be "a third-world experience." And it didn't matter that former Health and Human Services secretary Kathleen Sebelius displayed a level of incompetence that was hard to believe, even if it was on the part of a federal government appointee.

All that mattered to the administration was that the legislation remained the law of the land. All that mattered was that they'd pushed us further down the road that leads to socialized medicine.

The Un-Affordable Care Act forever changes the way medicine is practiced in America. And in the most devastating ways you can imagine.

Don't believe the avalanche of positive news stories generated by the administration's crony journalists.

Ultimately, should things continue the way they're headed, "ObamaScare" will deny tens of millions of Americans even the opportunity to receive health care. This will be especially true of the elderly and the poor, who, thanks to the ACA, are being refused health care because doctors are no longer paid enough to cover their expenses. They're simply refusing to take patients on Medicare, while those too poor to afford health insurance are shunted to Medicaid, where they were already overwhelming hospital emergency rooms with their need for treatment.

Which might have been the plan all along.

Is it too farfetched to believe that the real purpose of the Un-Affordable Care Act is to remove undesirables like the sick and the elderly from the rolls of the insured?

Well, consider this: Medicare Part D was passed into law under George W. Bush. It let the insurance companies compete for the business of insuring the cost of drugs for those over the age of sixty-five. It's the one federal program I know of that didn't cost as much as it was projected to cost. Part D offers seniors a choice of from twenty-eight to thirty-nine different plans, depending on which state they live in. Upward of 40 million seniors and disabled people signed up. More than 90 percent of them are happy with their plans.[1]

So what does the Centers for Medicare and Medicaid Services (CMS), the lead agency of Obamacare, plan to do with Part D? It plans to block seniors from enrolling in the most popular programs, the ones that charge them less for patronizing pharmacies that offer the lowest cost for their drugs.[2]

When Healthcare.gov, the website that Americans were supposed to use to sign up for their government health-care plans, was revealed to be a catastrophic failure, the anti-Obamacare chorus was louder than ever.

But I have news for you: Obama and his minions are ten steps ahead of the screaming anti-Obamacare chorus. Obama, Valerie Jarrett, David Axelrod, and the others may actually have wanted the website and the system to fail.

Why? So that the people who want free health care will demand a government-run, single-payer system. Call it "Government Medical Insurance, Inc."

One state already has single-payer health care. Vermont passed the first single-payer health-care law in the United States. It's known as Green Mountain Care. Vermont is known as the Green Mountain State because of the Green Mountain Boys. They were a militia group headed by Ethan Allen, and they were organized to help control a boundary dispute in what would become New England. Allen's group served in the Revolutionary War, and his name has become synonymous with independence of spirit and commitment to freedom. That's why it's so devastating that his state has become a hotbed of statist government activities. Green Mountain Care was supposed to provide health care for all Vermont residents. Now the state's lawmakers are calling for the repeal of the law. It's estimated that the cost of the program will be as high as $2 billion annually. That's the equivalent of the entire tax revenue of the state of Vermont.[3]

It's also exactly what will happen on a national level if Obamacare is allowed to stand. We need a national group of Green Mountain Boys.

Ted Cruz was right when he said that Obama is abusing his power. But what president hasn't? People were saying Obama lied. And Bush didn't lie about weapons of mass destruction?

I like Ted Cruz. I think he has guts. But he and the others are missing the point. It's not that the president is simply abusing his power—he's reaching for more.

My friends, we are in not the first stages, not the infancy stages, not the adolescent stages quite yet—we are in the childhood of socialism in the United States. And ObamaScare is the most important tool in advancing the president's goal of turning our country into the United Socialist States of America and the president himself into the American Castro.

As incompetent as this administration appears to be, it may well be engaging in purposeful incompetence. Remember that phrase; you read it here first. Like *planned obsolescence*, used to explain the 1970s automobile industry in Detroit, years from now they'll be using the phrase *purposeful incompetence* to describe the current administration. The administration's missteps in rolling out Obamacare could actually be part of a devious but ingenious plan that would reduce the best, most advanced health-care system in the world to one that rivals Venezuela's.

Let me tell you what's happening in Venezuela. The South American country's centrally planned socialist economy is collapsing, its citizens are rioting in the streets, and there's not enough money to provide drugs for patients of the state-run health-care system. As the Venezuelan economy implodes and the country's health-care system runs out of money and doctors, people are dying from easily treatable diseases.

The government stopped publishing health-care statistics in 2010, but estimates are that three-quarters of Venezuela's twenty thousand cancer patients are no longer receiving treatment. The ones who are have been forced to buy their own medical supplies.[4]

There are indications that the same thing is beginning to happen here. The mother of Ralston College president Stephen Blackwood had been battling cancer for years, and her Blue Cross/Blue Shield plan paid for her medical treatments and the drug Sandostatin, which was enabling her to continue her fight against the disease. When Obamacare eliminated her coverage, she shopped around and bought insurance from Humana. Only days before she was scheduled for another surgery, she was informed that her new plan would not pay for the drug that was keeping her alive. Thanks to Obamacare, she and her family would have to pay $14,000 out of pocket just so she could continue on Sandostatin. Her son explained it clearly to a journalist reporting the story: "Obamacare made my mother's old plan illegal, and it forced her to buy a new plan that would accelerate her disease and death."[5]

Why aren't there voices raised in outrage? How in God's name can a country that has set the world's medical standard for fifty years allow this to occur? Because the administration won't allow anyone to speak out.

Do you know what happens if you publicize the problems people are experiencing because of Obamacare? The Democrats threaten to revoke the licenses of radio and television stations that might be broadcasting these stories. Heading into the midterm elections, which will be loaded with ads that are critical of Obamacare, Dems are out to stop their political opponents from running any that talk about the disastrous plan. In a letter to the editor of a local paper, Michigan Democratic Senate candidate Gary Peters warned broadcasters that they could lose their licenses for airing what he called "false and misleading advertising," also known as what sane people would call the truth about Obamacare.[6]

From lunatic lefty Paul Krugman to Senate Democratic leader Harry Reid, Democrats are doing whatever they can to stifle the truth that Obamacare is sentencing us to a Venezuelan-like health-care system.

In Venezuela, two-thirds of the three hundred state-run hospitals have been reduced to walk-in clinics run by Cuban doctors. These clinics do not treat serious illnesses.[7] In the United States, the same thing is already beginning to happen: Four Georgia hospitals have been forced by Obamacare to shut down in the past two years, because Obamacare cuts payments for emergency services so drastically that they were on the verge of bankruptcy. The same thing is happening in half the states in the United States, which have rejected the expansion of Medicaid that Obamacare called for.[8]

With its medical system continuing its collapse, the Venezuelan government seized a major retail chain, ordered a military occupation of the chain's outlets, and lowered the prices of everything in the stores. What followed was described as "government-sanctioned looting."[9]

Our collapse will very likely mirror Venezuela's if Obamacare is not repealed.

Think it can't happen here?

In March 2013, Henry Chao met with an insurance industry lobbying group called America's Health Insurance Plans. Chao's job was pretty straightforward: Create an easy-to-use database with a user interface that enabled people to go online, enter some information, have the information verified, and present them with options for health insurance programs they could sign up for.

During the insurance conference, Chao did his best to make sure the representatives of the health insurance community didn't expect much. He said that he'd long since given up expectations of creating "a world-class user experience." It was in this conversation where he made his now infamous comment of just hoping that Obamacare wouldn't be "a third-world experience."[10]

I've told my radio audiences over and over that Obama is intent on reducing the United States to just another third-world country through his attempts to destroy our capitalist economy. Finally, one of Obama's own lieutenants—the leader of software development, no less—validates me!

The evidence is overwhelming. The Affordable Care Act was written, perhaps intentionally, in such a way that the best health-care system in the world would be reduced to the level of Venezuela's. Pay rates for doctors who accept government health-care insurance are cut dramatically from what is necessary to run a medical practice. Both insurance industry professionals and physicians agree that this is already leading to a two-tiered medical system, with many doctors opting out of Obamacare, while those who remain will be overrun with hordes of new patients they're unable to treat, thanks to the fact that there is already a shortage of primary care physicians in the United States.[11]

New York is one of a number of states in which the best hospitals are not available to ACA patients. Not a single Obamacare insurance plan includes the Memorial Sloan-Kettering Cancer Center in New York City among the hospitals covered, for instance. Since the list of hospitals and doctors you can choose from is limited to your local area, you won't even be allowed to go to a hospital that isn't just around the corner from you, and most hospitals in your state won't be available to you anyway.[12]

It's not only New York City cancer patients who are finding their primary sources of treatment unavailable. Doctors, hospital administrators, and insurance regulators are seeing this happen all around the country. A survey conducted by the Associated Press revealed that, for instance, the Seattle Cancer Care Alliance is not available in policies offered by five of the eight insurance companies in the state of Washington. Fewer than half of the insurance plans in the Houston area include the MD Anderson Cancer Center. Only four of the top nineteen comprehensive cancer centers said that Obamacare patients have access to their services in their responses to a national questionnaire.[13]

The four that are included are the Kimmel Comprehensive Cancer Center at Johns Hopkins in Baltimore; Fox Chase Cancer Center in Philadelphia; Duke Cancer Institute in Durham, North Carolina; and Vanderbilt-Ingram Cancer Center in Nashville.

There's a catch, though. They're not included in low-cost Obamacare plans.

There are also inevitably limits of some sort on who can receive cancer treatment under Obamacare plans. Buffalo's Roswell Park Cancer Institute is not covered by eleven of the sixteen Obamacare insurers in New York State. St. Louis's Siteman Cancer Center is included in a number of insurance plans, although none of them are included in Obamacare. Huntsman Cancer Institute in Salt Lake City is not included in Obamacare plans underwritten by Humana.[14]

Obamacare was sold as health insurance that would take care of people who have pre-existing medical conditions that would have caused them to be denied insurance before the ACA was passed. What's happening, though, is the exact opposite. As many people who are sick are finding out, they're not covered by their Obamacare policies. It's healthy people who are covered.

Are you in good health and want to get a "free" mammogram or a "free" colonoscopy? No problem. Are you sexually active and want "free" contraceptives? Obamacare welcomes you. You've got them.

Have cancer and want to get the best treatment available? It's a completely different story.

Do you know what happened when Dr. Katherine Albrecht tried to get treatment for her Stage 3c breast cancer through Obamacare in the state of New Hampshire? Her doctors told her to "get her affairs in order." They told her to resign herself to death. Her private insurer, though, took a different approach. It paid for her to go to Dana-Farber Cancer Center in Boston, and later to Weill Cornell Breast Cancer Center. She was treated successfully and recovered. When Obamacare became law, her private policy was canceled. She was one of the fortunate ones who received treatment before Obamacare became law.[15]

It's not only hospitals that are disappearing from health insurance plans. UnitedHealth dropped thousands of doctors from its network of providers. The insurer explained that the reduction in the number of doctors was because Medicare Advantage plans for the elderly were drastically underfunded by Obamacare, with cuts in payments from the government reduced to the point where medical practices and hospitals were experiencing cash flow problems. Doctors in at least ten states have been notified that they are no longer in United-Health's provider networks.[16]

Obamacare is the president's signature piece of legislation for a reason: It's designed to accelerate the transformation of this country into a socialist dictatorship. It's one of the signs we're heading toward civil war in this country between Americans who support the Constitution and the freedoms we have enjoyed throughout our history and the forces aligning behind a federal government that is rapidly assuming control over every aspect of our lives.

Let me tell you about an Obama connection that is not a coincidence.

For the Obamacare rollout, Obama worked with the same public relations specialists who also did the publicity for Venezuelan dictator Hugo Chavez. Celinda Lake and American Environics, the leftist pollster who advised the Obama campaign to make contraception for women one of the central issues in the 2012 presidential campaign, offered data that was useful. But the driving force in developing the strategy behind branding Obamacare was the Herndon Alliance. They're the ones who came up with the now infamous line, "If you like your health-care plan you can keep it."

The Herndon Alliance is a radical leftist group that has partnered in many projects with radical leftist, anti-American groups including MoveOn and La Raza.[17] But here's the punch line. Herndon had used the same reimaging strategy that they used for Obamacare before. The same American Environics that provided support for the Obamacare project had created and maintained Venezuelan dictator Hugo Chavez's public image.

Still don't think Obama visualizes a Venezuelan scenario for America?

Obama's health insurance legislation was never designed to be a brokerage for insurance plans that were provided by private insurance companies. It's my opinion that the ultimate goal of the Affordable Care Act is to eliminate the private health-care insurance market altogether and bring another large portion of our economy under a single payer: the dictatorial socialist government that is assuming power in the United States.

I see it as one more element in this president's attempt to destroy our capitalist economy and turn us into a member state of a globalist government ruled by a political and economic elite.

The act was passed into law illegally, and without a single Republican vote. Democrats rigged the election of Minnesota senator Al Franken in order to get a majority, then skirted the Constitution and used obscure congressional work-arounds to pass a law without even getting approval from the House.

The Obama administration defended the law, saying that it in no way represented a tax. Then Chief Justice Roberts rewrote the legislation by deciding it was a tax and not an attempt to regulate interstate commerce. Since any legislation that creates a tax must originate in the House of Representatives, and since the ACA hadn't originated in the House, the law immediately became unconstitutional.

After he had overstepped his constitutional limits, Roberts then disregarded the Constitution a second time when he voted to uphold the law.[18]

Roberts' swing vote in favor of Obamacare plunged America into one of the darkest, most dangerous periods in our history. The fact that ObamaScare legislation was allowed to stand by the chief justice of the Supreme Court marked the legitimizing of Obama's ongoing takeover of the United States of America.

The NSA has been spying on U.S. senators, members of the House of Representatives, and journalists for over a decade, according to NSA whistleblower William Binney. If they can spy on the Pope and foreign leaders like German chancellor Angela Merkel, why shouldn't we assume Obama didn't spy on Roberts, find something he's hiding somewhere, and blackmail him into giving Obamacare the Supreme Court's seal of approval?

Am I allowed to ask the question?

Has anyone in the media analyzed it from this perspective? I haven't heard it.

By the time the health-care law was ready to be implemented, it pitted Republicans against Democrats. It further divided the Republican Party into factions, with strong Tea Party conservatives like Ted Cruz and Utah senator Mike Lee standing up against the administration's takeover, while establishment Republicans like Karl Rove, John McCain, and Lindsey Graham wanting only to maintain the status quo. They presented no alternative to the Democratic agenda, because they're actually in collusion with the Democrats. Divide and conquer. The current administration's goal is to create chaos and further the ongoing U.S. economic collapse, leading us to civil war, a socialist society, and enslavement to an elitist world government.

I know that's difficult to accept, but you have to realize we're talking about the world of the leftist agenda. Let me give you an example of how the left works to help you understand their ultimate goals.

In the late 1960s, two radical leftist Columbia University professors, Richard Cloward and his wife, Frances Piven, developed a plan that had a strikingly similar goal to that of the current administration. It entailed signing up as many low-income Americans as possible—primarily American blacks—to the welfare rolls. They believed the financial burden of this would crash America's economy. It was part of a grand socialist revolution scheme they wanted to create in America.[19]

The strategy didn't achieve its ultimate goal of economic collapse, but it nearly bankrupted New York City, which had 150,000 welfare cases in 1960, and nearly 1.5 million ten years later. Like so many leftist movements, it also added members to the permanent African-American underclass that the Democrats have created in the United States. It contributed to destroying blacks' independence and their initiative to work and helped keep them enslaved in the inner-city ghettoes the liberal left had razed and rebuilt as part of its Great Society legislation of the 1960s.

In my opinion, the administration's intent with the Affordable Care Act is no different than the intent of Cloward and Piven forty years ago, except that this time the left is not just targeting African-Americans. The current administration's aim is to complete the collapse of the American economy and social order. This collapse would pit those who have lost their livelihoods and property against the political and economic oligarchy that is assuming control in the United States. Ultimately, the goal of the Obama administration might well be to make us vulnerable to a takeover of the United States by a globalist elite.

As I see it, Obamacare has five major objectives: the massive redistribution of wealth; the collection of vast amounts of personal data; the elimination of jobs and ultimate destruction of the middle class; the expansion of graft and corruption to further cripple social order; and a cash windfall for the president and his cronies.

If we're ever going save ourselves from total ruin, first we have to fully understand what we are being subjected to. Here, I explain the five major goals I believe Obamacare is meant to achieve.

Obamacare: Engineering a Massive Redistribution of Wealth

The left is the enemy of the middle class.

Obamacare targets the middle class, small business owners, professionals, individuals, and families whose annual incomes are in the $60,000-to-$175,000 range. These middle-class Americans are finding that under Obamacare they can no longer keep the health insurance policies they were happy with, as they were once promised by the president. The policies they were instructed to buy had premiums that were in many cases higher than the ones they had, with annual deductibles that ran as much as $10,000 more than they were paying.

They are the victims of the *purposeful incompetence* of Obamacare.

By eliminating the individual health insurance market, the administration is using Obamacare to bring into being a massive redistribution of wealth from the middle class to the poor. Deprived of health care they can't afford, the middle class will become totally dependent on the federal government for their medical care.

What was needed was a rationale. Enter MIT's Jonathan Gruber. I can't believe the level of insanity coming out of once-great universities. Gruber is the genius who said: "Genetic lottery winners should pay more for their health insurance."[20]

You understand how twisted this Gruber is, right? Saying that our health-care system is discriminatory, that if you're healthy you should pay more, and if you're sick you should pay less.

The problem is that there are any number of reasons you might be sick.

I've tried to take good care of myself. I've lived a healthy lifestyle. So don't you think I should pay less for my health care? Shouldn't people who live right, who don't take drugs, who don't have hyper-multiple sexual partners, shouldn't they be rewarded instead of ObamaScare charging me more so people who haven't lived healthy lifestyles can pay less?

I say people who indulge in risky behavior should pay more. I don't want to pay for their behavior.

I engage in the riskiest behavior on earth. I sleep eight hours a night. I eat a clean, healthy diet. I don't smoke. I don't do drugs.

I am a Normo-path.

I don't sleep with fifty people a week. We're not allowed to mention that promiscuity spreads sexually transmitted diseases? For instance, one of the consequences of providing contraception is that it can encourage people to engage in risky behavior. So with Obamacare we get to pay for people who get STDs because of their own irresponsible behavior?

There used to be a discount on your health insurance if you didn't smoke. You paid less for your health insurance if you followed a healthy lifestyle. And if you smoked, they wouldn't give you insurance, or they'd charge you more. They'd put you in a risk pool. With Obamacare there are no risk pools.

Everybody's in the risk pool now.

Do you think private insurance companies wanted to lose money on you because you didn't have any self-control? Only the government is that perverse.

So this guy Gruber from MIT says, *You're the genetic lottery winner because you're healthy.*

I watch my health. I take care of myself. And I should pay for an idiot who's injecting heroin? I should pay for a guy who smokes? I should pay for a prostitute riddled with disease?

I don't want to pay for them. That's how I feel. You pay for your own liver transplant if you drank like a fool. I'm not in favor of people who want the middle class, folks who live with morals, scruples, and integrity, to pay for those who live debauched lives. But that's where the collective wealth of America's once great middle class is headed.

Putting Your Private Information at Risk

Every American who is forced to go onto the Healthcare.gov website and enter personal information is immediately handing over their personal data—from their Social Security numbers, to their incomes, to their private health histories—to the enemy. But that's only what you give them voluntarily. Thanks to the raft of documents released by Edward Snowden, we now know that the NSA can gain access to your computer through such things as Windows error messages and your purchasing of apps. Even the popular Angry Birds app can give the NSA a portal into your privacy.[21] So if they can get into your computer and e-mail through apps and error messages, why can't they get in through a website application that they administer? Think about that.

As a report from the General Accounting Office explains, the information they gather goes to two main destinations. First it's channeled into the Federal Data Services Hub. The mission of the Data Services Hub is to pull together into one place your personal data from the IRS, the Departments of Homeland Security and Defense, the VA, the Social Security Administration, Medicaid, the Peace Corps, and any other government agency with which you've had even a passing relationship. Once it has the information, it distributes the data "to state and third party data sources needed to verify consumer-eligibility information."[22] In other words, your most private and personal information is allowed to leak out into the web, where it's fair game for any identity thief or political adversary.

Why is this allowed?

The federal government has hired fifty thousand new employees and given them the responsibility for administering this massive data grab. They're called navigators, and they aren't vetted during the hiring process or at any other time. No one knows how many petty criminals, sexual deviants, illegal aliens, and tax evaders have been hired as navigators.

These potentially rogue, highly partisan federal employees have access to all of your personal information.

One thing we do know: A terrorist from the country of Jordan worked briefly as an Obamacare navigator in Illinois. He got hired because virtually all governments—in this case, the Illinois state government—are incompetent to vet their employees and make sure they're not subversives or criminals. It turns out that Rasmieh Yousef Odeh, the navigator I'm talking about, had been convicted in Israel for her role in several bombings, including an attack that killed two Hebrew University students. Odeh had hidden a bomb in a candy box she planted on a shelf in one of the stores in the Israeli Shufersol supermarket chain. It wasn't until after she'd been hired and had worked as a navigator that the Illinois Department of Insurance finally discovered that "she had been convicted in Israel for her role in the bombings of a supermarket and the British Consulate in Jerusalem and failed to reveal the conviction on her application," as it stated in a disciplinary report.[23]

James O'Keefe, the activist whose stealth videos helped expose the corrupt practices of ACORN, turned his cameras on several groups of Obama's navigators. O'Keefe found that the people running Obamacare at the state and national levels are not only incompetent, they're often corrupt partisans. The supposedly nonpartisan group Enroll America inadvertantly revealed its true nature. When one of its officers, Brian Pendleton, was introduced at a speaking engagement, the person introducing him described the organization as "the official group for the DNC [Democratic National Committee]." The regional director for another group, Battleground Texas, a group which shares data and works directly with Enroll America, describes his organization's mission as "turning Texas blue."

One of O'Keefe's investigators posed as an applicant. When he told the navigator he smoked, he was advised to keep that information to himself. "Lie," he was told; "if you don't, your premiums will be higher." Another of O'Keefe's journalists told the navigator that he'd lied on his tax return. "Don't get yourself in trouble by declaring now," he was told.[24]

Guess which government agency the navigators report to?

If you guessed the IRS, you win.

The fact that your private information is collected in a central government database means that it provides the perfect opportunity for Obama supporters like Enroll America to use that data to conduct a get-out-the-vote operation for Democratic candidates. One of the results of this? Conservatives may never be able to successfully run for political office, because their personal information will be immediately given to their Democratic opponents so they can smear the opposing candidate. This means that if you oppose a government policy, the IRS can do precisely what Lois Lerner, the former director of the IRS Exempt Organizations Unit, did to Tea Party groups.

How does the president respond to the incompetence and corruption that is rampant in state health-care exchanges?

He issues a health-care "fix" by executive order.

Many state-run websites flounder, unable to provide even a reasonable chance to sign up for their residents. In those states, the Democratic governors have faced sharp criticism for their states' enrollment procedures because they decided to run their own websites. Those governors are the ones who will benefit from this new order.

In Oregon, the health-care exchange had failed to sign up a single person for health insurance by the end of 2013. The state's website did not function at all, so it was of no use in enrolling people. The state went to paper applications and hired four hundred new employees to process them. That hasn't worked very well, either, although Oregon does claim that some twenty-three thousand people had signed up by mid-January 2014. The state has spent more than $165 million of a $300 million budget to get its exchange up and running, to no avail.

Over half of its budget!

A cost of nearly $7,200 per person signing up!

No one has been fired, although two people did resign. There is an ongoing investigation, but as of this writing no charges have been filed.[25]

Oregon governor John Kitzhaber was ecstatic when he heard that Obama was going to bail him out. He said, "Today's news means that many more Oregonians will be able to access better coverage at a more affordable cost."

Here's what the executive order promises: Residents who can't sign up because of the incompetence of those running state exchanges can still get federal tax credits even though they bought private insurance policies other than those provided through the exchanges. Under the law, you weren't eligible for these subsidies unless you purchased from one of the exchanges.[26]

In other words, as he has done so often, when it's convenient, the president ignores the law.

Let me get back to the subject of Healthcare.gov's assault on our Fourth Amendment right to privacy.

I've told you about the Obama administration's penchant for purposeful incompetence. Well, there's no better example than the Obamacare website.

How vulnerable is Healthcare.gov? Programmers included language in the source code that explains that applicants have "no reasonable expectation of privacy."[27]

That's the equivalent of a bank having the slogan, "Your money's not safe with us!"

The website is so defenseless that cyberthieves are lining up. One of the ways hackers invade the privacy of website users is to create websites with similar names to the one they're trying to hack.

By the time Healthcare.gov was rolled out, more than seven hundred cybersquatters had set up websites with names like www.obama-care.us.

Obama-care.us presents itself as part of the "Obamacare enrollment team," and offers an "Obamacare enrollment form." The only purpose of the form that I can see is to steal your information. The site had more than three thousand visitors by mid-November 2013. The company that owns Obama-care.us owns nearly two hundred other cybersquatter sites designed to redirect visitors from locations with similar names.

The federal development team didn't bother to perform even the most rudimentary security checks before the roll-out of Healthcare.gov. If they had done what every competent development team does—check whether their website name was already in use—they would have discovered that Health-care.us had been registered nearly twenty years ago. That website, which has an image of the White House on its home page, was designed to deceive users into thinking it was sanctioned by the federal government.

In Website Building 101 they tell you to purchase domain names that are similar to the one you're developing to reduce the chance of cybersquatting. In the words of one cyber-security expert, "I was shocked to find out that they have not picked up any of these other top-level domains."[28]

Another security expert was shocked to find that the code,

which is used to transfer personal information to third parties, including advertising companies, was unencrypted.[29] CNN News hired a computer expert to test the security of the website. Their expert was able to guess at a user name, and then use unencrypted source code to access the password resetting function. After he had changed the user's password, he was able to display the three answers to the user's security questions. With this information, he could not only hack into this user's account on Healthcare.gov, he could also hack into other websites accessed by the user, since many systems use identical security questions.[30]

Computer security expert David Kennedy, CEO of Trusted Sec, explained that you don't even need to be an experienced computer user, let alone a hacker, to access records. Using a technique called passive reconnaissance, he was able to recover the personal data of more than seventy thousand people who had enrolled using the Obamacare website. He said that the website was like a car with doors and windows open. "That's basically what they allow you to do and there's no real sophistication level here," he said. It took him less than four minutes to get the data on the seventy thousand, and he could have gotten the private information of hundreds of thousands more if he'd wanted to.[31]

Another group of hackers known collectively as Anonymous took advantage of a flaw in Adobe Systems software that enabled them to break into thousands of Obamacare records. In doing so, they left back doors in the software that would enable them to return whenever they wanted to.[32] U.S. intelligence agencies issued a warning that Healthcare.gov had been infected by malware that had been created by computer experts in the nation of Belarus. They needed help from the Belarus government to remove it.[33]

Add to that the fact that the back end of Healthcare.gov—the code that actually enables people who enroll in Obamacare to pay their premiums—had not even been built by the end of March, when the open enrollment period for Obamacare ended, and you've got a recipe for total disaster. Henry Chao, the same guy who hoped Obamacare wouldn't be a third-world experience, said the payment software would be operative by mid-January 2014, but that date passed and you still couldn't pay your premium online.[34]

Healthcare.gov captures and stores all the important personal data of those who access it, then makes it easily available to other government agencies and hackers who crack the almost nonexistent encryption.

The hackers are nowhere near as corrupt and dangerous as the government agencies that have access to this data. For instance, the government agency that brought you Lois Lerner now has even greater access to your private medical and financial records than you could have ever have thought possible.

It's my opinion that Healthcare.gov may represent the most massive violation of our Fourth Amendment right to privacy ever committed in U.S. history.

The ACA: Designed to Eliminate Jobs and Increase Dependency

Even before the official rollout began, Obamacare had already begun to shrink the American middle class because it changed the definition of full-time work from forty to thirty hours a week. Employers everywhere began to reduce their employees' hours and eliminate many jobs.

The reason government officials gave for redefining full-time downward was so that more employees would be eligible for employer-paid health insurance. But in my opinion the real reason was to further decimate the U.S. economy. Because of the reduction in the number of full-time jobs, long-time middle-class employees saw their hours reduced and jobs eliminated.

The plan is working. It's moving us rapidly toward the next civil war, as middle-class Americans are being forced into the have-not category by a government dominated by the haves.

A report issued by the Congressional Budget Office, which in my opinion should also be known as the Democratic Party's mouthpiece, finally began to come clean on Obamacare's impact on jobs: The Affordable Care Act will cost the U.S. economy 2½ million jobs over the next several years.[35] In other words, as millions of people come into the labor market, millions of jobs will disappear thanks to Obamacare alone. It means that the real number, including lost jobs and new job seekers, is easily greater than five million. That's five million more Americans who will be forced onto the government dole as the administration's dream of creating a socialist hell right here in America is advanced. If there are any taxpayers left by that time, they'll be the ones footing the bill for this takeover.

Because Obamacare reduces the definition of full-time work to thirty hours a week, fewer employers will be willing to hire full-time employees and pay for their health insurance. A Duke University survey found that nearly half of all major U.S. employers are no longer going to provide health benefits for their employees, forcing them out into the Obamacare wilderness as they search for coverage. Some 40 percent say they'll reduce hiring new full-time employees for the same reason, adding to the job loss Americans face.[36]

Another consequence of the job-decimation component of Obamacare is that it encourages employers to consider reducing the number of people they hire. Because of the Affordable Care Act, full-time workers have to be paid an average of $1.79 more an hour. Companies in New York and New Jersey, where health-care plans are more expensive, are especially hard hit by this increase. The businesses that suffer the most? It's not the big law firms, banks, and manufacturers—the few of them that are left in the United States—it's small business such as restaurants, shops, and mom-and-pop stores where employees' wages eat up much of the operating budgets. The owner of one dog-grooming business in New York State says that Obamacare doubles his insurance cost per employee. Owners of small businesses—and these businesses taken together employ more than 30 million workers across the country—will face paying twice the current rate to insure their employees.[37]

How many times do I have to tell you how dangerous this administration has become? How many of their disastrous policies will it take before we say "enough"?

Operation Incompetence

You didn't have to be a detective to know that there was something suspicious about the Obamacare website from day one. Only four companies were even considered for the job of creating Healthcare.gov. By the time the rollout began, the total amount of compensation for the work awarded to the developer was over half a billion dollars.

The company chosen to take advantage of what amounts to a government handout, considering the abject failure of the launch, was the Canadian vendor Conseillers en Gestion et Informatique[38] (CGI; English translation: Information Systems and Management Consultants). CGI was one of the sixteen companies being considered, and while three other companies were invited to bid, I've been unable to find a good explanation of how and why the Canadian company was chosen for the massive project.[39]

Don't think that CGI was somehow chosen for the project on the merits of its past performance as a website developer. An online registry the company tried to build for an Ontario government health agency was a complete debacle. After three years of blown deadlines, the company was fired. Less than two years later, the Obama administration hired them.[40]

Toni Townes-Whitley, a Princeton classmate of the First Lady, is a senior vice president at the company that failed miserably to deliver Healthcare.gov. Both Michelle Obama and Townes-Whitley just happen to be members of the Association of Black Princeton Alumni.

Now, I am not implying in any way that the First Lady benefited. In any case, Michelle's Princeton classmate is a senior vice president of the company that won the contract to build the Obamacare website, but CGI has denied that Townes-Whitley was involved in any way with the company's selection as the developer of the Affordable Care Act website, saying, "Ms. Townes-Whitley is not currently and has never been responsible for the CMS contract as a CGI employee."[41]

Anyone with any real-world experience in any industry

knows that a project as massive and complex as developing a website that will enable tens of millions of people to sign up for health insurance is a difficult job. In fact, though, there are hundreds of such websites created and run by companies in the private sector.

With that in mind, isn't it curious that Obama gave Canada the Obamacare job with all the talent in our own backyard?

If then-HHS secretary Sebelius had even consulted company officers and software developers from organizations such as Google, Amazon, YouTube, or Facebook, she might have understood how you could actually develop and launch such a project in the allotted time. But even though the contract had been open for competitive bidding, the rules governing those bids were so arcane and difficult to follow that most companies couldn't even figure out how to submit bids.

The Small Business Association publishes a ten-step process explaining how to secure a federal government contract. Among the things it advises those seeking a contract to do are these:

• Seek out somebody who actually knows what they're doing to help you navigate the process.

• Utilize others, including consulting firms, to help you understand the rules governing the writing of a bid.

• Use data analysis tools to find the appropriate contracts to bid on.

• Consider partnering with another business, especially those owned by minorities and women.[42]

What it doesn't say is that you need to be a political insider even to be considered for a government contract.

It didn't stop there.

In a case brought by a nonprofit agency in Billings, Montana, Christa Ann McClure, the director of the Colorado health exchange, was indicted on eight counts of alleged fraud, including stealing from her previous employer, the nonprofit group Housing Montana, and paying herself hundreds of thousands of dollars for consulting services for projects she was in charge of. Nevertheless, when she was vetted for the Colorado job, she passed with flying colors. McClure failed to mention those potential charges to her new employer. After she was indicted and faced up to twenty years in prison,[43] she reached a plea agreement that called for her to make restitution of $33,000 for misdemeanor theft of public money. Eight felony counts against her were dismissed.[44]

In California's Covered California health exchange, people are finding they can't keep their doctors, and the hospitals they've become accustomed to aren't available to them. The companies providing policies under Covered California have cut down dramatically on the number of doctors and hospitals available to those insured under Obamacare in order to hold down their costs.

It's happening all over the country, as I've told you.

But in California, it's worse than most. California insurance commissioner Dave Jones stated the obvious: "There are a lot of economic incentives for health insurers to narrow their networks," he said. "But if they go too far, people won't have access to care. Network adequacy will be a big issue in 2014."[45]

The bigger issue is why such patent corruption and incompetence is allowed to continue.

Cash for Cronies

Do you remember the president's funding of green-energy companies like Solyndra? Companies that had no prospect for success but would cost taxpayers billions of dollars, cash that somehow found its way into the pockets of the Obama fundraising bundlers?

Healthcare.gov makes Solyndra look like lunch money.

The stock price of health insurance giant UnitedHealth is predicted to rise 40 percent in the future; it anticipates an increase in profits thanks to the increased insurance premiums users will have to pay under Obamacare. One of the company's subsidiaries, Quality Software Services Inc. (QSSI), was given large contracts to help with the website rollout. UnitedHealth executive vice president Anthony Welters raised half a million dollars for Obama in 2012.[46] Then, after QSSI bungled its part in developing the website, the administration gave them the job to fix their own mistakes. QSSI was chosen to be the general contractor in charge of repairing Healthcare.gov.[47]

It doesn't stop there. Technical specialty company Qualcomm specializes in developing products that transfer data securely among wireless health-care devices. Qualcomm expects that "wireless solutions are going to be looked at more prominently" under Obamacare. Let me just say that the company's former chairman, Irwin Jacobs, raised more than half a million dollars for Obama's reelection campaign.

As Fox News has reported, Obama bundlers David Friedman (nursing homes and long-term care) and Jay Snyder (investment specialist in health-care and pharmaceutical companies), each of whom raised $500,000 for Obama's reelection campaign, stand to make millions for their companies, both of which are positioned to benefit, assuming Obamacare survives.[48]

The president was finally forced by pressure from all sides to hold a press conference where he told another lie to Americans who wanted to keep their current health insurance plans.[49]

The bad news is that he didn't say anything that indicated he knew how to fix Obamacare.

When he came out a half hour late on November 15, 2013, instead of talking about the disaster of his signature legislation, the first thing he did was divert attention away from the ACA by talking about the Philippines disaster.

Do you even remember what the "Philippines disaster" was?

When he finally got around to talking about Obamacare, he told Americans he'd decided they can keep their healthcare plans for another year. He didn't say how he was going to make that happen. He didn't acknowledge that he didn't have the authority to make it happen. He didn't bother to explain that it would take the insurance companies months and months to reanalyze what it would do to the rates they need to charge.

More than five million people had had their health insurance canceled by early November 2013. The "insurance cycle"—the amount of time it takes for insurance companies to develop and test the plans they will offer to their customers—is about nine months. Those five million people will not even be able to buy a one-size-fits-all policy that would at least keep them covered, even at a higher cost and with coverage they don't need.

The issue of cost is finally coming to the fore. Health industry specialists are predicting that as the elections of 2014 get nearer, rate hikes will skyrocket. Kathleen Sebelius, who has since resigned, tried to downplay concerns over the coming rate hikes. Her analysis? In her words, "The increases are far less significant than what they were prior to the Affordable Care Act." This had those in the know scratching their heads. All they could say is that they—the people who run the insurance industry and who actually know something about health insurance—disagree. One senior insurance executive whose company expects to triple its rates on the Obamacare exchange next year said, "It's pretty shortsighted because I think everybody knows that the way the exchange has rolled out...is going to lead to higher costs."[50]

With his press conference announcement, Obama created what amounts to an insurance refugee crisis. Five million American health insurance refugees will be faced with potential disaster unless someone steps in to intervene in a way that will change their fate.

Let me give you a short list of some of the things you'll be losing when you switch to an Obamacare policy.

Obamacare won't pay for nongeneric drugs. That means that most people with illnesses being treated through the use of new drugs that are not sold as generics simply will not be able to afford treatment. If you suffer from a disease such as lupus or multiple sclerosis, you'll be dealing with what's called a "closed drug formulary." That's ObamaSpeak for "you're out of luck." As Dr. Scott Gottlieb of the American Enterprise Institute explains, "If the medicine that you need isn't on that list, it's not covered at all. You have to pay completely out of pocket to get that medicine, and the money you spend doesn't count against your deductible, and it doesn't count against your out of pocket limits, so you're basically on your own."[51]

Even if your drug is available generically, Obamacare will drive up the cost of generic drugs dramatically. Obamacare does require that exchange plans cover generic prescription drugs, but the demand may be driven up so much that the price of generic prescriptions could skyrocket. It's already happening. The prices of the generic cholesterol drug Pravastatin and the antibiotic Doxycycline have already spiked by nearly 1,000 percent in the months following the Obamacare rollout. More than three-quarters of pharmacists surveyed said they've seen the prices of two dozen or more generic drugs go higher. How many pharmacies will go out of business when people can't even afford generic drugs?[52]

There's still a lot that we don't know about Obamacare. Significant sections of the bill are still subject to regulatory action, and there's no way to predict what effect that might have on the consequences of this monstrosity. And there are still plenty of other consequences we haven't felt because the administration can't get core parts of the bill—like how people can pay their premiums—operative.

Big businesses still have no idea what the employer mandate might entail, and insurance companies have no idea what sort of benefits this behemoth is going to require them to provide in the future. There are still dozens of rules that are scheduled to be made public within the next year or so, some of which were expected by the middle of 2013 but have not yet been formulated and released. They include everything from non-discrimination standards to the Obamacare requirement that restaurants and food vendors put calorie counts on their menus and vending machines. Obama is not about to let individual citizens manage their own food intake without its attempting to influence their choices based on information that has already proven not to influence the food choices of overweight Americans despite the fact that it has been provided on virtually all other food packaging.

On April Fools' Day, the president took to the podium and announced that—miracle of miracles—Obamacare had signed up 7.1 million subscribers. Coincidentally, this was a hundred thousand more than were needed to make the rollout a "success."

In other words, Obama was trying to get everyone to believe that more than seven million people had managed to navigate the faulty website, get through the Healthcare.gov maze without having their identity stolen, and decipher the rules that change all the time. And now they think they've got health insurance. The problem is, they haven't paid for it yet. The back end of the website still can't accept their credit card information.

Facing the risk of rising insurance rates in the months before the 2014 midterm elections, the Obama administration essentially offered a bribe to insurance companies to keep their rates low for the next several years. Hidden in hundreds of pages' worth of new regulations issued in late May 2014 was a provision that pledged to bail out health insurance companies by compensating them with taxpayer money if they will keep rates low. It's another crooked Obama move to hold on to power despite the fact that Americans and U.S. insurance companies face devastating losses of coverage and money thanks to this legislation.[53]

You've probably followed the disturbing Veterans Affairs medical treatment scandal. Our returning and longtime veterans are put on secret waiting lists that are meant to hide the fact that they're not able to see doctors. The waits they must endure before they receive treatment often are a year or longer. Hundreds of veterans have died because they were unable to see a VA doctor. What's happening with the VA typifies what is going to happen with all medical care in the United States: Those who are ill and need treatment will be shuttled to the back of the line to endure long waits before they receive treatment. The fact that in the VA case it's those who have sacrificed their health fighting for our freedom makes this ineptitude only more egregious.

The White House isn't releasing any genuine data, because there isn't any. Sebelius has resigned, and the administration has hired another incompetent who can mismanage what's left of Obamacare. All they can provide is a made-up number to tell the public how many people are covered to try and make it sound like they know what they're talking about. We're starting to understand they have no idea what's going on.

CHAPTER 7

The War on Civil Rights

During the Civil War, Lincoln rerouted telegraph lines through the War Office to spy on reporters and editors to make sure their stories were sympathetic to his war views. Obama's FCC has pressured newsrooms to report what this administration wants reported. Those who don't are taken off the White House A-list—pushed to the back of the reporting bus.

By using the phrase "the war on civil rights" as the title of this chapter, my intent is to show you how serious I find our own government's depriving us of our civil rights to be. But before we go one sentence further I want to make sure you know what I mean by those words.

If you ask a sophomore in high school to define the term, you'll usually get an answer that includes names from the liberal Mount Rushmore: Martin Luther King Jr. or the Rev. Jesse Jackson or Bobby Kennedy. Or they'll bring up the Thirteenth and Fourteenth Amendments and how they pertain to slavery. It's not the high school students' fault that they have such a narrow view of words that are so encompassing. From the second grade on, they're limited to a one-sided version of what civil rights means. They're taught to think that civil rights is about one group, one movement, or one era in American history.

In other words, they're not getting the complete picture.

By definition, civil rights are political and social freedoms for all citizens and not simply for one group. And it's these civil rights, the ones to which we're all entitled by the U.S. Constitution, which are now disappearing.

Among the signs of that is the fact that race-based violence is on the rise in America today. I'm sure you've heard of this epidemic. It's called the Knockout Game, and it mostly involves a defenseless person and a group of aspiring young men, often associated with a gang. Sometimes the incident is captured on video and uploaded to YouTube so the world can see just how inhuman American cities have become. In one of the more notorious of these videos, filmed in Jersey City, New Jersey, you can see a man killed by the sucker punch. Over a million people have watched the video.

While I see the emergence of the Knockout Game as a sign of the racial division that is deepening in our country, that's not the only reason I recount it here. I tell it to you to bring your attention to a similar assault that recently happened in our most powerful legislative body. I tell it as a prime example of how vulnerable our civil rights are to the gang of leftists who now run this country.

Let me give you a little background.

If you're old enough, you might remember a movie called *Mr. Smith Goes to Washington*. Its director was Frank Capra, a man who made films so syrupy you could get diabetes just watching them. The simple premise of the movie is this: A naïve freshman U.S. senator introduces a bill that would set aside land for a camp in his home state to be used by the "Boy Rangers," Capra's lightly veiled version of the Boy Scouts. What the freshman senator doesn't know is that legislation for a graft-funded dam project on the land is already in the works, orchestrated by a crooked senator and unscrupulous businessmen.

To try and stop the legislation, Mr. Smith stages a one-man filibuster, holding the floor of the Senate to delay the vote on the dam project until his voice is raw and he's near collapse. Of course, Mr. Smith holds on just long enough. As the movie ends, mailbags filled with letters in support of the camp and carried by members of the Boy Rangers are dumped on the Senate floor. The principled politics behind *Mr. Smith Goes to Washington* not only made Jimmy Stewart a star, it also made a star out of the Senate filibuster, the single most effective defense against the overreach of corrupt power when it comes to presidential appointments.

The Filibuster Fiasco

Frank Capra is dead. So is Jimmy Stewart. And now so is the filibuster.

The filibuster had been around since the late 1700s. Harry "Reid 'Em and Weep" played the Knockout Game, successfully ending the filibuster without even bringing it to a vote.

And the American people are the defenseless victims.

Even Lamar Alexander, who has trouble making sense when

he tells you what he had for breakfast, said that Reid's removal of the filibuster is the "most dangerous and consequential change in the rules since Thomas Jefferson wrote them."[1]

The rule that Reid invoked is known as the "nuclear option." It allows the Senate to approve presidential nominations to the court and executive-level appointments with a simple majority. In March 2013, Rand Paul played the Jimmy Stewart role, filibustering for thirteen hours against the use of drones against Americans on American soil. A month earlier, Ted Cruz filibustered against raising the national debt ceiling.

Thanks to Reid's unilateral action, no longer can a filibuster be applied to force a supermajority vote. Rand Paul and Ted Cruz were the last of the Jimmy Stewarts in the Senate.

As I've told you, the Democrat-controlled Senate has pushed through a group of their handpicked policy cronies disguised as judges to forward the liberal agenda. Here's just one example of the damage the repeal of the filibuster rule can do. The president appointed three new members to the seven-member Federal Reserve Board of Governors. Janet Yellen, the new chairman of the Fed, now needs only a simple majority to have new board members approved.

But that's not something you have to worry about, right?

All that board does is to decide what the government is going to do with your money.

It didn't start out that way. The Federal Reserve Bank was created a little over a hundred years ago. Originally charged with creating monetary policy that would ensure economic stability, the Fed's mandate has expanded to the point where the presidentially appointed regional Federal Reserve Bank Board of Governors—known as the Federal Open Market Committee, or FOMC—is considered a "bank." Its influence and reach have extended far beyond that role. It now colludes with other major banks in doing everything from dictating interest rates to helping those banks hide such debt as valueless financial derivatives off their books.

But let me get back to the topic of Harry Reid's knocking out the filibuster.

Even Carl Levin, the outgoing Democratic senator from Michigan, was appalled by Reid's actions: "Once again [we] are moving down a destructive path," Levin said. "Pursuing the nuclear option in this manner removes an important check on majority overreach which is central to our system of government."[2]

So let me ask you, where will this governmental overreach end? Will the president and the Senate use this newfound power to seize your guns? Will the Senate, bowing to the president's will, use the nuclear option to help grant amnesty to tens of millions of illegal aliens who shouldn't be in the country in the first place? Will executive orders, immune to Senate scrutiny, continue to dole out entitlements that ensure poverty for life? Will the Obama administration continue to strangle the voice of reason and truth by appointing commissioners to the FCC who are intent on annihilating the First Amendment?

To those who support him, the president is the benevolent dictator they've been calling for. But where there is a dictator, there is inevitably gross injustice and the trampling of basic rights for all.

What is benevolent about our attorney general's choosing which laws he will uphold based on his leftist ideological leanings?

What is benevolent about a Department of Homeland Security that allows our southern border to be overrun by Mexican cartels bringing drugs and violence into the country while it stores up weapons and ammunition and tries to prevent American citizens from owning guns?

What is benevolent about a president whose signature legislation is single-handedly leading to the demise of the greatest medical system in the world?

And what is benevolent about Mrs. Obama's obscenely expensive and too-frequent travels with her mother and daughters along for a multi-million-dollar free ride at the expense of American taxpayers? This while her demands of a press blackout meant that even the lapdog U.S. journalists were not allowed to travel with her and her enormous entourage on her March 2014 "Spring Break" jaunt to China?

Guns and Globalists

Let's begin with guns. In early 2013, after the Newtown tragedy, we were being bombarded with ideologically skewed misrepresentations of the importance of gun control in reducing such tragic events. As I said after Newtown, I don't believe that psychopaths and other people with severe mental disorders should own guns. But I also know that the Democrats who want to take away our right to defend ourselves use the blood of innocent children to forward their agenda and take away all guns owned by private citizens. This does not include the guns that the Democrats themselves own. It's a direct assault on one of our most precious civil rights.

At the same time Democrats are preaching gun control and trying to deny us our right to bear arms, they're secretly reaping the spoils of their gun-control hypocrisy. Prominent

California Democratic state senator Leland Yee, a guy who hails from San Francisco, where I live, has tirelessly crusaded for gun control, preaching to grab our guns.

While he was shamelessly badgering his constituents about the need for them to give up their guns, Lee was allegedly working with gun smugglers in the Philippines in order to buy automatic weapons from them and bring them into the United States. He allegedly planned to sell them here.

The state senator who wanted to make sure that private citizens couldn't own handguns pled not guilty to "five counts related to influence peddling and one count of arms trafficking."[3] He was caught when he allegedly bragged to an undercover FBI about his smuggling operation. Lee's response after his arrest? "I'm just trying to run for Secretary of State. I hope I don't get indicted."[4]

While the antigun propaganda on display in every media outlet controlled by the left was being shoved down our throats, one of our public servants was up to something even more sinister. It's the old shell game—look at this hand while I fleece you with the other one.

While the federal government continues to work to limit the amount and type of weapons and ammunition private citizens can own, the Social Security Administration and the Department of Homeland Security has purchased *billions* of rounds of ammunition—more than enough to shoot every American citizen five times—including hollow-point bullets so lethal they're banned by the Geneva Convention.[5] In addition, DHS ordered 2,700 light-armored tanks to complement the billion-bullet march toward its impending war against American citizens.[6]

When asked by members of Congress about the purchase

of the ammunition, then-DHS secretary Janet Napolitano, aka "Big Sis," declined to answer.[7]

Then, almost a year later, DHS put out a notice that it was seeking bids for its intended purchase of more ammo, in this case 141,000 rounds of the most powerful and efficient sniper bullets.

It gets worse. One of the firms DHS dealt with produces targets called "no more hesitation" that are used by agents in practice. Some of the depictions on these targets are of pregnant women, children, old folks in residential settings, and other "non-traditional threats."[8]

At the same time, the Ohio National Guard is training its troops to target Second Amendment supporters with what they call "antigovernment" points of view. They call these patriots "domestic terrorists." Earlier, the same National Guard unit participated in a similar drill that targeted left-wing terrorists. The unit apologized for having the bad judgment to target a left-wing political group, but there was no hint of an apology for the targeting of conservatives.[9]

I'm not sure that patriotic American citizens, like the ones in the crosshairs of the Department of Homeland Security and the Ohio National Guard, are aware of how dire this situation is. In his 2008 campaign speech, Obama told us that a U.S. government under his presidency should create a "civilian national security force that would be just as powerful, just as strong, just as well-funded" as our military.

What he didn't say in his speech is that, as Abraham Lincoln had done at the time of the American Civil War, he envisioned this civilian military as his palace guard, policing our towns and our neighborhoods for any sign of insurrection against his assault on our fundamental freedoms.

If you think I'm exaggerating, consider this: The U.S. Army has a 300-acre site in Virginia where they practice a large-scale military takeover of an American city, which they've re-created. This "Anytown USA" contains a bank, a sports stadium, school, and even an underground transportation system that looks strikingly like the one in Washington, D.C. This fake town cost American taxpayers nearly $100 million.

A U.S. Army manual describes maneuvers like the ones practiced in the fake city as "Civil Disturbance Operations." The manual also includes directions for internment camps and a guide for internees to be "re-educated" until they develop "an appreciation for U.S. policies." This is what the Soviet Union did to its dissidents. An academic study that dovetails with the Army manual details the aggressive military response to an insurrection by Tea Party members who take over a town like the one built in Virginia.[10]

Do you realize what this means?

Do you realize the preparations that are being made by our federal government to stop any resistance to their increasingly dangerous and far-reaching denial of our civil rights?

The Savage Truth of the matter is that our government is preparing for nothing less than the next civil war. It's marshalling forces to be used against the American people, but the very divisions that the government is creating are causing many Americans to think about what we must do to resist this government takeover.

This administration is doing everything it can to turn America into the world capital of illegal immigration. The Department of Homeland Security is under orders not to prosecute aliens who are in the country illegally and instead to open our borders to another wave of non-English-speaking illegal immigrants, many of whom will swell the rolls of an eternal welfare state and guarantee a Democratic-majority voting bloc while they continue to undermine our language and our culture.

Our president and the government agencies at his behest are doing everything they can to ensure that a wave of illegal immigrants continues to cross our southwestern border with Mexico. On top of that, they're offering illegal aliens benefits that make them beholden to the Democratic Party for life. The U.S. Department of Agriculture, in conjunction with the Mexican government, has assured illegal immigrants in a Spanish-language brochure distributed in Mexico that their immigration status will not be checked when they apply for free food once they're in the United States, and that they "need not divulge information regarding [their] immigration status" in order to receive food stamps.[11]

Obama suspended the deportation of millions of young illegal aliens by executive order because Congress would not pass the DREAM Act. His Justice Department refuses to enforce the antidrug laws in states with antimarijuana laws. His administrators have gutted federal welfare-for-work requirements by defining *work* in terms so convoluted, states have trouble interpreting the meaning of the word.

And you wonder why I get mad?

Through such acts as suspending the insurance mandate of the Affordable Care Act by executive order, Obama has effectively made the rule of law irrelevant in this country.

As one commentator has expressed it, Obamacare "is a perversely self-inflicted, man-made disaster that replaced the efficiency of the private markets with the tangle, confusion, and ideological bias of government bureaucracy."[12]

This administration is making a blatant power grab. It makes virtually every decision on the basis of politics and not on the basis of the Constitution it's pledged to uphold. Every agency of the administration is infected with this corruption and hunger for power.

From the policies and practices of Attorney General Eric Holder to former Health and Human Services secretary Kathleen Sebelius to "retired" director of the tax-exempt division of the IRS Lois Lerner, there is not a single policy or decision that is made for the reason it should be made. Every decision smacks of leftist politics and sympathy for America's enemies both outside and inside this country. Every decision is made to carry out what I see as the administration's true agenda: undermining America's position as the most powerful nation in the world for the purpose of advancing the establishment of a global world order.

America's Constitutional Crisis

Below is just a partial laundry list of this administration's recent actions overriding the Constitution:

• The Labor Department issued a mandate in February 2013 that delayed the Affordable Care Act limits on individual health-care spending for a year, a procedure that requires legislative action.

• The administration explained in a blog post during the 2013 Fourth of July weekend that it was unilaterally delaying the employer mandate, again without congressional cooperation.

- In August 2013, the federal Office of Personnel Management issued a declaration of change to the Affordable Care Act that released congressmen and their staffs from having to buy their health insurance from the federal health-care exchanges.

- The Department of Education, in conjunction with Eric Holder's Justice Department, issued an order to the University of Montana demanding that the school restrict freedom of speech. Among other things, it denied students their legal rights by suggesting that anyone violating the university's speech codes be punished without having their cases heard before a committee of students.[13]

Eric Holder's Justice Department, populated as it is with attorneys who have defended accused terrorists and other anti-American clients as they pressed their leftist agenda, consistently did everything in its power—and often well outside its power—to trample the rule of law.

Nothing has changed since Holder took office.

In fact, it's gotten worse.

From our right to own property, to our religious freedom, to our ability to purchase and own stock, the Department of Justice has used every bit of its power to expand government and limit civil rights. In 2013 alone, the Supreme Court intervened and denied the Department of Justice's arguments nine times.[14]

Let me give you some examples of what the Justice Department is still doing to deny us our civil rights.

For starters, it's relentlessly prosecuting the administration's political enemies.

Former Virginia governor Robert McDonnell has been indicted on charges of corruption, and an aggressive criminal investigation into the activities of New Jersey governor Chris Christie has been launched.

McDonnell is accused of corruption charges stemming from gifts he received from a Virginia businessman. The great treasure the governor is accused of taking amounts to about as much as they give you at a golf outing: golf shirts, clubs, and shoes. The former attorney general of Virginia—who's a Democrat—conducted an in-depth investigation and found no crime had been committed. He called the whole matter "political niceties."[15]

But Holder is going after McDonnell as if he's a serial killer. If this isn't a political witch hunt, I don't know what is.

The real reason for Holder's attack on McDonnell?

Before the "scandal" broke, he'd been a top contender to run against Hillary Clinton in 2016.

It's the same reason the DoJ is going after Chris Christie. Christie appears to be another likely candidate to oppose Hillary Clinton, and the Democratic Party needs to do all it can to nip Christie's potential candidacy in the bud.

And what's Christie's offense? Traffic on the George Washington Bridge. The DoJ goes after Chris Christie for traffic on a bridge that always has a traffic jam? I know that there were some issues that happened as a result of the traffic jam, but nothing resembling evidence that Christie was involved in making it happen has been presented. I grew up in New York City. I've driven over the George Washington Bridge countless times. I can count on one hand the times there weren't cars lined up bumper-to-bumper at the toll plaza in Fort Lee. Instead of inventing crises over which to investigate politicians of the opposing party, investigate the real crises, the real corruption that is occurring all around us.

Holder's Department of Justice does not defend the law of the land; it holds itself above the law. When he was questioned in a congressional hearing about the legal and constitutional basis on which the president had delayed the employer mandate of the Affordable Care Act, he couldn't come up with an answer. Looking confused, he stammered, "I'll be honest with you, I have not seen...I don't remember looking at or having seen the analysis in some time, so I'm not sure where along the spectrum that would come."[16]

When he was questioned about the fact that he appointed Barbara Bosserman—a Justice Department trial attorney who just happens to be an Obama political donor—to head the investigation into the IRS targeting of conservative political groups, Holder showed his inadequacy as a liar: "I don't know anything about the political activities of any of the people who are involved in this investigation."[17]

More than ten thousand attorneys work at the Department of Justice. And Holder wants us to believe that it just so happened that the one he picked was also the best possible candidate to protect the administration's political interests?

Let me ask you, how many months have passed since the IRS targeting of conservative groups was exposed? And in that time, how much have you heard about the federal investigation? How many people have been indicted? How many have been fired? Has there been one single action taken to get to the bottom of this extremely important case?[18] Don't bother to look it up. I'll save you the time. There hasn't been any.

And in the meantime, all the e-mails that Lois Lerner sent during the time the targeting of conservative groups was going on have suddenly, nearly a year later, been found to have gone missing![19]

After True the Vote founder Catherine Englebrecht applied for tax-exempt status, she received no fewer than fifteen visits from four different federal agencies over a two-year span. The IRS audited Englebrecht's personal and business tax returns four times. She was questioned over and over about her political beliefs.[20]

Our rights are being trampled, and the top lawyer in the land claims he doesn't know the law or the political affiliation of the people he appoints to uphold the law.

Let me tell you what Eric Holder is doing in Louisiana to the rights of the very minorities he claims to be defending.

After Hurricane Katrina, the New Orleans school district decided to convert all of the city's public schools into charter schools. These schools are publicly funded, but independent school boards govern them.

By 2014, 85 percent of New Orleans students attended these charter schools.[21]

Now the DoJ is aggressively trying to prevent the parents of Louisiana minority school children from being able to choose the school they can attend. He's doing everything he can to make sure that the children who would most benefit from being able to use the state's school voucher program are denied.

Louisiana governor Bobby Jindal described it correctly when he said that the president and his attorney general "are trying to keep kids trapped in failing public schools against the wishes of their parents."

The DoJ is arguing that Louisiana schools that are still operating under desegregation laws passed in the 1970s should *not* be allowed to issue vouchers to children because the vouchers might upset the racial balance of the schools. In one instance, the Justice Department claimed that a school that had lost six students because they chose to attend other schools had become "too white." Another had become "too black."[22]

Nearly 90 percent of the students in the New Orleans public school system are African-American. The Justice Department is arguing that allowing 570 of them to attend the schools of their choice would "create a racial imbalance."[23]

Is Holder saying that 88 percent black students is not racial imbalance?

Or is he really saying that keeping minority students in failing schools will mean that they're unlikely to be able to go to college and escape being dependent on federal welfare for the rest of their lives?

Of the mountain of questionable moves he's made, among the attorney general's most questionable was naming Debo Adegbile to the position of assistant attorney general for the Civil Rights Division of the Justice Department.

Let me tell you who Debo Adegbile is. He's an attorney who defended cop killer Mumia Abu-Jamal.

On December 9, 1981, a young Philadelphia police officer named Danny Faulkner pulled over a car that was going the wrong way on a one-way street. Quickly, the routine traffic stop turned cold-blooded. Danny, an Army veteran and a newly married husband, was shot once in the back and, as he lay dying, four more times, including once in his face. Mumia Abu-Jamal, a radio personality and Black Muslim, was literally holding the smoking gun when police backup arrived. Abu-Jamal was convicted of murdering Danny Faulkner in Philadelphia in 1982.[24]

When Holder was trying to push Adegbile's nomination through the Senate, the Judiciary Committee chairman,

Democrat Patrick Leahy, refused to let Faulkner's widow, Maureen, testify at Adegbile's confirmation hearing.[25] The wife of a murdered cop was denied the right to testify at the appointment hearing of an attorney who had defended the murderer.

Despite Leahy's intransigence, the Senate, including seven Democrats, staged a victory for principled government, voting by a simple majority of 52–47 to defeat Adegbile's appointment.[26]

Harry Reid's own change of the filibuster rules, which now requires only a simple majority to defeat a filibuster, was forced back down his throat. Without Reid's unilateral change, the Senate likely would not have had the votes to block Adegbile's appointment without a filibuster. Reid himself, hoist by his own petard, was furious. Nonetheless, Reid is planning to ask the Senate for another vote on the appointment at some time in the future.[27]

New York, New York

Let me change the focus from the corrupt politics of the federal government to those of the city I grew up in. What's happening in New York is mirroring the takeover of our nation, as a committed leftist is trying to seize control of the city.

I grew up in the Bronx. I remember my grandfather well. I call him "the astronaut," because he was the one who left the old country to come to America, which might as well have been Mars for all he knew. He's the one who first learned the language that his grandson would later master and make his living from. He's the one who assimilated and worked so hard that he dropped dead at forty-seven.

I also remember living in a family with a hardworking father and a stay-at-home mother. I remember sitting on my father's lap as we listened to the radio. There were no satellite dishes, Netflix, or SmartTV. It was simple, hard, and wonderful all at once. Because we knew there was opportunity if we worked for it.

I know New York City. It's in my blood. I've lived through the disastrous administrations of left-of-liberal mayors like John Lindsay and watched from a distance as David Dinkins—even worse than Lindsay, if that's possible—almost destroyed the city. New York City has many great people. There are even a few good conservatives there. It just has lousy leaders.

And none of them is worse than Bill de Blasio.

Here is how I see Mayor de Blasio: he is following the same socialist path as that being taken by the federal government. This includes expanding benefits for illegal aliens.

This is what de Blasio said in one of his first press conferences as mayor: "To all of my fellow New Yorkers who are undocumented, I say, 'New York City is your home, too, and we will not force any of our residents to live their lives in the shadows.'"

Then why, Mr. Mayor, don't you send bus tickets to the ones streaming over Arizona's border carrying bundles of pot? You can meet them at the Port Authority Bus Terminal with a book of food stamps, a Jimmy Buffett T-shirt, and a frozen margarita. The New York City mayor fancies himself a modern-day Robin Hood, taxing the rich to help the poor. But how does he help the poor? By using tax revenues to fund social crutches like pre-K schooling, which will be about as helpful in stopping the cycle of poverty as was Al Gore's Midnight Basketball. Remember that beauty?

Just two months into his term, de Blasio called a press conference to announce a sweeping plan to crack down on moving violations in order to eliminate pedestrians being killed by motor vehicles. Okay. I don't think his idea will make much of a difference, but okay. Then, two days after the press conference, a news van following the mayor clocked his SUV going at sixty miles per hour in a twenty-five-mile-an-hour zone while it committed no fewer than thirteen moving violations on a trip from Queens to City Hall. The violations included blowing through stop signs and changing lanes indiscriminately.[28]

His hypocrisy is inexcusable. The new mayor calls himself a New Yorker, but he grew up in Cambridge, Massachusetts, in the shadow of Harvard University. The very definition of a limousine liberal, he eats pizza with a knife and fork and spouts the liberal line about income equality while all the time emboldening social entitlements like food stamps, minimum wage, and illegal-immigrant ID cards that increase inequality.

And where do you think de Blasio came up with these ideas? He calls his policies "government with a soul," but even his words aren't his own. Fiorello La Guardia came up with that chestnut when he was mayor back in the 1930s.

I thank my lucky stars every day that I no longer live in New York. I love the city, but I can't stand its politics.

Take charter schools, for instance. De Blasio is in lockstep with Eric Holder, and he's using the power of his office to try to enforce regulations that are a blueprint for killing the expansion of charter schools.

In what amounts to a prison sentence, poor and minority schoolchildren in New York City are relegated to a second-class education and permanent status in the American underclass as de Blasio goes about ending a $210 million subsidy for charter schools when they operate in the same buildings as public schools. This would raise costs enormously and make it nearly impossible for these schools to meet operating expenses. De Blasio is doing everything he can to eliminate charter schools by denying them the opportunity to locate in the same buildings as public schools.[29]

In other words, he's taking away free choice for the families of seventy thousand New York City students who already attend charter schools and fifty thousand more who want to go to them. Like others in positions of power in the Democratic Party, de Blasio is determined to make sure American poor and minority students remain trapped in the American leftist educational gulag.

And the reason is simple: A racial minority citizen who depends on the U.S. government for his or her food and shelter is a guaranteed Democratic voter for life.

Each day this man is in office, he makes the city worse.

Anybody who's visited Manhattan will tell you that Fifty-Ninth Street between Fifth and Eighth Avenues, also known as Central Park South, is lined with lovely horse-drawn carriages. They're iconic. They've been there forever. You've seen them in dozens of movies. One of de Blasio's first campaign promises was to get rid of them. "[I'll] aggressively move to make horse carriages no longer a part of the landscape," he said.

In their place he wants to put electric cars, presumably to run over the pedestrians that he doesn't hit with his own speeding SUV.

Let me just give you one more example of de Blasio hypocrisy. In February 2013, New York City police pulled over a Lincoln Continental in Brooklyn for making an illegal turn. Orlando Findlayter, the self-ordained "bishop" of a church that's located over a bodega, was the driver of the car. When police checked, they discovered that the bishop's driver's license had been suspended for failure to buy auto insurance, and he was wanted on several outstanding warrants stemming from an immigration protest. Because it was one o'clock in the morning, Bishop Orlando was being processed into the system and was about to spend a night in jail, just like anyone else arrested at that time of night in New York.

Then the phone rang in the precinct commander's office.

It seems that Orlando Findlayter was more than just a warrant evader and bodega bishop. He was also a member of Bill de Blasio's transition team and had delivered thousands of black votes for the mayor. When the precinct commander picked up the phone she was quite surprised to hear Mayor de Blasio's voice.

If you guessed that Orlando didn't spend the night in jail, you guessed correctly. Because in New York City today there are two sets of rules: one set for the friends of the mayor, and one set for everyone else.[30]

Since before the days of Abraham Lincoln, New York City has always been the center of media. In Lincoln's day, of course, newspapers were the main form of professional news delivery. And like the president and the swooning press of today, Lincoln had the editors of the big papers of New York in his watch pocket. In no small measure, those editors and the newspapers they worked for catapulted Lincoln onto the national stage and were perhaps the primary reason he was elected president the first time.

Among the things Lincoln found it necessary to do early in the Civil War was to have the telegraph wires rerouted through the office of his secretary of war, Edwin M. Stanton. Lincoln knew which stories he felt needed to be withheld from publication. Stanton was also in charge of what amounted to Lincoln's secret police. During the Civil War, this covert squad arrested dozens of reporters and editors who weren't faithful to Lincoln's message.[31]

Obama seems to be following Lincoln's path, perhaps based on his sense that we're heading toward a second civil war.

As I told you in chapter 3, the Federal Communications Commission proposed a plan to interrogate television and radio newsroom employees in order to gather information on how they choose the stories they run, although the plan was never implemented. The plan was called Critical Information Needs, and the FCC planned to target newsrooms across the country. Obviously, none of these news organizations would have been able to operate without the FCC's approval. I ask you: How far away are we from the FCC dictating what the stations can or can't say?

Here's how Democrats, along with the FCC—the federal administration group that is looking to steal away even the news we receive in our newspapers and broadcast media—plan to save American citizens in case they have their cell phones stolen: They propose to require by law that phone manufacturers put a "kill switch" in cellular devices so they can be disabled and their personal information wiped out in case their owners lose them. The bill would give the FCC the right to require that this feature be included in new smartphones, and it would likely cost consumers $30 billion... every year.

Pardon my sarcasm, but of course there's no possibility that the FCC could use this capability to shut down the phones of anyone it thought was engaged in subversive or criminal activity, is there? No chance it might share this capability with, say, the NSA?[32]

The FCC is only one of the federal agencies this administration uses to attack its enemies.

Filmmaker James O'Keefe had exposed the radical leftist voter-fraud group ACORN by secretly filming ACORN agents explaining to clients how they could game the system. After O'Keefe released the footage to the public, ACORN was effectively disbanded.

That didn't sit well with the president, who had had close ties to ACORN throughout his political career.

O'Keefe is now having his tax returns audited in New York for the second time.[33]

While the IRS has singled out O'Keefe and other conservative political individuals and groups for scrutiny, it has intentionally refused to look at the finances of labor unions and business groups who support Obama.

Instead, it's focusing on the people and organizations that oppose this administration politically.

In November 2013, the IRS changed its regulations regarding 501(c)(4) groups. The new regulations eliminate tax-exempt status for organizations that engage in activities such as educating citizens, holding candidate forums, and political lobbying. The groups targeted include those whose officers have made any public statements that so much as refer to incumbent political figures and candidates.

Labor unions are exempt from these new regulations.

The IRS developed this plan in secret. Lois Lerner, the former head of the IRS's tax-exempt division and a liberal operative, began to formalize the IRS attack strategy, in conjunction with the Treasury Department, against the administration's political enemies while Lerner's own targeting of conservative tax-exempt organizations was at its peak. E-mails between Lerner and Treasury Department officials clearly reveal this.

Treasury Department attorney Ruth Madrigal sent an e-mail to Lois Lerner and other key IRS officials in June of 2012 that referenced "addressing [the political activities of 501(c)(4) organizations] (off-plan) in 2013, I've got my radar up and this seemed interesting."

The targeting of conservative organizations was intentional from the start, and it began as far back as 2011.[34]

And it was not "rogue" employees, as the president claimed in a national interview, who were carrying out this widespread attack. It was, and continues to be, the collective effort of the administrators who now populate the current administration and threaten our freedoms.

The Four Horsewomen of the Apocalypse

As I've told you, the Four Horsewomen of the Apocalypse are the ladies who make most of the decisions that come out of the White House. Secretary of State Hillary Clinton, who shouted "What difference does it make?" when she was confronted about the four Americans killed in the Benghazi terrorist raid during a Congressional hearing, is one of them.

Two is Susan Rice, who lied to the American people on five national television shows about the Benghazi massacre.

Three was Kathleen Sebelius, now the former Health and Human Services secretary. Sebelius presided over the Obamacare debacle.

And four is Valerie Jarrett, the most powerful and dangerous of them all.

Jarrett's official title is senior advisor and assistant to the president for public engagement and intergovernmental affairs. Jarrett was the one who advised Obama to go ahead and pass the Affordable Care Act despite the fact that he didn't have the votes to do so. She's also the person who advised Obama to loan half a billion dollars to Solyndra, the failed green energy company that cemented the administration's reputation for crony capitalism and unworkable projects.[35]

But despite her disastrous record as a decision maker, Jarrett is the key advisor to the president.

When the American consulate in Benghazi was under siege, it was Jarrett who is said to have ordered the stand-down.[36] She's also reported to be the one who was instrumental in negotiating the infamous deal with Iran that has allowed that country to continue developing nuclear weapons.

Though Jarrett may be the most dangerous person in Washington, D.C., John Podesta is one of the most destructive leftists I know. Podesta was allegedly brought on to help right the foundering administration by rescuing it from the Obamacare disaster and the scandals I've just gone over.

Podesta, a former Bill Clinton advisor, is the founder of the Center for American Progress. This group was formed to promote the ideas of the left, and it functions thanks to donations from subversives like George Soros. Podesta's Center for American Progress is a tax-exempt corporation that I'm sure will never face problems with the IRS.

Podesta, a card-carrying leftist, has dedicated his life to developing policies and programs in the United States and internationally that undermine capitalism and freedom. In addition to working on the PR job of rebranding and selling Obamacare to an unwitting public, Podesta is taking his show global by working with the United Nations on something called the "universal sustainable development agenda," which is gobbledygook for "food stamps for the world." The plan is slated to begin in the year 2020.[37]

Podesta is also focused on stopping global warming for the world. As I'll explain to you in the next chapter, beneath its bogus "science of climate change," the climate change movement is actually an international leftist attempt at a worldwide wealth transfer, not from the rich to the poor but from the middle-class taxpayers around the globe to the über-wealthy.

This is not a book devoted just to bashing our president. Our freedoms are being undermined by anti-American forces that include many in the U.S. government, in our education system, our press, and our military. From economic advisors to foreign enemies, we're fighting against a broad-based coalition that wants to see us fail. Nonetheless, I'd be remiss if I didn't bring what the president is doing out into the open.

Let me start with this: In his 2014 State of the Union speech, Obama told America that he wasn't even going to go through the pretense of legislation anymore. "I've got a pen and I've got a phone," he told them.[38]

In other words, he's not changing his style of governing a bit.

He made it clear he was going to rule by executive order and by having his Cabinet secretaries issue regulations that do not need congressional approval in order to move what many see as his antibusiness, anti-energy, anti-America agenda forward.

And there is practically no one left to stop him. Up to now, there's been a small group of conservatives who are willing to stand up to him. They've been enough, but just barely enough, to make it difficult for the president to get laws passed that support his agenda.

Two Texas Republicans spoke out strongly against Obama's executive-order presidency. Representative Randy Weber tweeted that the president is a "socialistic dictator."[39] Senator Ted Cruz published a *Wall Street Journal* op-ed in which he described what he called "the president's persistent pattern of lawlessness, his willingness to disregard the written law and instead enforce his own policies via executive fiat.... The president's taste for unilateral action to circumvent Congress should concern every citizen, regardless of party or ideology."[40]

It bothers me when I hear politicians and political commentators explaining that there's not really very much the president can do as far as setting policy and making law without the approval of Congress.

Texas Republican congressman John Culberson said that if Obama tries to advance his agenda by using illegal executive orders the House has the power to stop him simply by withholding funding for the projects and policies he announces. In Culberson's words, "The power of the purse is the secret to this guy—the most illegal, unlawful president in American history."[41]

Culberson may be right about the illegality, but the "power of the purse" hasn't even slowed the president down.

Obama single-handedly implemented what amounts to his DREAM Act through a 2012 executive order that allows young illegal immigrants to remain in the United States indefinitely.

He's initiated regulations through the Environmental Protection Agency that have shut down oil exploration on the coast of Alaska and stalled the Keystone XL Pipeline, severely damaging America's energy industry, along with the U.S. economy.

He showed his sympathy for terrorists by unilaterally lifting immigration restrictions on people who have provided "limited material support" to terror groups.[42]

Rather than protect our borders and our citizens from allowing terrorist supporters into the United States, Obama has effectively granted immunity from deportation to known terrorists.[43]

If you think Congress can stop this administration's subversive undermining of the Constitution and the laws of the United States by cutting funding, you're in a fantasyland. Republican "leaders" like John Boehner and former Republican vice presidential candidate Paul Ryan just don't get it. They refuse to understand that they're the victims of a master of legislative sleight-of-hand who has already taken over many governmental functions that should be handled by the other branches of our federal government. Both of these leaders have engaged in discussions with the president about a new immigration law that would effectively grant amnesty to the illegals already in the country.

The power of the purse has not been mentioned in these discussions.

Even political liberals are beginning to see the danger we face. One Constitutional scholar described the president's agenda as the very danger the Constitution was designed to avoid. "We have what many once called an imperial presidency model of largely unchecked authority," he wrote.[44]

Here is a short list of the policies and actions the president has initiated by executive order:

• He's unilaterally modified the Affordable Care Act without consulting Congress, despite the fact that Congress alone has the power to change the law.

• He's bypassed the Senate in confirming several of his nominees for federal posts.

• And he's effectively eliminated the welfare work requirements that Bill Clinton and the U.S. Congress had implemented and that had been so instrumental in reducing the number of Americans receiving welfare benefits.[45]

As one commentator has said, "The ultimate check on presidential lawlessness is elections and, in extreme cases, impeachment."[46]

The latter may be the only solution to end this imperial presidency.

I started this chapter by telling you how Obama and his henchman, Harry Reid, used the Knockout Game to take away our civil rights by getting rid of the filibuster. I went on to tell you how this administration, both by overt and subversive methods, is systematically stripping us of the rights and freedoms that the U.S. Constitution guarantees. I'll admit I've painted a pretty dire picture. Our enemies within outnumber us and out-finance us. And they have a head start.

CHAPTER 8

The War on Science

Yes, the Obama administration has lied to us consistently about global warming. They try to draw the eyes of the nation away from the real threats and calamities, like what's happening in the Middle East and in Ukraine, with nonsense about rising seas and shrinking ice caps. The president champions regulations that cripple our energy output while he delights the warmists and the windmill farmers. But don't be fooled.

I want to start this chapter by telling you a story. You might remember it. In late November 2013, a research vessel carrying Australian scientists and academics left New Zealand and headed to Antarctica on a fact-finding expedition. The expedition had set out to gather evidence of global warming. If you know anything about me you know that I know something about such types of voyages.

The ship, the *Akademik Shokalskiy*, was of Russian registry and was specially outfitted for polar navigating. But on Christmas Eve, the *Shokalskiy* sailed into a blizzard off the coast of

Antarctica and in no time was literally encased in ice so thick it was frozen in place. Two icebreakers, one Chinese and one Australian, which were in relative proximity, received the SOS. En route, the Chinese vessel, called the *Snow Dragon*, an icebreaker so powerful it's capable of navigating through ice as much as fifty feet thick, got stuck in the ice.[1] Ice thickness and blinding snow caused the Australian ship to turn back. A U.S. Coast Guard cutter named the *Polar Star*, one of the most technically advanced polar icebreakers ever made, headed to free the scientists. But six days later the Russian research vessel was still frozen as stiff as a box of spinach in an old freezer.

There was plenty of food and supplies onboard, so it wasn't exactly a life-or-death situation. E-mailed videos showed high spirits among the passengers on the isolated ship. But as the days went by and the weather cleared, it became obvious to the scientists that they weren't alone. Penguins lined the frozen shores to get a look at the icebound ship. Ten years or so ago, *March of the Penguins*, an Academy Award–winning documentary about the mating journey of emperor penguins, was filmed in this area. The penguins certainly knew more about their neighborhood than the scientists did. Perhaps some on board realized the irony of their situation.

Finally, two weeks later, helicopters dispatched from the Chinese icebreaker were able to rescue the passengers of the *Akademik Shokalskiy*. Chris Turney, the Australian college professor who led the expedition, admitted to a reporter that the research team "got stuck in our own experiment."

The New "Cold" War...on the Climate

In late February 2014, our secretary of state, John Kerry, said that "climate change" was the "greatest challenge of our generation." He added, "We should not allow a tiny minority of shoddy scientists and science and extreme ideologues to compete with scientific fact." Kerry—remember, he's the secretary of state—uttered these words while Russia was amassing military assets in Ukraine as part of the expansion Russian president Vladimir Putin was carrying out at our expense. For his part, Obama stood behind a microphone saying that the "international community" would issue a statement outlining the "costs" to Putin if he went any further.

A week later, while both Kerry and Obama were on vacation and Putin was ramping up his Crimea annexation and threatening to crash the U.S. economy if we tried to stop him, a "policy guidance statement," the first of Kerry's tenure, was released by the State Department. The statement urged his staff of seventy thousand to make climate change a top priority, saying, "Protecting our environment and meeting the challenge of global climate change is a critical mission for me as our country's top diplomat."[2]

In other words, after Putin had annexed Crimea and was moving troops to the Russia-Ukraine border in preparation for invading Ukraine, Kerry was delivering the full faith and power of the U.S. Department of State into the hands of the nutty warmists of the world.

While Putin was reigniting the Cold War, Kerry was focused on ecosystems.

Meanwhile, on the home front, Obama has been using

the climate change canard as a reason to stop all legitimate energy production. One of his more contemptible moves was the appointment of John Podesta. In earlier chapters, I told you about Podesta, an Obama lieutenant whom I consider one of the most dangerous leftists in this country. Podesta promised that Obama would not hesitate to use executive orders in regulating energy production. He would gladly bypass Congress to impose his will on the American people. Podesta guaranteed that his boss would move "forward on his climate change and energy transformation agenda."[3]

Obama's appointment of Podesta is perhaps the clearest indication that this administration is ignoring the separation of powers on which our republic is based. White House mouthpiece Jay Carney promised, "Podesta will help implement executive actions where necessary when we can't get cooperation out of Congress."[4] For his part, Podesta doesn't even try to hide his contempt of Republican members of Congress who oppose the Obama agenda. He calls them "a cult worthy of Jonestown."

It's been clear for more than a decade what the international left is up to. The wealth-transfer specialists bent on implementing a new world order have used climate change as a shell to move money from hardworking, responsible people to the über-elites. If it weren't so diabolical, their plan would be a parody: the domination of the global economy and the reduction of the planet's citizenry to nothing more than the welfare clients of the international oligarchy.

The best part about making a case against the fraud of global warming is you don't have to make a case. You can just sit back and watch the left make the case for you.

So let me introduce you to a few members of the global warming debate team.

Let me begin with Ottmar Edenhofer. Edenhofer was the co-chair of Working Group III of the Intergovernmental Panel on Climate Change (IPCC). That group's 2010 United Nations Climate Change Conference, known as COP-16, was held in Cancun, Mexico.

Edenhofer, in a startlingly candid interview with a German newspaper, let slip the true motives behind the climate change mafia: "[O]ne must say clearly that we redistribute de facto the world's wealth by climate policy," he told the German reporter. "This has almost nothing to do with environmental policy anymore, with problems such as deforestation or the ozone hole."[5]

Edenhofer's admission that global warming is nothing more than a political issue totally undermines the "science" that the left invented to justify global warming. The sole reason for the theory that man-made global warming exists at all is to help its proponents gain political and financial power over the money generated by capitalist economies.

In November 2013, 132 poor countries walked out of the United Nations climate talks during discussions of transferring wealth from richer countries—read "Western democracies"—to poorer ones. The discussion was about how wealthier nations would compensate those not so developed. The poorer nations insisted that developed countries give them $100 billion a year so they could prepare for natural disasters such as typhoons, heat waves, droughts, and other weather consequences of global warming. It was even suggested that rich countries pay for the fact that they had emitted greenhouse gases into the atmosphere as they developed their industrial base.[6] This is the true agenda of the climate change movement.

Another beauty is Christiana Figueres, the so-called

climate chief of the United Nations. Let me give you an idea of how much Figueres knows. Communist China, according to her, is the ideal model for government's role in fighting climate change. One has to wonder if Ms. Figueres is familiar with the giant digital billboards the Chinese have erected. These advertisements feature a picture of the sun and the message "Protecting the atmospheric environment is everyone's responsibility." China's pollution levels are more than 25 times higher than even the World Health Organization says are safe. Undoubtedly, the signs are there to remind citizens, who are unable to see the sun for weeks at a time because the airborne particulate matter blocks it out, that the golden orb around which the Earth revolves still exists.

Citizens in China are regularly notified that the air they breathe is "very unhealthy" and can cause "significant aggravation of heart or lung disease and premature mortality in persons with cardiopulmonary disease and the elderly." Citizens are often advised to avoid all physical activity outdoors.[7] Although it is the greatest emitter of carbon dioxide into the atmosphere in the history of mankind, China is "doing it right," according to the U.N. climate change czar.[8]

There is no more powerful testimony, however, than evidence that comes from someone on one side of an issue who has seen the error of his ways. Such is the case with Patrick Moore, one of the cofounders of Greenpeace, the radical leftist climate change advocacy group. Greenpeace is one of the reasons Barack Obama hasn't, as of this writing, approved the Keystone XL Pipeline. Moore was a member of Greenpeace from its earliest days, in 1971, until the time he left the group fifteen years later, as Greenpeace became focused not on global warming but on the politics of global warming.

"There is no scientific proof that human emissions of carbon dioxide (CO_2) are the dominant cause of the minor warming of the Earth's atmosphere over the past 100 years," Moore said in front of a Senate committee on the environment. He went on to explain that even if the planet is warming up slightly, that's not necessarily a bad thing for human beings, who according to Moore are a "subtropical" species.[9] He went on to explain that "we evolved at the equator in a climate where freezing weather did not exist. The only reasons we can survive these cold climates are fire, clothing, and housing."[10]

Even more important, though, he talked about one of the primary reasons he left Greenpeace: The group aided and abetted those who established fraudulent computer models in order to scare people into believing that human activity actually had a negative impact on the climate. In other words, the "science" itself is a hoax. And you don't have to take Moore's word or my word for it. The people who practice it have admitted as much.

The entire climate-change movement is now in shambles, thanks to serial scandals about faked research, consecutive record cold and wet winters in much of Europe and the United States, and the conflict-of-interest get-rich schemes of prominent global-warming preachers such as the global warming debate team captain, Al Gore.

But you can only laugh at them for so long before it starts to sicken you. A graph created by these climate change researchers showing what they reported was a dramatic rise in temperature has been the subject of controversy when different e-mails were brought to light. One of the most potentially incriminating of these e-mails reads like this:

I've just completed Mike's [Michael Mann's] Nature trick of adding in the real temps to each series for the last 20 years (ie. from 1981 onwards) and from 1961 for Keith's [Keith Briffa's] to hide the decline.[11]

The e-mails that Mann exchanged with his pro-global-warming cohorts were made public through leaks; Mann himself has never released all of his e-mails. Recently seventeen news outlets got together to demand that he release them under the Freedom of Information Act.[12]

Mann had an answer to his critics. He made his opinion of at least one of them clear by filing a defamation-of-character lawsuit against a journalist who had criticized him in language Mann thought was overly harsh. The blog post over which Mann is suing described him as "the man behind the fraudulent climate-change 'hockey-stick' graph, the very ringmaster of the tree-ring circus." Mann claimed that the blog post in which the words appeared falsely implies that he engaged in academic corruption, fraud, and deceit.

In other words, he may have been behaving like a typical twenty-first-century academic.

When I say "typical academic," I mean it. Was another college prof, Lawrence Torcello of the Rochester Institute of Technology, saying in effect that anyone who disagrees with the fact that global warming is occurring and threatens life on this planet *should be jailed*?[13] Here are his words:

What are we to make of those behind the well documented corporate funding of global warming denial? Those who purposefully strive to make sure "inexact, incomplete and contradictory information" is given to the public? I believe we understand them correctly when we know them to be not only corrupt and deceitful, but criminally negligent in their willful disregard for human life. It is time for modern societies to interpret and update their legal systems accordingly.[14]

Speak what you see as the truth, and it's not out of the question that academics will sue you for defamation and suggest that you be thrown in jail. It's what the global warming movement has become.

In the midst of all this, the UN released its latest "climate change" report. It predicted that hundreds of millions of people will be displaced by the effects of climate change, from rising sea levels to droughts, and the result will be an increase in the risk of violent conflict around the globe. The report asserts that global warming will be responsible for food production being reduced by two percent annually, and the result will be a 20 percent increase in malnutrition in children.[15]

I'm not buying it, and it appears to me that the public isn't buying it, either.

But just when you think you've seen it all, they pull a stunt that tops the rest.

John Beale was one of the many agents at the Environmental Protection Agency (EPA) committed to advance the Obama climate agenda. To give you an idea of Beale's character, he applied for and was issued a handicapped parking permit because he claimed he suffered from malaria that he'd contracted while serving in Vietnam. Beale never served in Vietnam, nor did he have malaria. He just thought that his convenience was more important than that of someone who really needed the access. And Beale wasn't some low-level clerk.

He was the top climate change expert at the EPA and helped reauthorize the Clean Air Act. He was also the highest-paid member of the agency, which was a pretty neat trick given that he took as much as eighteen months off in a row.

The reason Beale was able take such extended leaves was because he convinced the EPA hierarchy that, in addition to his duties at the EPA, he was a CIA operative. The people running the EPA believed him. When he'd return from his sojourns—which were usually spent on Cape Cod, in his northern Virginia home, or at a variety of vacation spots to which he'd fly first class, stay in four-star hotels, and rent limousines, all on the company dime—he'd tell his environmental pals that he'd been on assignment in Pakistan or at CIA headquarters in Langley.

How long was Beale able to pull his con off? For decades. When he retired in 2011, the agency gave him a farewell dinner cruise on the Potomac. They also forgot to take him off the payroll. Beale received and cashed his full-time paycheck for nineteen months before the agency finally realized the mistake.

Beale was convicted and sentenced to thirty-two months for his crimes in late 2013.[16]

Beale's ruse might even be amusing if he didn't hold such influence in the EPA. In meetings with Gina McCarthy, head of the EPA's Office of Air and Radiation, Beale said he wanted to develop proposals, ones that could be introduced through legislation or through EPA regulation, that would enable the administration to increase its stranglehold on American energy production. In testimony Beale admitted he wanted to "modify the DNA of the capitalist system."

Responding to Beale's testimony, Dan Kish, senior vice

president for policy at the Institute for Energy Research, explained that "the real agenda behind this administration's energy and environmental policies is just what President Obama has said it is: to fundamentally transform America."[17]

The Environmental Pilferage Agency

By the way, you might have heard the name Gina McCarthy before. McCarthy was issued a subpoena that demanded she hand over data from taxpayer-funded EPA studies that had been conducted nearly twenty years ago. Based on these studies, which assert microscopic airborne particles kill thousands of Americans every year, the EPA put in place new ozone regulation standards that would cost the U.S. economy an estimated $90 billion a year. That would make them the most expensive regulations in U.S. history. McCarthy has refused to comply with the subpoena. Her reason for not releasing the data? Maybe it's because an *independent* study has found "no statistical correlation" between airborne microscopic particles and deaths in the state of California.[18]

I use the term *independent* in the most facetious way I can convey. The EPA is one of the most corrupt agencies in modern American history. As I see it, its only rival is the IRS.

The agency's latest attempt to expand its power over the release of greenhouse gases by automobiles has been expanded to include those released by power plants and other facilities, which in my opinion are already overregulated. A coalition of thirteen state attorneys general, industrial groups, and utility companies is challenging the EPA's regulatory power grab, and the case, *Utility Air Regulatory Group v. EPA*, has gone to the Supreme Court.[19]

Louisiana senator David Vitter had this to say: "This case marks an extremely critical point in clarifying just how far the Obama Administration can extend their regulatory overreach, including by rewriting the Clean Air Act to suit its needs."[20]

Vitter has cause to be concerned. The EPA said in its defense against the suit that emissions standards for passenger cars should be applied also to gas pollutants from stationary facilities. In other words, the EPA is expanding its power over the release of pollutants by automobiles to include those released by power plants and other facilities. Kentucky congressional representative Ed Whitfield went even further, saying the agency's move to broaden the scope of its regulatory powers reflects "an unprecedented expansion of regulatory control over the U.S. economy."[21]

E-mails also document the collusion among environmentalists and EPA officials as they work together to kill the Keystone XL Pipeline. Wyoming senator John Barasso says it this way: "These damning e-mails make it clear that the Obama administration has been actively trying to stop this important project for years."[22]

One of the e-mails in question was sent by Sierra Club radical environmentalist Lena Moffitt to Michael Goo, an EPA policy administrator who himself had been a stalwart of the environmental movement before he hired on with the EPA. Moffitt thanked Goo for meeting with her and her colleagues about the Keystone XL Pipeline and how to "engage" so that they could further disrupt plans to go ahead with Keystone. Barasso went on to say, "Despite the fact that Keystone XL has bipartisan support in Congress and from governors, environmental extremists inside and out of the administration are working behind closed doors to kill it."[23]

In addition to appeasing environmental radicals, the Obama administration has another reason to hold up approval of the Keystone XL Pipeline: Wealthy Democratic backers of the president have a great deal of money invested in companies who are in competition with the company that will build the pipeline. Virginia Democratic senator Tim Kaine opposed Keystone approval, saying, "In my view, there is now enough evidence to conclude that construction of this pipeline is not in America's long-term interest." What Kaine didn't mention was his conflict of interest. He has as much as $50,000 invested in Kinder Morgan Energy Partners, a company that is looking to build a pipeline that would compete directly with Keystone to transport oil from Canada through the United States.[24]

Obama's anti-energy policy came home to roost during the Ukrainian crisis that began in February 2014. Let me explain to you how the actions of this ideologically blinded president—who has clung to an energy policy based on fabricated data and his own and the radical left's use of energy policy to cement their power grab in the United States—have not only come home to roost for Americans who suffer economically from his policies but for America's allies from Europe to the Middle East as well.

In 2012, I made this prediction concerning the Keystone XL Pipeline:

Simply by relaxing the EPA stranglehold on oil and gas production, we would begin to economically isolate rogue regimes in the Middle East in a way no vague "economic sanctions" of the kind Obama has talked about but never instituted could ever do. If we go ahead with what I'm calling for here—approval of the Keystone XL Pipeline—within as little as a decade I predict we would be able to supply not only all of our own oil and gas needs, but those of our European allies as well.[25]

I'd like to make an addendum to those prophetic words. Not only would it isolate rogue regimes in the Middle East, it would isolate Vladimir Putin.

I never trusted Putin. I don't know why anyone who lived through the Cold War would. But I respect his savvy. He knows both his limitations and what he is not limited by. And our president doesn't limit him. He ignored Obama's threats—that his takeover of eastern Ukraine would cost him—and why not? The truth is that Putin supplies Europe with a significant amount of its energy, as much as half of some countries' total energy supplies. You see, Putin has for the past decade and more been exploiting Russia's substantial oil and natural gas resources through an aggressive exploration and drilling policy. He built pipelines to transport the enormous lode of energy he tapped from Russia through Ukraine to European customers.

In other words, while Obama was delaying the Keystone XL Pipeline project for more than five years on the basis of phony environmental standards and appeasing his green-energy cronies, Putin cornered Europe's energy market.

If Obama had moved ahead with approval of the Keystone XL Pipeline in the first year or two of his administration, we would have been able to step in and ship natural gas and oil to our European allies. Had that been the case, the

Russian dictator might not have acted as he did in Ukraine and Crimea, given that he would not have had the energy leverage that Obama's reckless and corrupt energy policy gave him. If Obama had given the go-ahead to Keystone even only two years ago, the United States would not have had to bow to Putin.

How could Obama not know this? That's the question. Is this another case of the current administration intentionally misusing our energy policy to weaken the U.S. internationally?

Is the situation in Ukraine part of a master plan the president has desired since he took office?

He certainly wasn't paying much attention to what was going on in Ukraine. Instead, he was out campaigning, outlining the next stages of his agenda in an attempt to distract America's attention from the domestic and foreign policy disasters—from Obamacare to the Middle East to Putin—that are unfolding before our eyes. Appearing in front of a group of political donors as Putin's military was advancing into Crimea and massing troops on the Russia-Ukraine border, Obama explained the situation in Ukraine this way: "We may be able to de-escalate over the next several days and weeks, but it's a serious situation and we're spending a lot of time on it."[26]

Not a word about the Russian and Ukrainian casualties or the military, financial, and energy crises Putin's actions are generating. As I see it, the only thing Obama seemed worried about was his being able to advance his agenda through incessant campaigning.

So is it that he doesn't care that his energy policy is making the world more dangerous? It certainly seems that way.

At home, his energy policy may be doing even more damage. Let me give you some examples of what I mean.

Obama has had no problems admitting that his energy policies would raise the cost of electricity for all Americans and would likely put the coal industry out of business. The president explained it this way:

> When I was asked earlier about the issue of coal, under my plan of a cap-and-trade system, electricity rates would necessarily skyrocket. . . . Because I'm capping greenhouse gases, coal-powered plants would have to retrofit their operations. That'll cost money; they will pass that money on to consumers.[27]

Two years later, his then soon-to-be-appointed secretary of energy, Steven Chu, said this: "Somehow we have to figure out how to boost the price of gasoline [in America] to the levels in Europe."[28]

He was setting the United States up for a conversion to green energy that he would engineer by throwing taxpayer money—billions' worth—to his green-energy cronies like Solyndra. Unfortunately, Obama ignores the fact that the energy from green sources like wind and the sun now provides only two-tenths of 1 percent of the U.S. electricity supply and are so diffuse that they will likely never provide more than 1 or 2 percent of the total energy needed to run this country.[29]

There are other considerations where green energy is concerned. For instance, wind-power installations kill more than 1.4 million birds and bats every year, and that number will only increase as windmill farms spread across the United States.

While the president makes a flourish about his pardon of a Thanksgiving turkey or two every year, he may be issuing a death sentence on our national bird. For the next thirty years, wind-power installations will be allowed to kill as many bald eagles and golden eagles as they want. The language of the imperative is cold: It calls what I see as the slaughter of the symbol of America the "non-purposeful take of eagles."

Take in this context means "murder."[30]

In other words, if you're building a wind-power farm, you don't have to follow the endangered species rules that other Americans must adhere to.

It's not just wind farms that kill birds. The glare from huge solar arrays that are often installed in remote areas can confuse migratory birds, including pelicans, causing them to think they are flying over bodies of water. When they attempt to land on what they see as water, they are often injured or killed by the heat generated by the solar panels.[31]

As he ignores the killing of eagles, under the endangered-species legislation Obama has diverted water from California farmers who desperately need it to maintain America's food supply in order to save the smelt. Instead of letting a few fish perish, Obama is sending California's drought-diminished water supply out into the Pacific Ocean.

The Real Cost of Our Climate Policy

Obama's purpose is to push alternative energy "solutions" that would compete with coal, oil, and natural gas. But there was something rather important that Obama and his climate comrades never bothered to find out. According to Prof. Larry Bell, renewable energy is not compatible with the existing power grid transmission and distribution system. It's costing Germany nearly $100 billion just to adapt its current energy delivery system in order to accommodate renewable energy, he says. The grid in the United States is hundreds of times larger and more complex than Germany's, and even planning to convert it to adapt to renewable sources would likely cost more than $100 billion. The cost of the conversion itself is so astronomical, it's not even raised in conversation.[32]

Guess what all of this time, energy, and money going into alternative sources has produced? According to the Bureau of Labor Statistics, the electricity price index in the United States rose to a new record high in January 2014. It's exactly what Chu claimed he wanted to happen. At the same time, Department of Energy data indicates that electricity production has declined since Barack Obama took office—it hit its peak in 2007 and has slid downward every year since. We've added 14 million people in the United States since then, and we're producing nearly 5 percent less electricity than we did only a year ago to supply their needs. The Obama administration doesn't even understand the law of supply and demand.[33]

Recently, Obama waved his executive-order wand and created what he calls climate hubs. Agriculture Secretary Tom Vilsack announced the creation of seven of these climate centers in January 2014. "Climate hubs are part of our broad commitment to developing the next generation of climate solutions," he said. Although Vilsack refused to directly answer reporters' questions on the cost of the hubs, estimates say that they will cost the taxpayer hundreds of millions of dollars. The hubs are supposed to help farmers and rural communities respond to the risks of climate change, including drought, invasive pests, fires, and floods. This type of information, as one strategist told Fox News, can also be found in the *Farmers' Almanac*, which you can buy online for $6.79. The proposed locations are at existing Agriculture Department facilities and/ or at agricultural universities, most of which have the same capabilities as the proposed hubs.

It's interesting to note that according to the U.S. Department of Agriculture, fires, specifically wildfires, are part of climate change. News to me. I thought wildfires were actually exacerbated by the federal government's unwillingness to go into forests and clear out debris. When trees and other vegetation die, they are currently left on the forest floor. This is done in the name of letting nature take its course instead of managing nature responsibly. Countless birds, animals, and humans suffer when the dead vegetation fuels forest fires. They kill people and destroy wildlife habitat and humans' homes. And then there is the amount of particulate matter that is spewed into the atmosphere as a result of these fires, matter that—if environmentalists are correct—exacerbates climate change. Even if they're right, they're wrong.

If the last decade's temperature data are any indication, we may be entering into another ice age. According to many scientists, the sun is in a period of what is known as "solar lull," which could predict a long period of global cooling. Dr. Richard Harrison, the head of space physics at Rutherford Appleton Laboratory in England, told the BBC he's never seen anything like this. "If you want to go back to see when the sun was this inactive…you've got to go back about 100 years," he said.[34]

So the problem isn't rising oceans that threaten to submerge coastal areas around the world after the polar ice caps melt from global warming; it's the onset of a new ice age. A similar phase of sunspot inactivity known as the Maunder Minimum occurred in the 1600s and triggered what has become known as the Little Ice Age. It lasted well into the nineteenth century—we've been pulling out of it gradually over the last hundred years—and it killed about a quarter of the people in northern Europe.

My question is this: Are we facing another Maunder Minimum? "There is no scientist alive who has seen a solar cycle as weak as this one," says Harvard-Smithsonian Center for Astrophysics researcher Andrés Munoz-Jaramillo. Another solar observer, David Hathaway, head of the solar physics group at the National Aeronautic and Space Administration's (NASA's) Marshall Space Flight Center, agrees: "I would say it is the weakest in 200 years."[35]

They're talking about the virtual disappearance of sunspots during the past year. Normally the number of sunspots rises and falls in eleven-year cycles, and we should currently be at the peak of the cycle, when the sun is producing the highest output of sunspots, a phenomenon that contributes to the earth's warming. Instead, the sun has effectively gone to sleep at a time when it should be producing sunspots at its maximum levels.[36]

One of the effects of the weakness of the current solar cycle can be seen in our weather here on earth. The global climate has been cooling for more than a decade, and the past winter—which was one of the coldest on record for the northern, midwestern, and eastern states—may be the precursor of temperatures to come. The data confirms this. In November 2013 alone, nearly 1,000 record low-temperature records were set in the United States.[37] At the same time, images from Europe's Cryostat spacecraft showed that Arctic sea ice coverage had increased by some 50 percent, from 1,400 cubic miles to 2,100 cubic miles by the end of the melting season when compared with the same time last year.[38] The Arctic, Antarctic, and Great Lakes ice masses have increased so greatly over only the past winter that even if the spring and summer warming in the northern hemisphere is normal, there is the risk of waters rising. It's not global warming but global cooling that is most likely to cause this to happen.

The climate statistics for 2013 were made public before NASA and the National Oceanic and Atmospheric Administration (NOAA) had a chance to tamper with them. The statistics revealed that 2013 was one of the ten coldest years in the United States since 1985, and it saw the largest year-on-year decline in global temperatures ever seen. Before the numbers are officially released to the sympathetic press, these two organizations will rework them so that they reflect the official U.S. position on climate change.[39] You can bet on that. When the *Akademik Shokalskiy* was frozen for weeks in the Antarctic, only Fox News mentioned the fact that the stranded climate crazies were out to demonstrate the existence of global warming.[40]

There is solid evidence that forces much larger than man's ability to spew carbon into the air are at work to change the climate. One climate scientist, Benjamin Santer, blames volcanoes. When volcanoes erupt, they inject large amounts of sulfur dioxide into the upper atmosphere, where it forms sulfuric acid drops that reflect sunlight back away from the earth. The reduced amount of radiant energy causes the lower atmosphere and the earth's surface to cool. There have been seventeen volcanic eruptions in the past fifteen years, and the mirror effect they create may be contributing to global cooling as well.[41] Unfortunately, although Santer correctly identifies the effect of volcanoes as reducing atmospheric temperatures, he is still working under the misconception that human activity significantly increases temperatures on our planet. Half right is better than nothing.

Volcanoes were implicated in another study that used ice-penetrating radar to discover an active volcano under nearly a mile of Antarctic ice. "Eruptions at this site are unlikely to penetrate the 1.2–2-kilometer-thick overlying ice, but would generate large volumes of melt water that could significantly affect ice stream flow," according to the study. The discovery explains why ice in the west Antarctic region is melting. But it also undercuts global warming frauds' arguments about man-made causes of the ice melt. Aside from a small region of Antarctica, the rest of the polar cap is experience record-breaking gains in the amount of ice over the past two years.[42]

Nothing has changed in the left's attitude toward climate change. Al Gore is still spouting the same tired rhetoric about the dangers of climate change. Like all climate change advocates, he ignores the fact that temperatures haven't risen in fifteen years. The NASA and NOAA interpretations of the latest official report on global warming still maintain—against the evidence—that their climate models are accurate and that warming is still occurring. A top MIT climate scientist said otherwise when he found the report had "truly sunk to the level of hilarious incoherence."[43] That should tell you all you need to know about the administration's climate policy.

One of the reasons the environmentalists have switched from using the term "global warming" to describe the earth's weather to using "climate change" is that although the temperature decline of the past fifteen years effectively disproves that we're in a warming period, it's easier to defend when warming doesn't happen. No matter what evidence crops up to the contrary, "climate change" is a one-size-fits-all term. Despite the fact that the environmentalist movement's computer models have been demonstrated to be unconnected with real-world activity, there's no way they can be disproven as long as we're just talking about a change in the weather.[44]

In spite of the administration's energy policies, in states where oil and gas production by private companies has been allowed to proceed without unnecessary government intervention, economies are booming and unemployment is at lows that reflect how responsible energy policy could impact the entire country if the leftists in power would step aside. In Texas, for instance, the oil and gas sector is setting new records and exceeding even the wildest of expectations. Oil production in Texas has skyrocketed by more than 140 percent in the past five years. At the same time, because of Obama's energy policy, the price of West Texas crude oil has increase by more than 150 percent. Even the corrupt International Energy Agency has had to take notice. Because of the dramatic increase in U.S. oil production, spearheaded by Texas and North Dakota, that organization has estimated that within the next year the United States will become the largest oil-producing country in the world.[45]

One of the reasons for the increase in oil and natural gas production in the United States is fracking. It's a clean technology that enables energy companies to extract oil and natural gas from shale. States that allow fracking have seen their economies reap economic benefits; states like California that won't even consider fracking or other technologically available methods of exploiting oil and natural gas reserves continue to risk teetering on the edge of bankruptcy.

In the meantime, while developing economies such as those in India and China are radically increasing their CO_2 output, the amount of carbon dioxide we release into the atmosphere has been reduced by 8 percent in the past two years alone. Not that it matters; carbon dioxide is such a small component of the earth's atmosphere that doubling our output would have no effect whatsoever on the planet's climate.

Another area in which fracking is proving to be an extraordinarily efficient technology is in the amount of water necessary to produce energy. One million BTUs of energy produced by fracking requires about three gallons of water, the lowest amount of any energy-producing source. Do you know how many gallons of water are required to produce one gallon of ethanol, the environmentalists' energy source of choice? 15,800! It requires nearly sixteen thousand gallons of water to produce ethanol that will generate a million BTUs, where fracking requires three gallons of water to produce the same results.

Even former leftist EPA head Lisa Jackson had to admit the effectiveness of fracking. In testimony before Congress, Jackson admitted, "I'm not aware of any proven case where the fracking process itself has affected water." From efficiency in the use of land to reduced negative impact on wildlife, fracking is proving to be one of the most productive technologies ever in producing energy.[46]

Forced by the overwhelming body of fact, climate change activists have been forced to concede that the average surface temperature on our planet has not increased in a decade and a half. But they describe this as a "pause." A fifteen-year pause! And during all of that time, so-called greenhouse gases have not stopped being emitted into the atmosphere, and in fact the amounts have increased over that time. The IPCC has known this for at least ten years, but that didn't stop them from beating the global warming drum. They still insist that those who actually look at real climate data are "denialists" and that the earth is still facing catastrophic consequences if we don't stop our current energy production practices.[47]

The Obama administration's climate change policy is actually endangering our national security. While China's state media were releasing that country's plans to conduct nuclear warfare on the United States, Barack Obama had more pressing concerns. He was issuing an executive order directing the government to prepare for the impact of global warming.

As our enemies become more and more emboldened by Obama's reducing our military readiness and allowing himself to be pushed around by what amounts to no more than international schoolyard bullies, the president, because of his mistaken notion of what's happening with our weather, has ordered federal agencies to "work with states to build 'resilience' against major storms and other weather extremes" that may be coming by reinforcing everything from bridges to buildings.[48]

Obama's energy policy continues to target reducing America's energy independence to as great a degree as possible. In my opinion, the president has demonstrated that he has no intention of lifting his shutdown of oil exploration and production on federal lands or of stopping his criminal delay of the building of the Keystone XL Pipeline, even as it becomes clear that if he had done so several years ago we would be in a stronger position to stop Vladimir Putin's attempts to rebuild the Russian empire. In North Dakota, energy production is creating an economic boom that has resulted in a state budget surplus and reduced unemployment to barely measurable levels while increasing wages in even the most menial jobs to upward of $20 an hour. Those working in the oil fields typically earn five times more than that.[49]

The administration's answer: Throw up new roadblocks that will continue to delay the building of the Keystone pipeline, even as Canada begins to ship oil to China.

As I've demonstrated in this chapter, not only is the green-energy initiative fraudulent—built as it is on unsupportable theories and nonexistent proof that releasing carbon into the atmosphere is dangerous to our climate—it is but one more way in which we are being divided into groups of private citizens and political and economic power mongers, the very groups who are likely to oppose each other in the coming civil war.

CHAPTER 9

The War on Our Schools

Already at a disadvantage because they've spent their time in school parroting leftist platitudes rather than thinking for themselves, graduates are now forced to compete for minimum-wage jobs for which they're overqualified. In the process, they continue to live with their parents because they can't afford a place of their own. The brick-and-mortar universities, which were once the cornerstones of free speech and educational inquiry, have become debt-ridden gulags of biased, agenda-driven indoctrination.

As many of you know, I grew up in the Bronx. My father was an immigrant and not an educated man. He was hard-working and intelligent, but he didn't have the opportunity or the money for college, though education was very important in my family. I went to public schools and City College. I wasn't naturally a good student, or rather I wasn't a good memorizer, which was the modus operandi in school back then. I was much more of a dreamer and a free thinker. And when I discovered jazz in my teens, I thought I needed to know nothing else.

What could be more important in life than Stan Getz or Charlie Parker?

Though jazz would remain the soundtrack to my life, it became evident that I couldn't live on music alone. I worked hard, became a good student, and would ultimately acquire several graduate degrees, including a doctorate from the University of California. My dissertation was published as a book, which is extremely rare. The child who had trouble memorizing the date of the Magna Carta and the multiplication tables is now a doctor and the author of twenty-eight books.

If you were lucky enough to have been born in the United States before about 1975—as I was, just barely—and if you were fortunate enough to have completed your public-school education by the mid- to late 1980s, you were the beneficiary of the best primary and secondary school system in the world.

But then Jimmy Carter became president and created the Department of Education in 1979. At the time, the United States was first in the world in the quality of education by every measure. Under Carter, instead of leaving education to people at the state and local levels, where it thrived, the federal government took over U.S. schools, and the quality of education began to sink, slowly at first, and gradually more rapidly. Now our international standing in education is trapped in the teens and low to midtwenties in virtually every ranking of every academic discipline.[1] American high school students' academic performances have sunk to fourteenth in reading, seventeenth in science, and twenty-sixth in math scores when measured against students in other countries around the world.[2]

Student performances on the 2012 Program for International Assessment tests revealed that Asian countries in particular provide their students with a much better education than the United States does. Chinese students, specifically those living in the city of Shanghai, posted the highest scores in the world in math and science. Students in Vietnam, which has been a third-world country since before we fought there in the rice paddies during the 1960s and '70s, now score higher than those in the United States.

Even current U.S. Education secretary Arne Duncan, an Obama lieutenant and leftist ideologue, characterized the flat scores as a "picture of educational stagnation."[3]

Let me give you a few reasons why.

Negative Outcome-Based Education

In 1979, the illiteracy rate among high school students in the United States was about 1 percent.[4] In other words, if you were in school before that time you were among the 99 percent of high school students who could read.

In the early 1980s, an approach to learning known as "outcome-based education" was introduced in the Chicago city schools. It was later expanded across much of the U.S. educational system.

This instructional methodology dictates that until all students have mastered the content in a given subject area, no student is allowed to advance to the next level. If you're an above-average student and know the subject matter, you have to sit on your thumbs until everyone has caught up with you.[5] If you ask someone who is a proponent of this method, they will give you a lot of double-talk about the outcome of the whole class being more important than the success of the individual student.

Do you know what happened in Chicago after this subversive approach was introduced?

Within five years, nearly half of all the public school students in Chicago dropped out.[6]

Literacy rates plummeted.

There is no question in my mind that Chicago's current inner-city violence and unemployment is caused in no small measure by the intentional destruction of the city's school system through the introduction of this leftist educational agenda.

And I have little doubt that, as Carter effectively nationalized education in this country through his creation of the federal Department of Education, this approach has been largely responsible for the dramatic drop in the national literacy rates of our elementary and high school students.

By 2010, although graduation rates were at an all-time-high 78 percent of high school students, 26 percent of twelfth graders could not read at their grade level. Put another way: *More than a quarter of today's graduating high school students are functionally illiterate.*[7]

According to the U.S. Department of Education, National Institute of Literacy, in 2013, *19 percent of high school graduates could not read at all.*[8]

Despite the decrease in our students' academic ranking around the world since the late 1970s, there are nearly 5,000 four-year colleges and universities in the United States with some 18 million students in attendance. That's more than double the number of students attending colleges and universities in the '70s.[9]

At the same time, in order to accommodate an increasingly ill-prepared population of college-eligible students, standards in higher education have dropped precipitously. Apart from the top-tier colleges and universities, most college curricula for incoming freshmen now consist of little more than remediation to bring students up to the standard of high school graduates of the 1970s.[10]

So how do our Ivy League leaders handle such a problem? They look the other way while our educational system becomes rife with cons and criminals.

For instance, a Dallas-based company that bills itself as a "custom writing service" creates papers for barely literate students to turn in as their own work. There's so much demand for the firm's services that it now employs more than one hundred writers. As the company's news release explains, students "no longer have to face the burden of academic coursework."

Students—and it breaks my heart to call them that—rave about the service. Here are some of the things they have to say:

> "The paper was written excellent...My professor was satisfied, and so am I."
> "I've sent the paper to evaluation first 'cause I wasn't sure if they can find a writer with a relevant academic background...But yes, they did! It seems like she read my thoughts and written the paper as if I did it myself, lol :-)"
> "Cool essay. Couldn't been done better. Just noticed a few typos, but that's okay."[11]

We were once a country that produced the likes of Mark Twain, Ernest Hemingway, and William Faulkner. Now we have this.

Compounding the diminished quality of the education they

received in our elementary and high schools, 18 million college students are living in an education bubble. Simply put, an education bubble is the same as a bubble in real estate or finance. As tuition goes up, the financial benefits of a college degree decrease. The student who takes a student loan is immediately underwater, just like the person who buys a house at the height of the market and the next week the bubble breaks. College graduates are underperforming so badly today that new legislation is in the works that would mandate colleges demonstrate the success or failure of the education their students receive by publishing data on the salaries their graduates earn.[12]

The number of high school students enrolling in colleges has increased by 47 percent since 1970, with 25 percent of the increase occurring between 2000 and 2008. During roughly the same time, tuition costs at four-year public colleges and universities rose by nearly 250 percent, while the median U.S. family income has dropped by more than 14 percent.[13]

Colleges have padded their faculties and staffs enormously as the education bubble has developed. Layer upon layer of management has been added.[14] It won't be long until some university will create a position called Dean of Deans.

A few years back, the University of Minnesota created a department called the Office of Equity and Diversity. According to a *Wall Street Journal* investigation, that department has ten people with the word *director* in their title. The school employs 353 people who make over $200,000 a year.[15]

This ugly and inefficient trend is made much worse by the introduction of hundreds of new pseudo-academic disciplines in response to the growing division of the U.S. population into groups—based on such characteristics as gender, race, and income—that political leftists have brought about.[16]

University coursework is overloaded with classes weighted heavily toward such soft disciplines as Conflict Resolution and Peace Studies, which can be molded to comply with their professors' political biases. Here are some of the more enlightened subjects that are being offered at our major universities today:

- GaGa for Gaga: Sex, Gender and Identity (University of Virginia)
- Philosophy and *Star Trek* (Georgetown University)
- God, Sex, Chocolate: Desire and the Spiritual Path (UC San Diego)
- The Feminist Critique of Christianity (University of Pennsylvania)
- What if Harry Potter Is Real? (Appalachian State University)[17]

If you're an English major, you very likely no longer study the writings of Geoffrey Chaucer, William Shakespeare, and John Milton. Those requirements are gone. Now, if you choose to major in English, in many universities you'll have to take at least three "literature" courses in one or more of the following disciplines: Gender, Race, Ethnicity, Disability, and Sexuality Studies; Imperial, Transnational, and Postcolonial Studies; Interdisciplinary Studies; or Critical Theory. The substance of courses in these disciplines is left up the professor's interpretation.[18]

There was a time when free speech was a fight that the left viewed as strictly theirs. But now on college campuses across the country, it is the conservative voice that struggles to be heard. Look no further than commencement addresses and whom the elite schools pick to deliver them. In 2012, out of the top fifty liberal arts colleges, only one asked a conservative, Governor Bob McDonnell from Virginia, to give a commencement speech. McDonnell spoke at the University of Richmond. Not a single conservative was asked to speak outside of his home state.[19]

As I see it, college textbook publishing has degenerated into something akin to a racket that is trying desperately to maintain its stranglehold on the extended-adolescence market that brick-and-mortar institutions of higher education have helped create.[20] According to a survey conducted by a public interest research group, textbooks cost college students over $1,200 a year on average, with the cost of many individual books soaring to $200 and higher. What's more, new editions, usually with little additional material, are published every two or three years. This effectively limits the market for used textbooks. The cost of textbooks is so prohibitive that students regularly decide their course schedule not on their hopes and dreams but on how much the books for the course will cost.[21]

Beyond that, American colleges foster the physical separation of people into racial, ethnic, and cultural groups, a purposeful result, I believe, of the president's agenda. As I see it, his plan is to drive wedges between us based on characteristics that include race, and college campuses are a perfect staging ground for this.

Let me give you some examples.

At many universities, blacks are offered the option of living in all-black dormitories or on all-black floors within dormitories. Even where colleges don't offer segregated housing, students often self-segregate. It's gotten so serious at the University of Massachusetts that the school claims it is trying to end the practice:

The self-segregation has become so entrenched that one resi-
dential area on campus preferred by Asian students is known
as "Chinatown." A residential cluster where many black stu-
dents choose to live is commonly referred to on campus as "The
Projects."... The university said that it plans to discourage
students from self-segregating with the rooming choices, but
it is unclear at this time how this will be accomplished.[22]

Bubble.edu

As I've mentioned, the education bubble that is reflected in the
radical increase in tuition and other expenses is made possible
by the same thing that led to the housing bubble: an increase
in debt offered to people who don't have the means to pay it
back, along with a takeover of the student loan industry by the
federal government.

Total student loan debt, which has reached more than $1
trillion, now exceeds credit card debt in the United States.[23] In
the wake of this, 33 percent of all "subprime student loans" are
more than ninety days overdue. Before the crash of 2008, that
number was 24 percent.[24]

With the Obama administration no longer requiring
repayment of unpaid student loans—why not let the American taxpayer shoulder the burden for student debt like they do
for pretty much all other U.S. debt?—we face another financial catastrophe. And this one will contribute significantly to
the radical takeover of America. This is fully in keeping with
Obama's intent to cause most Americans to become dependent
on the federal government for the needs of their lives. This,

in turn, exacerbates the possibility of the coming civil war in our country.

As the federal government commandeers the student loan business and college tuition rates soar, many students graduate with debt beyond their ability to pay. That's largely due to the fact that the current administration's economic policy has driven most of the jobs that were traditionally filled by college graduates out of the country.

Already at a disadvantage because they've spent their time in school parroting leftist platitudes rather than thinking for themselves, graduates are now forced to compete for minimum-wage jobs for which they're overqualified. In the process, they continue to live with their parents because they can't afford a place of their own. By the way: Thank you, Mr. President, for raising the federal minimum wage to $10.10 an hour. At that rate, college grads may be able to pay back the school loans they owe by the time they're eligible for Social Security—if Social Security is still around by then.

Here's how I see it: The brick-and-mortar universities, which were once the cornerstones of free speech and educational inquiry, have become debt-ridden gulags of biased, agenda-driven indoctrination.

The indoctrination of students begins early in the American educational system.

One of the reasons is Common Core.

In 2010, a set of standards that had been developed by a committee selected by state governors was released. It prescribes for educators what students should learn at each grade level, K through 12.[25] Education Secretary Arne Duncan—who formerly headed up the Chicago school system that was a pioneer in destroying American education during the late twentieth century—provided incentives for states to adopt the standards by promising Race to the Top grants to those who did.

What emerged was another program that solidified the political left's hold on progressive education in the United States.

Common Core is designed and implemented by vacuous and unseeing leftist functionaries. It's full of educational bureaucratic language that even most educators can't understand. Many call it "Corespeak."

How about having your children's education designed, not on principles of learning important skills and absorbing information that will help them succeed in the real world, but on leftist "values" embedded in language that includes words such as *globalism, empathy, benchmarks, automaticity, collaborative partner, rigor, relevancy,* and *relationship.*

The stewards of Corespeak are banking on parents and students being too embarrassed to ask to have the terms explained to them. As one commentator put it, "You don't want to be 'that parent' who asks, 'What are they talking about?' And they know it."[26]

So why would educators come up with a whole new language that confuses those they're supposed to be serving? It's as simple as it is subversive: Baffle parents and students with words that cover their inadequacy, criminality, and the advancement of their leftist agenda. Remember Bill Clinton's "It depends on what the meaning of *is* is"?

What do those committed to real education think about Common Core?

A Hillsdale College professor slams Common Core's dictum to eliminate the study of classic literature and replace it with "informational" books that are nothing more than communist manifestos. He singles out textbook publisher Prentice Hall for creating "clearly ideological" books for use in America's schools.

Describing Common Core, which recommends teaching politically driven non-subjects like global warming, as "superficial, biased, and embarrassingly dumb," he comes to this conclusion:

> *Either there exists no coherent philosophy of education governing the arrangement of texts within the document, or there does exist a coherent philosophy: that of obscuring the high, powerful truths about virtue, freedom, suffering, and happiness found in great works of Western literature.*[27]

So how can we fight back?

One way is through the funding of school vouchers that enable parents to choose the schools their children attend according to the quality of the education they receive and not where they live.

Let me expand on the subject of Louisiana's charter schools.

Louisiana governor Bobby Jindal has promoted the use of educational vouchers, and Louisiana schools after Hurricane Katrina have made a remarkable turnaround in the quality of education they provide for their students and the educational outcomes their students achieve. It is a phenomenon that frightens the wits out of the Obama administration. So much so that the president dispatched Attorney General Eric Holder to intervene in Louisiana's promotion of educational success.

Holder's Justice Department filed a lawsuit to block the

school voucher program in twenty-two Louisiana school districts.

Because the Louisiana voucher law limits vouchers to families with incomes below five times the poverty level whose children attend schools that fail to meet federal standards, black children are overwhelmingly the beneficiaries of the program.

Nearly seven thousand students received school vouchers in Louisiana, and 83 percent of them were black.

In other words, Holder is essentially making a race-based case *against* black students being able to get a quality education. Do you know what Holder's reasoning was on this? *The voucher program might lead to a return of segregation by leaving many of the state's schools with too many white students.*[28]

"We've got Eric Holder and the Department of Justice trying to stand in the schoolhouse door to prevent minority kids, low-income kids, kids who haven't had access to a great education the chance to go to better schools," said Jindal.[29]

Governor Jindal chose those words carefully and wisely. The "schoolhouse door" reference evokes the South of the 1960s and Governor George Wallace trying to block black students from integrating the University of Alabama.

We have a black attorney general doing the same thing.

Let me ask you, How could that be?

How could we have the top law enforcement officer in the country, an African-American, trying to sabotage a successful educational program that primarily benefits African-American children?

How can that happen unless bigger forces are at play?

Except for the run-up to the Civil War, the rhetoric for secession was never louder than it was in George Wallace's time.

The division in our country was never angrier, although right now it's a close second.

And nowhere are anger and distrust more easily provoked than when the education and the fate of our children are at stake.

What I see as Holder's war against the schoolchildren of Louisiana is part of a calculated timetable. And the clock is ticking.

At the same time Holder is making a race-based argument against black children in Louisiana schools, he's complaining about what he sees as another racist conspiracy in America, this one in our preschools.

Holder's issue? Black children are singled out for discipline more frequently than their white counterparts. While black kids make up only 18 percent of America's preschool population, nearly half of black preschoolers were suspended more than once.[30]

This new issue has already generated a response. Education Secretary Arne Duncan has set forth a framework of what he calls educational equality of outcome. New York City has its own version of the national Dignity in Schools Campaign. The framework calls for keeping students who disrupt classes in the classroom. According to this plan, minority students are unfairly targeted when they're disruptive. Notice that it's not the disruption that is the focus of the plan, but the targeting of the unruly and sometimes violent students.

It's called "disparate impact," and it's one of the guiding principles of Eric Holder's tenure as attorney general.

It doesn't matter what they do in the classroom. The only thing that matters is that they're impacted "disparately" for their behavior. Make the other students and the teachers suffer because of bad student behavior, but don't deal with the behavior itself.[31]

Under the principle of disparate impact, teachers and administrators risk being branded as racists if they lodge a complaint against a minority student. The disparate impact principle also discourages schools from calling the police, even when behavior threatens the safety of students and teachers.

The disparate impact rule is the guiding principle in Eric Holder's denying Louisiana students a good education. Of course, Holder's real intent has nothing to do with the welfare of disadvantaged students trapped in the leftist educational ghetto that the public schools have become. It has everything to do with the current administration's further centralizing control of an already centralized and ideologically corrupt education system in the United States.

The Justice Department is demanding that the federal government has the final say on whether or not students get vouchers and, if they do, who gets them.

Holder is eying more than just control over the twenty-two school districts in question. He's determined to take over the entire state of Louisiana's voucher program. In doing this, he would also gain control over the state's private schools. And do you really think he'll stop at the Louisiana border?

Let me give you an idea of how seditious Obama is when it comes to education. Just before he was reelected, his Education Department instituted something called Race to the Top. Obama dangled $4.3 billion in stimulus funds in front of governors to prod them into enrolling their states in this federally run contest. Ostensibly, the states posting the highest testing scores would get the biggest parts of the cash. Now, you have to understand, these governors were desperate for school funding. So they didn't bother to look at the price that their states would have to pay for money that came out of the pockets of regular Americans anyhow.

They didn't know they were signing on for a nationalized core curriculum.

They didn't know they were turning over local control of schools to federal bureaucrats.

They didn't know they were agreeing to a lower national standard.

They didn't know that their education funds would be redistributed.

They didn't know that the option of private schools and home schooling would be taken away.

It was bait-and-switch in the most destructive sense of that phrase. And governors across the nation fell for it, hook, line, and sinker.

The hopes and dreams of millions of American children now rest in the president's hands. Out of all the power grabs this administration has perpetrated, this is perhaps the most sinister.

Our president's plan for a complete and merciless takeover of education was in the works even before he ran for president. And the plotting of it involved the usual Chicago suspects.

In the late 1990s and early 2000s, Obama was the chairman of Chicago Annenberg Challenge (CAC). Purportedly an education foundation formed to improve Chicago's public schools and founded by none other than bomb thrower Bill Ayers, the CAC was a strong-armed front that raised hundreds of millions of dollars and funneled the cash to organizations like the South Shore African Village Collaborative, the Dual Language Exchange, and ACORN.[32]

CAC in Chicago was a microcosm of a bigger plan and sowed the seeds for the president's nationalized education agenda. Just like the plan this administration has in the works for the nation, in Chicago education "wealth" was redistributed, local control was abolished, and private schooling defunded. In spite of the millions raised by CAC, testing scores remained stagnant and would soon plummet. Much of this came on the watch of Arne Duncan, who was CEO of the Chicago public school system at the time.

The government takeover of education is best illustrated by what's happening in a tiny minority school district in Marin County. The single school in the Sausalito district has only about 150 students. Because it's known as a "basic aid district," one which gets an inordinate amount of property tax money to fund it, the district spends about $30,000 per student every year. That amount of money will buy you a year at a good university. It's more than three times the $9,000 spent per student in the average California school district.[33] Even so, owing to grotesque administrative salaries, school board "expenses," and patronage teaching positions under the guise of aiding "minority" students, they can't make ends meet.

Can you say "disparate impact"?

If it all sounds suspiciously incestuous, it is.

The older generation likes to talk about how school was much harder when they were children. "I walked five miles to school and five miles home—uphill both ways!" is the old saw. But it wasn't that school was harder, it was better. It was staffed by dedicated teachers who didn't take any guff and knew their subject. It was the center of the neighborhood or community, and not under the thumb of some big, faceless government bureaucracy. It was where kids learned not only the three Rs, but what's right and what's wrong. They learned how to fend for themselves, and how to become productive members of society.

Doesn't seem like much to ask for, does it?

Now, though, our schools have become places where students are indoctrinated into leftist thinking. In the most fundamental and important sense, they're now the agencies for separating the youth of our nation from their parents and other Americans who grew up when the Constitution meant something and most Americans held values that the left now denigrates. Our schools have changed into the spawning grounds for young people who may no longer have any source for the truth and who may be among the first victims in the coming civil war.

CHAPTER 10

The War on Our Allies

With the announcement of public negotiations with Iran, the rift between the United States and Israel grew into a chasm. In one of the great understatements of all time, Israeli prime minister Benjamin Netanyahu called a possible agreement between the United States and Iran, "a bad deal, a very, very bad deal." Netanyahu went so far as to travel to Russia to try to get Putin to weigh in against the U.S.-Iran nuclear weapons deal. Can you image a prime minister of Israel traveling to Russia for help? Only in Obama's Middle East could that happen.

There is popular cable television program called *The Americans*. If you haven't watched it, I'm sure you've heard about it. Set in Ronald Reagan's 1980s, the show is about sleeper Soviet spies hiding in plain sight as a typical American family. The premise is brilliant in its small way because not only does it evoke the cloak-and-dagger drama of the Cold War, it also plays on fears that are much more recent. Russian president Vladimir Putin has restarted the Cold War with a vengeance. As the Middle East peace process falls apart, Iraq is overrun by a small Islamist terrorist army, and China becomes more militantly aggressive, we're retreating from our position of world power.

If nothing else, the Obama foreign policy is falling apart before our eyes.

Let me begin with what's happening in the Middle East. While the left was celebrating the wonderful Arab Spring, I coined the phrase "Arab Winter." I saw that the uprisings meant our influence and ability to protect our allies in the region were facing extinction.

Sunni and Shiite sects hate each other now more than they ever did. Egypt remains in turmoil. The situation in Syria has caused fissures that may drive the world into war.

As I see it, it is evident that the administration's pro-Muslim-fundamentalist foreign policy weakens our allies and assures that Muslim radicals will gain enough power to at least take over North Africa, while a weakened Iraq is also ripe for the taking. We have all but destroyed our relationship with our most important ally, Israel.

As we were leaving Iraq with no status of forces agreement in place, the power vacuum caused by the departure of our military there was being filled with Islamic chaos. Islamist radical forces took over Fallujah and Ramadi, two key western Iraqi cities that hundreds of American lives had been sacrificed to gain. Sunni radicals continued on the march in the early summer of 2014, beheading Christians and Shiite Muslims as they drove toward Baghdad.

The Middle East is returning to the Ice Age of Islamic Fundamentalism.

I've written twenty-eight books and I could write twenty-eight more on just what's wrong with this administration's handling of the Middle East alone and still have plenty of material left over.

In late August 2013, after chemical weapons were used in the Syrian civil war, the United States had every intention of firing Tomahawk missiles—the same missiles the military is now planning to eliminate from our weapons arsenal—at Syrian president Bashar Assad's forces. Make no mistake. We were going to war. John Kerry and John McCain both wanted us to go to war, as did many others tied in to the U.S. military-industrial complex.

I don't know about you, but I haven't forgotten our history of going to war based on bad information. And yet our commander in chief, who won the presidential election in 2008 on his antiwar stance, was going to fire Tomahawks into Syria in support of Syrian rebel forces that are rife with fighters from al Qaeda and other radical Islamist groups.

Only an unscripted remark by Secretary of State John Kerry, the intervention of Vladimir Putin, and a promise by Assad to turn over his chemical weapons kept Obama's finger off the trigger.

Had we attacked Syria, we might well have drawn the Russians into an expanded Middle Eastern war.

But we didn't shoot any missiles at Syria, and everything worked out fine, right?

Well, not exactly.

Did I miss something? I haven't seen a whole lot of sarin gas changing hands.

Meanwhile, the civil war there continues to escalate, a dangerously aggressive Russia has emerged as a major player in the

Middle East and Ukraine, and the crimes against humanity in Syria and Iraq continue to pile up.

Not bad for a couple of weeks' work on the part of the administration.

They were just getting started. A month after signing a chemical weapons pact that Assad had no intention of abiding by, the United States announced it was also going to negotiate with Iran. Easing economic sanctions on Iran, the State Department promised, would ensure the terrorist state would stop its development of nuclear weapons.

As it turned out, the public negotiations with Iran had very little to do with the real deals being struck. While Obama announced his "historic nuclear deal" with Iran, according to sources ranging from *Investor's Business Daily* to *Haaretz*, the United States had already secretly reached an agreement with the Iranians. By the time photos of the world's leaders arriving in Geneva for the talks with Iran appeared on the front pages of newspapers, we had already eased economic sanctions against the Ayatollah Ali Khamenei regime. We had already effectively given Iran the go-ahead to continue enriching uranium with virtually no limitations.

Obama's operatives had put together the deal with Ali Akbar Salehi, the head of Iran's Atomic Energy Organization.[1]

Months later, Abbas Araqchi, the chief Iranian negotiator in the agreement talks, admitted that there was a "nonpaper," an informal side deal agreed to by the participants but not included or even mentioned in the text of the agreement. Among the guarantees that were part of the nonpaper was a guarantee of "Iran's right to continue nuclear research and development during the next several months."[2] Although the State Department denied the existence of the nonpaper, Araqchi didn't back down. He was smug when he talked about the secret side deal. "We will in no way, never, dismantle our [nuclear] centrifuges," he said.[3]

In the wake of the signing of the agreement, Iranian president Hassan Rouhani bragged via Twitter: "Our relationship w/ the world is based on Iranian nation's interests. In #Geneva agreement world powers surrendered to Iranian nation's will."[4] The Iranian army's commander, Maj. Gen. Ataollah Salehi, boasted to the Iranian news agency that "given their weakness in the military dimension, they have opted for the political arena and we will certainly succeed in this area too."[5]

So the questions I pose are these: Is the reason we received nothing—no assurances for our allies, no halt of nuclear enrichment, no signal at all that the Iranian leopard had changed its spots—because of the ineptness of our State Department and other negotiators? Or did we actually get what we wanted all along: the empowerment of Iran?

We got the answer not much more than six months after we reached agreement with Iran in Geneva. Iran's Supreme Leader, Ayatollah Ali Khamenei, made it clear that Iran would not rest until the United States was wiped off the map. Here are his words:

Battle and jihad are endless because evil and its front continue to exist.... This battle will only end when the society can get rid of the oppressors' front with America at the head of it, which has expanded its claws on human mind, body and thought.... This requires a difficult and lengthy struggle and need for great strides.[6]

Do you wonder why we've given in to the Iranians on every front?

I've mentioned the name Valerie Jarrett earlier in this book. Jarrett is the president's most trusted advisor, the true power broker in the White House. She's the one who orchestrated the one-sided secret deal with Iran.

Put just about every pro-Muslim move this administration has made under a microscope and you'll find Jarrett's fingerprints on it.

So what is her allegiance to America?

Maybe her rise to the very pinnacle of power is just a series of unbelievable coincidences and circumstances?

Playing devil's advocate in the truest sense of that term, let's give her the benefit of the doubt. Maybe she is devoted to the red, white, and blue. But if that's the case, she may be the most incompetent negotiator since Neville Chamberlain.

With the announcement of public negotiations with Iran, the rift between the United States and Israel grew into a chasm. In one of the great understatements of all time, Israeli prime minister Benjamin Netanyahu called a possible agreement between the U.S. and Iran, "a bad deal, a very, very bad deal." Netanyahu went so far as to travel to Russia to try to get Putin to weigh in against the U.S.-Iran nuclear weapons deal. Can you imagine a prime minister of Israel traveling to Russia for help?

Putin, a supporter of Iran, had this to say: "A real chance has now emerged for finding a solution to this long-standing problem."[7]

One of the few trump cards we held in our relationship with Iran was the threat of partnering with one or more of the countries that are rapidly becoming our former allies—these include Saudi Arabia, Jordan, and Egypt—in a military strike against Iranian nuclear production facilities.

But we don't hold that card anymore. Our participation in any attack would be in violation of the agreement that we negotiated with Iran.

With her secret agreement in place, Jarrett left our former allies looking around to find other ways to protect themselves against a nuclear-armed foe.

The idea that Jarrett was given even a small role in negotiations with Iran—let alone leading a team of negotiators—is an indication, I believe, of how suspicious the negotiations were in the first place. She has absolutely no qualifications to be involved in high-level discussions of such critical importance to our foreign policy.[8]

Jarrett's father-in-law, Vernon Jarrett, and Frank Marshall Davis, Barack Obama's mentor, were colleagues in Chicago. Both Vernon Jarrett and Davis were covert members of the Communist Party during the 1940s, and they influenced Jarrett's political beliefs significantly. Valerie Jarrett grew up in the leftist incubator of 1960s Chicago, and she's known Barack Obama since his radical days at Columbia.

I'll ask again: Could the fact that Valerie Jarrett is Iranian possibly color her political and foreign policy views? Certainly Americans born in Israel are overwhelmingly sympathetic to Israel's policy positions.

Jofi Joseph, a member of the White House National Security Council, once tweeted that Jarrett was a "vacuous cipher" and that her relationship with the president "concern[ed]" him.[9]

I repeat my question: Does the fact that she's Iranian have

anything to do with the emerging Middle East policy of the United States?

Does the fact that former secretary of state Hillary Clinton's personal assistant, Huma Abedin, "worked for many years at a journal that promotes Islamic supremacist ideology that was founded by a top al Qaeda financier, Abdullah Omar Naseef"[10] in any way influence our policy regarding Islamist extremism?[11]

Is it possible that the current administration's foreign policy, controlled as it is by Valerie Jarrett, has been designed to encourage the emergence of what amounts to a new power alignment across the Middle East?

Sources in Israel described the United States as promoting "erratic" policies throughout the Middle East.[12]

I don't find our policies erratic at all. I find them consistently on the side of supporting Islamist radical forces. The United States sided with Islamist insurgents during the "Arab Winter." The United States supported the overthrow of the governments in Egypt and Libya, despite the fact that neither country was a direct threat to the United States.

Egypt was once our strong ally. Egyptian president Hosni Mubarak helped maintain border security between Egypt and Israel. He kept in check the Muslim Brotherhood, the radical terrorist group responsible for the assassination of Egyptian president Anwar Sadat in 1981 and the seed group for other Islamist terrorist organizations, including al Qaeda.[13] The Muslim Brotherhood, which has been declared a terrorist group by Egypt[14] and Saudi Arabia,[15] seeks nothing less than a government based on Islamist principles, including the implementation of Shariah law and waging jihad against the West.

What I called the Arab Winter resulted in the institution of a government run by Mohamed Morsi and the Muslim Brotherhood. Less than two years later, the Egyptian people realized their mistake in electing an Islamist president, and the Egyptian military rose up to throw Morsi out, a move, one would think, that should have aligned nicely with America's foreign policy. But instead of giving the new Egyptian government our support, we interrupted sending them foreign aid.

We followed much the same path as we did with Hosni Mubarak when dealing with Libyan dictator Moammar Gadhafi.

Gadhafi had given up being an enemy of the United States, and for all his faults, was able to keep political order and restrain the chaos that is now engulfing Libya. Yet, after Gadhafi's death at the hands of a mob, Hillary Clinton joked, "We came, we saw, he died,"[16] no doubt to the shrill laughter of her friends in high places.

In fact, if Gadhafi was still in power, four Americans who lost their lives in the Benghazi attack might well be alive today. It's my conviction that their blood is on this administration's hands. The administration's handling of the Benghazi massacre has had devastating implications for America's foreign policy and our ability to be the world's leader in the fight against terrorism and for freedom. As one commentator put it, "The longer the Obama presidency continues, the more America's status as a superpower ebbs away."[17]

Is it so far-fetched to believe that the administration knew that Libya was a tinderbox of insurgency and terrorism and that Gadhafi's removal was the spark that would set it ablaze?

On a related note, why does the administration keep supporting Palestine?

While he was meeting with Palestinian president Mahmoud Abbas, Kerry announced that the United States was sending Palestine an additional $75 million in aid. The announcement came only hours after an Israeli soldier was stabbed to death by a Palestinian terrorist as the soldier was riding on a bus in the city of Afula, Israel.[18]

Meanwhile, in the midst of the political, military, and economic chaos brought about by the lack of U.S. leadership in the Middle East, the president told the United Nations General Assembly that the world is more stable today than it was five years ago.

Do you know how many wars are going on in the world today? More than sixty. And there are more than five hundred different armies and militias and separatist groups that are conducting these armed engagements.[19]

That's the administration's idea of "stable."

Pick just about any country in the Middle East, and you'll see that America has looked the other way or outright supported the rise of Islamic fundamentalism and the increase in terrorist activity that goes hand in hand with it.

Sunni rebels stage terror attacks because the Obama administration couldn't be bothered to develop a status of forces agreement with Iraqi prime minister Nouri al-Maliki that would have kept U.S. troops in Iraq.[20]

Baghdad is the scene of terrorist attacks and bombings almost every day, and the level of violence has been growing steadily since the current U.S. administration turned its attention away from Iraq. More than eight thousand Iraqis were killed in 2013 alone as the level of insurgency, supported by Iran, skyrocketed.[21]

In the early summer of 2014, the terrorist group ISIS, which some call more violent that al Qaeda, staged an offensive that saw them overrun several Iraqi cities and move aggressively toward Baghdad.[22]

Do you remember when the president announced that the United States would not install the missile defense system that we had promised to Poland? When he did that, he not only left our Eastern European ally without a way to stop potential Iranian missile attacks, he sent a message of weakness to Russia as well.

Now he's done it again. Israel, working with the U.S. company Raytheon, has developed a missile defense system called David's Sling, and our former Middle East ally had contracted to sell the system to Poland. That was until we stepped in and vetoed the sale of David's Sling to Poland.[23]

The reason?

One U.S. official said this: "The decision was based on a very simple factor—Israel was a major player in the deal."

It was a $13 billion deal.

Once again, we prevented our allies from stopping the spread of Islamist and communist aggression.

Our reputation in the Middle East shrinks, and the rest of the world takes notice.

The same thing is happening in the Far East.

North Korean dictator Kim Jong-un thumbed his nose at the president when he restarted his nuclear reactors and moved ahead with his country's development of nuclear weapons.

China, through state-run media outlets including China Central TV and the *People's Daily*, has publicly announced its plans to use its submarine fleet to launch a nuclear attack on the United States. They went as far as releasing a map that shows how much damage the attack will bring to the western

United States.[24] By early 2014, reports released by Chinese state media indicated that they were preparing to use force to seize the island of Zhongye, one of the Senkaku Islands whose ownership is disputed by the Philippines and China.[25]

Because of this, and because of America's weak foreign policy, Japan is now contemplating transferring its weaponry to other Asian countries in order to work with them as allies against China's growing militancy. In a meeting with representatives of the ten member states of the Association of Southeast Asian Nations, Japan addressed the question of China's "unilateral attempts to change the status quo by force."[26]

To give you a sense of how much the balance of power in the world has shifted away from the United States, when the United Nations Security Council—the United States, China, France, Great Britain, Germany, and Russia—began to participate in negotiations with Iran, which country do you think actually stood up and spoke out against the pending Geneva agreement? It wasn't the United States. The normally meek and unassertive French negotiators assured Israel that they would stand firm against an Iran deal.[27]

Adding to the mess of U.S. foreign policy is the spreading scandal at the National Security Agency. German chancellor Angela Merkel, leader of Europe's most economically powerful nation, vented her anger at the administration for turning the U.S. spy agency against America's allies. This was in response to the revelation that the NSA had been tapping Merkel's private phone conversations for years, even before she became chancellor.[28]

It doesn't stop there.

The day before talks were scheduled to begin in Geneva in mid-February 2014, Iran declared once again, "The Zionist regime is an illegitimate and bastard regime." At the same time, Pakistan was said to have nuclear weapons ready to deliver to Saudi Arabia so that it could defend itself against a possible Iranian nuclear attack.[29]

With the foreign policy of the United States in shambles, our traditional enemies, from Iran to China to Russia to North Korea, are emboldened. To them we appear weak, uncertain, and unable to decide whether we support our traditional allies, including Israel and the European Union nations, or not.

Even the Pentagon is concerned.

Chinese military technology advances are proceeding at an alarming rate. It recently tested an ultra-high-speed missile that will enable it to send nuclear warheads to targets around the world at hypersonic speeds. The technology amounts to what one U.S. official describes as a "jet-powered, atmospheric cruise missile" which can reach speeds of nearly 8,000 miles per hour.

Although we're still far and away the number one military power on the planet, China has its eyes on our perch, and with the advances it's making in military technology, we may not hold that position for much longer.[30]

Sir Hew Strachan, a senior security advisor from Great Britain, said this about the United States' foreign policy: "Obama has no sense of what he wants to do in the world."[31]

We know that Saudi Arabia has been supporting Pakistan's development of nuclear weapons and that the Saudis have already ordered nuclear missiles from Pakistan. Pakistan is prepared to deliver those weapons to the Saudis at a moment's notice. The Saudis have found it necessary to develop a new source for protecting their borders from invasion, because the United States has effectively deserted Saudi Arabia as we move toward what appears to be a U.S.-Iranian alliance against Israel, Egypt, and Saudi Arabia in the Middle East.

Our negotiations with Iran—our secretly lifting sanctions against our avowed terrorist enemy—represent the clearest indication of how far we've moved from being an ally of Israel, and yet the Jewish community in the United States is silent today.

In fact, with the United States seeming to desert Israel, the Jewish state is left with only one choice: to exercise its military strength against Iran. Such an attack—which, because of the U.S.'s secret negotiations with Iran, would have to be done on its own—would make Israel look like a warmonger. It would make the Israelis outcasts among the nations of the world.

Israel had the chance to attack Iran and stop that country's development of nuclear weapons years ago, but it failed to exercise that option. I believe that the reason Israel did not attack Iran was that they feared they would insult and offend their American ally.

Look what that loyalty got them.

In my view, that American ally has turned its back on Israel and formed an alliance with the most dangerous terrorist nation in the world.

While the administration effectively neutered an Israeli military response to Iran, it is entirely possible that U.S. foreign policy has set the stage for a confrontation between Saudi Arabia and Iran. If that happens, Saudi Arabia—formerly protected by its alliance with the United States—may well have to respond alone to an Iranian military attack. If that scenario occurs, Saudi Arabia will surely lose. It would likely lose because Iran would not hesitate to use its nukes against the Saudis. It is also possible that with the Saudis' possessing nuclear weapons, the Middle East could be the staging ground for a broader nuclear war.

Couple the sectarian violence between Sunni and Shiite factions with the dramatic increase in radical Islamist violence against the West and the United States's ongoing withdrawal from the region, and you have the ingredients for a cataclysmic event. With a future that includes a nuclear-armed Iran, that event could be biblical in scope.

The NSA and American IN-Security

If there is anything to the old adage that information is power, and I think there is, then the NSA is already the most powerful entity known to man. Its mission is to simply achieve and maintain control over the private information of every citizen and every business and governmental organization in the world.

The question is: Despite the fact that we're capturing so much information, much of it about the activities and communications of Americans, are we actually decreasing the chances of terrorist attacks against America?

In early 2014, California senator Dianne Feinstein claimed that 54 terrorist "events" had been "interrupted" by the NSA, including 13 on American soil, 25 in Europe, 11 in Asia, and five in Africa.

Even then-NSA director general Keith Alexander couldn't let that lie stand. He corrected Feinstein, admitting that at most one terrorist plot had been thwarted.

Do you know the details of the "terrorist event" that the NSA had intervened on? It involved a cab driver in San Diego who sent $8,500 to a group in Somalia that had been identified as a terrorist group.[32]

The NSA is defining *terrorism* downward in order to justify its existence as an illegal data-grabbing behemoth.

As information is said to be power, power is said to be intoxicating. Barack Obama campaigned initially on "transparency in government." Now he oversees and defends an illegal entity that gathers Americans' private information and has a budget three times the size of the CIA's. Let me tell you again how big the NSA is. It can intercept and capture communications that contain as many words as there are in the Library of Congress. It does that incomprehensible feat every six hours. The agency's Fort Meade headquarters consists of a campus that covers five thousand acres, and its electrical bill is over $70 million a year.[33]

That's the transparency that the president promised.

To put the administration's priorities in perspective, while it was collecting and stockpiling our most personal information, it didn't spot a convicted terrorist who attended a meeting in the Cannon Office Building on Capitol Hill—even though he was still under house arrest.

It happened on December 5, 2013.

A group called the Egypt Freedom Foundation held a conference protesting the ouster of Egyptian president Mohamed Morsi. Ahmed Bedier, the group's president, had long been associated with the Council on American-Islamist Relations (CAIR), another group that has gained a foothold with the current administration.

Here is what several prominent U.S. public figures have to say about CAIR:

Sen. Charles Schumer (Democrat, New York) describes

it as an organization "which we know has ties to terrorism." Sen. Dick Durbin (Democrat, Illinois) observes that CAIR is "unusual in its extreme rhetoric and its associations with groups that are suspect." Steven Pomerantz, the FBI's former chief of counterterrorism, notes that "CAIR, its leaders, and its activities effectively give aid to international terrorist groups."[34]

And this infiltration of Capitol Hill pales in comparison with what's going on in the White House itself.

In 2004, the FBI uncovered the intentions of Muslim Brotherhood members in the United States to infiltrate our government and undermine it "from within" in a document seized during a raid on the home of a suspected terrorist.[35]

Ten years later, as many as six suspected Islamist sympathizers are advising this administration on foreign policy.

One of these advisors is a member of the Homeland Security Advisory Council who attends meetings in the White House despite the fact that he supports the Muslim Brotherhood and has tweeted that he considers "the United States of America an Islamic country with an Islamically compliant constitution."[36]

My take is that we have an Islamically compliant administration.

And in February 2014, Barack Obama held a meeting in the White House with a Muslim Brotherhood member with connections to Hamas. He was ostensibly attending the meeting to serve as a translator for another attendee, but it's difficult to see the need to let a man with such connections into the White House just so another Muslim can make himself understood.

When asked about the presence of a person who has strong

associations with the Muslim Brotherhood, the White House referred the question "to the Iraqi government."[37]

There are at least four others working in the administration on sensitive antiterrorist projects who are alleged to support and associate with Islamist terrorist organizations.[38]

There is a great body of evidence that suggests the Obama administration gives preferential treatment to Muslim Brotherhood members when they travel to the United States. These people were given "port courtesy" at Minneapolis Airport and at New York's John F. Kennedy and Washington's Dulles airports. According to a State Department directive, these Muslim Brotherhood members could "not be pulled into secondary [screening] upon arrival at a point of entry." In other words, they were not to be subjected to what any American might encounter when boarding a flight: TSA pat-downs, secondary screening of carry-on luggage, and hand inspection in order to uncover possible explosives.[39]

While Muslim Brotherhood members are granted free travel access anywhere in the U.S., the United States is rejecting Israeli applications for tourist visas and denying Israeli tourists membership in the U.S. Visa Waiver Program. In 2013, nearly 10 percent of Israelis applying were rejected, almost double the 2012 level and nearly four times the number of rejections in 2007 during the Bush presidency. And Israel still hasn't been granted the same rights as thirty-eight other countries who are members of the Visa Waiver Program have received. The reason Israel has been denied membership is because of the way it treats Arab-American travelers to its country and because the current administration feels Israel is slowing down progress in Middle East "peace talks."[40]

This was made clear when an e-mail from White House

deputy national security advisor Ben Rhodes explained the message the Obama administration would be sending out to the public in Susan Rice's Sunday morning television appearances immediately after the Benghazi killings:

> *We've made our views on this video crystal clear. The United States government had nothing to do with it. We reject its message and its contents. We find it disgusting and reprehensible. But there is absolutely no justification at all for responding to this movie with violence. And we are working to make sure that people around the globe hear that message.*[41]

As the White House routinely plays host to people with Islamist radical ties and sympathies, its surveillance activities indicate that it's redefined who our enemies are.

Do you need proof of this?

The U.S. secretary of state threatened to boycott Israel, our strongest ally in the Middle East. Doing the rounds on Sunday morning TV, Kerry insisted that a campaign to ostracize Israel would grow if peace talks with the Palestinians failed. In other words, if Israel refuses to give up its own borders, language, and culture and refuses to allow itself to be overrun and conquered by Arab neighbors who will never enter into a peace agreement with Israel.[42]

At the same time, Kerry admitted in a behind-the-scenes meeting with members of Congress that U.S. policy relative to Syria was a failure. In late December 2013, it was revealed that Syria was far behind schedule in its promised removal of chemical weapons that the Kerry-inspired "breakthrough" agreement promised.[43]

Given Kerry's statements, should Israel consider the United

States its enemy? Our secretary of state has been decidedly one-sided in the negotiations between Israel and the Palestinians—and the side he's on isn't that of our longtime ally. "Does Israel want a third intifada?" Kerry said. Are these the words and policies of a friend?

Meanwhile, in Syria we know that forces fighting Assad are rife with terrorists who hate the United States. How do we know this? Because the administration admits it.

In February 2014, newly appointed DHS secretary Jeh Johnson declared that Syria had become a matter of homeland security. His rationale? U.S. and Canadian citizens are going to Syria in order to fight on the side of Syrian rebels against the Assad government.[44]

In other words, once they're finished in Syria, they may return to the United States and Canada and try to stage terrorist attacks against us. Johnson is admitting that those fighting against Assad are likely to be Islamist terrorists.

When Afghanistan president Hamid Karzai was asked what he thought would be the best outcome of his country's relationship with the United States, he replied, "It is favorable if they surrender to us."[45]

Karzai's contempt for and his refusal to cooperate with the current administration by immediately signing a status of forces agreement with the United States is an indicator of how far U.S. prestige has fallen among world leaders, whether they are enemies or friends.

"You're not to be trusted" is the message we're getting back from them.

It's the message American citizens themselves are sending to the administration as they realize that they're being treated with the same level of suspicion as known terrorists are treated.

But the corruption and ineptitude that mark what I see as this administration's national security failures pale in comparison to how we handled Vladimir Putin's Ukrainian aggression. Let me make it clear from the start: It was the United States, and not Russia, that engineered the uprising against the elected Ukrainian government. The Obama administration spent billions to enable radical right wingers to stage a phony revolution in Ukraine, then complained when Putin stepped in and drew a real red line in the sand, daring the United States to challenge him.

Let me make sense of what happened in Ukraine for you. The legitimately elected Ukrainian president Viktor Yanukovich was ousted and the country placed in the hands of rebel forces spearheaded by Chechen Islamist radicals.

Assistant Secretary of State Victoria Nuland, along with Obama advisor Susan Rice, are neoconservatives. The neocons don't care which side you're on, as long as they can work with you to create a political situation that they can grow into a war from which they will profit.

The Ukrainian "revolution" was fostered and encouraged by Nuland, Rice, and U.S. ambassador to Ukraine, Geoffrey Pyatt. Over the weeks leading to the February 2014 uprising, these three were instrumental in staging a destabilization campaign. Working with Ukrainian rebels, they fostered the Ukrainian uprising that caused Yanukovich to flee from Kiev.

In fact, it was Nuland herself who selected the new Ukrainian prime minister. She had this lined up three weeks before the insurrection in Ukraine started. Nuland's famous "f—— the EU" was leaked early in February, and it was a covert admission made public that we were on the side of the insurgents. That recording revealed that the administration favored installing Vitali Klitschko—referred to as "Klitsch" in Nuland's phone conversations—as their choice to be deputy prime minister of Ukraine, with Arseniy Yatseniuk—"Yats" as they referred to him—being their choice as Prime Minister.[46]

Arizona senator John McCain was also part of this duplicity. McCain went to Kiev in December 2013 and helped incite the mobs who would ultimately overthrow the legitimately elected president. If there were such a thing as a Nobel Anti-Peace Prize, McCain would win it hands down for his work in Egypt and Syria, topped off by what he's done in Ukraine. McCain was proposing nothing less than that we stage a military intervention in Ukraine, as he's done many times before. McCain was in Syria, secretly backing rebels there, rebels who turned out to be Islamist radicals, supposedly our sworn enemies. McCain also made a covert trip to Libya, where he received an award from the military. This happened on the very day Shariah law was declared in that country, the same day McCain arrived. While he was in Ukraine, he met with a number of rebels who were intent on regime change in that country, and he expressed regret that he wasn't having success, saying, "I do not see a military option and it's tragic."[47]

The U.S.-supported insurgents took over Kiev and held the Ukrainian people hostage as the United States stood down and Putin amassed forces on the Russia-Ukraine border. As this was happening, Barack Obama mouthed the emptiest of words—there would be "costs" to Russia for military action against the insurgents—while the United States found that its hands were tied.

In the early days of the rebellion, former Ukrainian president Yanukovich met with the rebels staging the uprising, and the two parties agreed to stop the violence and make an orderly transition to a new government chosen in a new set of elections. Instead, the right-wing rebels ignored the agreement and took over Kiev by force, with their armed patrols maintaining control through violence.

The situation in Ukraine has been painted as a conflict between Vladimir Putin's Russia (the so-called bad guys) and Ukrainian rebels (the so-called good guys) who seek to oust Russia from a position of influence in Ukraine and install a new government that will be responsive to the Ukrainian people.

Don't believe a word of it.

The Ukrainian nationalists are fascists. Washington's original purpose for staging a coup in Ukraine was to move Ukraine away from Russia and bring Ukraine into the EU. In other words, the neocons and the bought-and-paid-for "moderates" in the Obama administration wanted to wrest control of Ukraine from Putin's hands and gain economic and energy control over the country. As one commentator has pointed out, Western nations, with the United States leading the way, have been provoking Putin for decades. We've expanded NATO to include former Soviet states—Ukraine looks like the next target—and we've attacked allies of Russia, including Libya and Iraq. The United States, along with other Western nations, through our incursions into the politics, economics, and national security of Russia and several of its allies, has effectively caused the situation that resulted in Putin standing ready to invade Ukraine militarily if necessary.[48]

Putin is certainly not a good guy, but he is not the villain in this. The Jews have always been the canaries in the coal mine of human rights in Russia, and Putin has been better to Russian Jews than any other Russian leader in the past century.

With the elected government now driven out of Ukraine, the anti-Semitic U.S.-backed fascist thugs who have assumed control are vandalizing synagogues and threatening the lives of Jews in Ukraine.

Do you know what Obama did only a week after his administration succeeded in engineering the takeover of the Ukrainian government by Islamist radicals? First, he made the empty gesture of restricting the ability of a dozen Russians to travel to the United States. In answer to this, Putin mocked Obama by restricting the rights of several U.S. politicians to travel to Russia. But more important, at the same time Obama has been relaxing the requirements on Islamist terrorists to travel to America, he's increasing his rejection of Israelis who want to travel to the United States.

Do you understand that?

Obama is increasing our ability to be infiltrated by terrorists while he's denying our allies, the Israelis, the ability to travel here.

It began when the United States restricted the rights of young Israelis who had completed their military service in Israel to travel here. By 2012, the ban had extended to all Israeli students. Even Sen. Charles Schumer complained, saying in a letter to John Kerry that the "State Department policy of categorically denying young Israelis tourist visas makes it nearly impossible for any young Israeli to visit the U.S."[49] For once, Schumer was right.

Obama's attempts at thwarting Putin have essentially forced him to deploy military assets to Crimea and to annex that country. Crimea is an important region that Russia ceded to Ukraine in the 1950s, when the USSR was reaching the height of its power and Ukraine was one of its puppet states.

Let me give you some background that will help you understand what went on in Russia, Ukraine, and Crimea after the
fall of the Soviet Union in the early 1990s. After Ukraine
achieved independence and Crimea was ceded to Ukraine,
state-owned assets of the Soviet Union were privatized. This
is where the term *oligarchs*, which you hear used so often in
discussions about the Ukrainian conflict, comes into play.
Those state-owned business and utilities were transferred into
the hands of a small group of powerful, politically connected
individuals, who effectively took control of Russia's economy.
Russia became a capitalist country in one sense of the word,
but the private ownership of the country's assets was transferred to a small group of cronies who quickly became among
the richest and most powerful businessmen in the world. The
Russian oligarchs continue in that role today.

The Russian oligarchs are a critical component in deter-
mining the outcome of the Russia-Ukraine situation, because
they essentially monopolize the precious metal, chemical, and
energy industries in Ukraine. While their power was weakened in Russia as the country's government became more and
more centralized, especially under Putin, no such thing happened in Ukraine. In that country, the oligarchs still hold tre-
mendous power and can sway the country politically. Every
major political hopeful, from presidential candidates to those
hoping for seats in parliament, are connected closely to one
or more of the oligarchs. Among the first people Ukrainian
presidential candidate "Klitsch" Klitschko met with was Rinat
Akhmetov, the richest man in Russia.[50]

Russia's annexation of Crimea is also important relative to
Ukraine. The majority population in Crimea is Russian, and

its warm-water Black Sea ports are critical to Russian military and trade interests. Russia could not afford to let the Crimean region fall into the hands of the insurgents who have taken over Ukraine, something Obama and his foreign-policy know-nothings seem not to have anticipated.

In addition to annexing and deploying military assets in Crimea in the face of the Ukraine insurgency, Putin has contacted his allies in at least eight other strategically located countries in order to assure that Russia has access to those countries' military facilities so Putin's forces can extend their long-range naval and strategic bomber capabilities. In other words, the U.S. interference in Ukrainian politics has resulted in Putin's expanding his military influence, while at the same time Barack Obama is bent on decimating our military in the middle of the Ukrainian crisis. The Pentagon is planning on reducing our military capacity to pre–World War II levels, shrinking the number of soldiers in uniform from its current 520,000 to as few as 440,000 soldiers.[51] As the U.S. military budget was once again being gutted, China announced it was increasing its annual military budget by 12.2 percent in order to fund its effort to continue to modernize the Chinese military.[52]

The president seems to be in the dark about what the conflict in Ukraine means. Nuland and Rice, two of the women who seem to make so many critical decisions of this administration, seem to have told him to blame Putin, and that appears to be what he's done.

It is my opinion that the Russian and Ukrainian people are at grave risk from the Ukrainian nationalists and Chechen Islamic jihadists into whose hands the United States has placed the fate of Ukraine, and Putin has called on his allies to assist him in expanding his military presence around the world.

That differs greatly from the way the United States handled the Ukrainian situation. Did John Kerry consult with Congress before he delivered his message to Russia? Were the EU and NATO countries consulted? They're the ones whose economies and political integrity are at risk here. And does Kerry even understand that the U.S. policy of taunting Russia raises the risk of war? And with that in mind, did he even bother to think of talking with our allies around the world—from Japan to Australia, from Canada to Mexico—who would be adversely affected if we were drawn into war?

The answer is no. A small group of insiders in the U.S. government who have strong allegiances to a powerful group that favors war are running our foreign policy. And it's our allies who are most likely to be damaged by it.

Where U.S. interests are open to being undermined, George Soros is never far from the action. Soros funds the Open Society Foundations, which provides grants to agencies in EU countries that are actively working to undermine Russia. In a piece he wrote recommending that the EU intervene economically to help keep Ukraine financially viable, Soros had this to say:

> *The EU, along with the International Monetary Fund, is putting together a multi-billion-dollar rescue package to save the country from financial collapse. But that will not be sufficient to sustain the national unity that Ukraine will need in the coming years.... Ukraine will need outside assistance that only the EU can provide: management expertise and access to markets.*[53]

The administration is sending the same message to American citizens themselves as he's sending to our enemies, and Americans are starting to realize that they're being treated with the same level of suspicion as known terrorists are treated.

Members of the Saudi royal family have issued the most accurate characterization of the state of U.S. international relations:

> *The U.S. has to have a foreign policy. Well-defined, well-structured. You don't have it right now, unfortunately. It's just complete chaos. Confusion. No policy. I mean, we feel it. We sense it, you know.*[54]

We're seeing American foreign policy at its nadir.

CHAPTER 11

The Savage Truth: Stopping the Coming Civil War

We will preserve for our children this, the last best hope of man on earth, or we will sentence them to take the first step into a thousand years of darkness.
—*Ronald Reagan*

The World Liberal Revolution

This book is not just about the coming civil war in America; it's also about the conflict that the current administration is pushing in the name of a broader worldwide liberal revolution. As I see it, the forces of the left are attempting nothing less than a socialist takeover of the world economy and global politics.

This world liberal revolution is what the tens of millions of conservative, law-abiding Americans are fighting against, often without even knowing it.

We are the equivalent of the anticommunists who fought Stalin.

The conservatives in our country, those who still believe in the family, in personal and religious freedom, in the Constitution of the United States, who are standing up to an increasingly overbearing federal government...we are the new resistance.

Everything is at stake.

Unless this power grab is arrested, we will all become serfs to the new world order.

In the Soviet Union, if a person did not comply with the dictates and politics of the Communist Party, at first they were ignored. That meant that any reference to them disappeared from the Soviet newspaper *Pravda*.

I, Michael Savage, am the most famous media personality in the history of the San Francisco Bay area. Starting with a local show twenty years ago, I became famous for my writings and my radio show, which is now syndicated nationally and carried by more than two hundred stations around the United States.

Yet in the San Francisco Bay area, I am ignored.

I'm almost never mentioned by the local newspaper or in the local media.

It's as though I don't exist.

I'm in the liberal gulag, a gulag in which the only things that are permitted to be talked about are actors, singers, sports figures, degenerates, anti-Americans, occupiers, and Democrats—these are the only "heroes" the American media will talk about. Those who oppose the individual freedoms championed by Western civilization are considered heroes, while those of us who uphold Western values are looked upon as the enemy.

Unless this liberal revolution is stopped, and turned back, there will be a civil war in the United States, which is more than likely to be crushed by a leftist government that is already preparing to quell what it anticipates will be massive civil unrest.

How Serious Has the Situation Become?

"You and I have a rendezvous with destiny," Ronald Reagan, the greatest president of this era, once promised. "We will preserve for our children this, the last best hope of man on earth, or we will sentence them to take the first step into a thousand years of darkness."

We're six years deep into the abyss that Reagan warned us about, and we have reached the point of no return. If we continue down this road to ruin, for even one year more, we may never see the light again.

Not since the run-up to the Civil War have we as a country been more divided. The battle lines have been drawn:

The haves against the have-nots.

The illegal aliens against hardworking middle-class families.

Liberals who hate the Second Amendment versus lawful gun owners, millions of whom are refusing to register their weapons and ammunition in states like Connecticut.

Climate activists whose policies cause forest fires and exacerbate drought against those who understand that the effect of human activity on the climate is negligible.

Anti-Christian communist educators against god-fearing families.

Republicrats against patriots.

Yes, you heard me. It was Brutus who stabbed Caesar, Judas

who gave Christ up to the Romans. It's always the ones closest who do the most damage when they turn.

Do you understand what I'm saying?

The see-through conservatives who rule the Republican Party are in league with Democrats, it's as simple as that. Why would they allow Lois Lerner of the IRS to plead the Fifth time after time and to destroy the hard drives on her computers? Why would they look the other way while Democratic operatives within federal agencies blatantly target patriots from the Tea Party with impunity? Why do Republican Party leaders cave again and again to Obama's agenda?

The answer is actually very simple.

They are on his side.

Listen to what Ted Cruz has to say: "At this point with grassroots conservatives around the country it's a close vote between who they distrust the most, the president, John Boehner, or Mitch McConnell."

Even if this criminal administration falls short of what I think is its goal of seeing Americans fighting Americans in all-out civil war on American soil, Obama's disregard for the rule of law marches us at the very least further along toward a mid-twenty-first-century dictatorship.

We are becoming the Union of Soviet States of America: the USSA.

I've mentioned the fact that most Republicans now agree that we should become members of the "global community." It's not a coincidence that the phrase "global community" is synonymous with the word *communism*, or that Barack Obama got his start as a community organizer. Communism has never been anything but a group of power-crazed leftists bent on depriving the citizens under their control of all of their rights and property while transferring those to an all-powerful central government.

Barack Obama, the Democratic Party, and establishment Republicans are bent on nothing less.

It begins, as most moves toward communism do, in our schools. It took the left a century to commandeer our education system, from grade schools to our universities.

From Franklin D. Roosevelt's starting the entitlement society to Lyndon B. Johnson's Great Society and the gradual degradation of the U.S. Supreme Court, the leftist takeover has continued relentlessly. Obama's election to the presidency in 2008 might represent the final nail in the coffin of freedom unless we continue to persevere against the threats that we now face.

What I see as Obama's drive to weaken America while he incapacitates the American people is not something that's in our remote future. We're living our future right now.

Like every communist country, we've become a surveillance state in which the NSA can track our every move. If the KGB had had the technology that is now being used to monitor every American's daily activities, we'd all be speaking Russian.

Obama has taken an economy that had been gradually moving toward socialism for decades and accelerated the process exponentially, driving it into the ground as his appointees now regulate everything from the press, to student loans, to spending on medical care. Like the oligarchs who took control of the Russian economy after the fall of the Soviet Union, Obama's political cronies have been given billions of our dollars in return for their support of his campaigns. The cash disappears down the rat hole of the bankrupt green-energy companies run by the president's cronies. Those who benefited from the Solyndra scandal have never been brought to justice.

Obama presents himself as the symbol of American pop culture, debasing the once proud and respected office he holds by appearing on TV talk and variety shows like *The View* and *The Tonight Show*. He does everything from slow-jamming the news to defending the mommy jeans he wore when he threw out the first pitch at an All-Star game. His "interview" with stoner talk show host Zach Galifianakis was a mockery of the presidency.

His administration has tightened its hold on Americans' freedoms by imposing limits on everything from political speech to gun ownership to running a business to how we educate our children. Instead of reinforcing "Life, Liberty and the pursuit of Happiness," government administrators are invading our privacy, censoring the media as no administration in our history has ever done, and confiscating and redistributing our wealth.

Stalin had his reeducation camps. Obama's got the U.S. education system.

Obama takes matters into his own hands, making and changing laws and policy unilaterally. And as he does, a compliant Congress sits quietly and does nothing. "There's not been a whimper of regret or opposition of any substance coming from Congress," said one constitutional law professor. "To watch their power usurped by another branch, you would think, would concentrate the minds of all members."[1]

From more than three dozen illegal and unconstitutional executive-order delays to his own health-care legislation to the political profiling of conservative groups by the IRS to his illegal recess appointments of judges and NLRB members to enacting the DREAM Act after it had been rejected by Congress, Obama's presidential corruption and his usurpation of congressional authority have surpassed what even those of us who understand Obama could have imagined.

His first lieutenant, DoJ head Eric Holder, leads an organization whose attorneys have committed more than 650 ethical violations, according to the DoJ's own Office of Professional Responsibilty.[2]

And when you look beyond his domestic policy, you find a foreign policy that makes Jimmy Carter look like Gen. George Patton. From the Middle East to North Africa to Ukraine, Obama has made every potentially fatal error you can imagine when it comes to protecting our national interests. Despots laugh out loud when Obama opens his mouth to chastise them for not adhering to "global community standards" as they commit terrorist acts that kill U.S. soldiers, Christians, and even their own Muslim brothers and sisters in the name of an Islamic jihad that Obama is unwilling to recognize, let alone admit, even exists.

He exclaims, "I can do whatever I want." He writes his own rules, and then sends out his Cabinet secretaries to impose these dictates on industries that are vital, not only to our national sovereignty, but to our very survival as a nation.

When Congress wanted to pass legislation that requires the president to follow the law by enabling them to "sue the President over whether he has properly discharged his constitutional obligation to take care that the laws be faithfully executed exceeds constitutional limitations," Obama's response was to threaten to veto such a bill.[3]

A list of Obama's disregard of the law could go on ad

infinitum. But I promised you that this book would also offer a way out of the perilous situation we're in. Heed the words that follow well. As a great man once said, they might be our last, best chance for survival.

My Questions for You

How did an unknown senator from Illinois become president of the United States?

How did an unknown cardinal, the first non-European in 1400 years and from a country with a Marxist history, become Pope?

How did an avowed Sandinista supporter with strong socialist leanings become mayor of the largest city in America?

Is this a sign of the times?

Or is it something more sinister?

This book is an attempt to alert the American people to inexorable forces that are moving the nation toward an alliance with the worldwide socialist movement.

There is no question in my mind that the emerging EU/United States axis represents the movement toward a new world order, that it is rapidly becoming the new US-EU socialist union.

What strikes me as ironic, even prophetic, is that the last bulwark against this rush toward socialism may be Vladimir Putin!

Russophobia seems to motivate both Obama and the EU leadership. Putin stands in their way.

We have the Pope appearing before the nations of the UN and calling for income redistribution.

He's trading on what he sees as the sins of the church by calling for income redistribution.

Amnesty for illegal aliens is nothing less than sovereignty redistribution in the form of land and resources redistribution.

What would you call that?

Is that not socialism?

The American people do not want to give up their sovereignty to people coming here from Mexico and other third-world countries.

And yet both parties in America are rushing over the cliff into the abyss of granting amnesty to at least 30 million illegal aliens. The true number, which we may never know, is likely to be much higher, possibly double that number.

Need I mention socialized medicine? We now have an emerging Cuban-style medical system thanks to the fact that Obamacare is now the law of the land in the United States of America and threatens to consume the once-greatest medical system in the world. Will we soon be seeing sets of double books and de facto death panels as we learned exist in the VA hospitals?

This book is both a warning and a plea.

If the people of the United States do not wake up and confront the forces that are moving us inexorably toward a world government, we may be entering a thousand years of darkness from which mankind may never emerge.

Just what might trigger a civil war is anyone's guess.

Could it be the call for reparations?

How many people have benefited from reparations in this country? My grandfather was an immigrant who died in his tailor shop at forty-seven from overwork.

Should I pay reparations?

It is my opinion that this administration is bent on crushing U.S. hegemony and power and rolling our country into just another card in the deck of cards called the new world order.

Winning the War

Despite the fact that the Obama administration appears to me to have no qualms about starting a second civil war, and despite what I've said about middle-of-the-road Republicans who too often side with their Democratic adversaries, I'm telling you that our resistance must be a peaceful resistance. It must be waged through the ballot box, or else this country will descend into chaos and violence.

I want to give you an overview of what we need to do in order to win both houses of Congress in 2014 and to elect a Republican president in 2016.

As I see it, we—and I mean Republicans and Independents generally—must return to being a nationalist party, a party that understands that such actions as cutting entitlement spending will spur us to take action against the leftist takeover that is occurring before our very eyes.

If you listen to my show at all, you know that I believe that Republicans—with a few exceptions—are unwilling to stand up and confront Obama regarding his legislation and policies. But if Obama is successful in regaining control of the House of Representatives while he retains the Senate, he will be able to fully control all legislation, and even the weak Republican opposition we currently have will vanish.

It's too early to tell if a committed Tea Party politician can become the Republican Party candidate for president in 2016.

Much as I like and respect most of what I hear from Ted Cruz, we must make sure that all Republicans will unite behind a candidate such as Cruz in 2016 before we choose him to represent the Republican Party in the 2016 presidential election.

The good news is that by the early summer of 2014, selection of candidates for the midterm elections indicated to me that the conservatives and the mainstream Republicans might be mending fences, that they may be trying to find a way to work together. I hope that is the case.

That's because, most important, we must find a way to unite Republicans and conservatives to develop a majority that can attain the presidency in 2016.

We must have someone in office after 2016 who can and will issue executive orders that reverse the damage that Obama's executive orders have done. Someone who can purge every last radical Obama appointee. We must find a way to replace them, not with Republican knee-jerkers, but with traditionalists and nationalists, if we are to save the nation.

Americans are crying for a return to patriotism and nationalism here, the same kind of national pride that we saw the Russians display at the Sochi Olympics.

We must somehow find a Republican candidate who is acceptable to the Republican mainstream—even as we gradually weed them out of the Republican Party over time—and yet who will uphold the Constitution and the rule of law.

Cleaning up the Republican Party and repurposing it to again become the party that is committed to true American values is something that must be done over time. We must unite Republicans for the 2014 and 2016 elections if we hope to topple the Obama administration.

And the time is right to do just that.

Democrats are in a panic as they watch the instruments of control that they've put in place, such as ObamaScare and the IRS, lose favor in the public's eyes, crumbling under the weight of their own corruption. The president's popularity and approval ratings are plummeting as millions of Americans lose their health-care insurance and their hope of surviving serious illness.

Proof of their panic can be seen in the way they're already attacking potential Republican candidates who might run against Hillary Clinton—or against Obama himself if he decides to discard even the illusion of giving up the control he has done so much to amass. They're trying desperately to create the appearance of a scandal with New Jersey governor Chris Christie. It's so far-fetched—creating a traffic jam on the world's busiest bridge—it just might work. Wisconsin governor Scott Walker has worked miracles in his state, and so Democrats are doing everything they can to try to prove some sort of campaign finance trickery by pinning a guilt-by-association rap on Walker because of alleged irregularities committed by one of his campaign donors.

I'm waiting to see how they might attack Dr. Ben Carson, who has emerged as a principled conservative who might run for the presidency in 2016.

Obama himself warned that his party might get "clobbered" in the midterm elections coming up. In a meeting with donors, Obama explained that "our politics in Washington have become so toxic that people just lose faith...and that's especially true during the midterms." What Obama is not admitting is that his policies have so badly hurt the blacks and Hispanics his party needs to turn out for elections that many of them are not even going to vote in the 2016 presidential election. The only thing Obama has in common with his core constituency is the color of his skin. Which is why he and his minions give one race-baiting speech after another. The president is an Ivy League elitist who cares for Americans' problems only when it serves his agenda.

I've mentioned the need to keep the Republican Party together for the near future if we are determined to win the upcoming elections. The problem with a third party is that it will absolutely destroy any chance of defeating the Democrats.

Of course we'd all like an honest third party that has a chance to win. I've talked about a nationalist party before, one that focuses on borders, language, and culture. And that is still the message that needs to be delivered. But right now, I don't think even Ronald Reagan could win as a third-party candidate. Look at what happened when H. Ross Perot came along in the early 1990s with his third party. All he did was suck votes away from the Republicans and get Bill Clinton elected.

I think the answer is a strong, truly conservative plank inside the Republican Party. It can be done.

First, we—and by "we" I mean the rapidly expanding number of Americans who understand that our freedoms are being taken away daily and that we risk the loss of every positive thing America has stood for—must win back control of the U.S. Senate and add to our control of the House. Only then can we even start the process of restoring the United States to greatness.

Beyond 2014, we must also begin to focus on the upcoming presidential election. And while I understand that Mitt Romney proved to be a weak candidate in 2012—and that we lost that election primarily because Romney would not even put up a fight after he demolished Obama in their first debate—it's likely that we'll get another Romney-like candidate in 2016, if not Romney himself, who has suddenly reappeared, mouthing the criticisms of Obama that he hadn't the courage to say during the presidential campaign.

As of this writing I'm not predicting who the Republican candidate might be, but whoever it is, we must get that candidate elected.

We must also understand the challenges we face even if we do elect a Republican as the next president.

The Republican Party is a compromised party. It has come to stand for little more than what the Democratic oligarchy stands for. As of the fall of 2014, we don't know whether Ted Cruz can win a presidential election. Whatever we do, we must select a Republican who can win the presidency and who will reassert the positions and values we stand for when he occupies the Oval Office.

Ultimately, if you do not stand for the principles on which this country was founded and on which it has risen to be the most powerful nation on earth, the whole house of cards will collapse. Neither the Republicans nor the Democrats have what's necessary to rebuild our country. They no longer have the trust of the American people.

If All Else Fails...

I began this book by expressing my fear of a war between Americans orchestrated by Barack Obama. Although I sought to draw a parallel between our sixteenth and forty-fourth presidents, it was not my intention to desecrate Abraham Lincoln or what he has come to represent. Though I vehemently disagree with his centralized-government policies, Lincoln owns a worthy place in the tapestry of our great republic. The American Civil War began only a month after his first inauguration. Unlike Obama's, Lincoln's war was not the result of an intricately planned and implemented agenda. Our sixteenth president was far more a victim of his circumstances than the person who occupies the Oval Office today.

And anyhow, the comparisons between Lincoln and Obama are not originally mine. They belong to Obama himself. If you feel the need to comment derisively about how I handled Lincoln's legacy here, call the White House, because that's where your anger should be directed.

The truth is, Obama doesn't come close to being the man Lincoln was.

Maybe the biggest difference between Obama and Lincoln is their oratorical talent. Given the chance, Obama would use all the syllables in the dictionary in a single speech, where Lincoln was a master of the economy of words.

Perhaps the most poignant words he ever uttered came at the site of the most devastating battle ever fought on American soil:

> *That we here highly resolve that these dead shall not have died in vain—that this nation, under God, shall have a new birth of freedom—and that government of the people, by the people, for the people, shall not perish from the earth.*

Lincoln spoke these immortal words on November 19, 1863, four and a half months after the battle of Gettysburg.

On the 150th anniversary of the Gettysburg Address,

Obama chose not to honor those who gave their lives in that battle.

Instead, he sent Sally Jewell to represent him.

Who?

Exactly.

Sally Jewell was the United States secretary of the interior.

While Jewell was carrying out the duty that the president himself should have attended to, Obama was speaking to a roomful of CEOs about his economic policies.

The president of the United States thought that speaking at a donor "meet and greet" was more important than attending the anniversary of the battle that began the end of slavery.

You shouldn't be surprised.

The devil once said that his greatest trick was convincing you he didn't exist.

Obama's greatest trick is convincing us that he has our best interests at heart.

As I see it, he has only a dictator's interests at heart. And he must be stopped.

How can that be done?

If only 10 percent—even 5 percent!—of those of you who voted Democratic in the last two elections vote Republican in 2014 and 2016, you can save this country.

Though I fear the worst, I also have the greatest faith in the patriotic resolve in America. According to a poll conducted in September 2013, more than 20 percent of Americans identify themselves as members of the Tea Party.[4] Another 42 percent of voters, many of whom may be Tea Partiers, identify as Independent.[5]

Most would consider them outnumbered in their quest

to bring our country back to its former glory. It's not a fair fight, the pundits say.

Not me. If this large block of voters actually voted against the treason, incompetence, and indifference, they could save the nation.

I hear the roar of those patriotic voices every day on my national radio show. I feel the conviction in their belief, I sense the soundness of their ideals, and I hear the strong beats of their patriotic hearts.

Notes

Chapter 1: Graduating to Treason?

1. "Transcript: Attorney general Eric Holder's speech to Morgan State University graduates," *Washington Post*, May 17, 2014 (http://www.washingtonpost.com/politics/transcript-attorney-general-eric-holders-speech-to-morgan-state-university-graduates/2014/05/17/d6b72284-ddd0-11e3-b745-87d39690c5c0_story.html).

2. "Jay Rockefeller Says Racism Behind Opposition to Obama," YouTube, May 8, 2014 (http://www.youtube.com/watch?v=fZLH7oxbReg).

3. Tapper, Jake, "Fellow Soldiers Call Bowe Bergdahl a Deserter, Not a Hero," CNN.com, June 4, 2014 (http://www.cnn.com/2014/06/01/us/bergdahl-deserter-or-hero/).

4. Szathmary, Zoe, "Now the White House Says Hagel Made Final Call on Bergdahl as Criticism of Obama over Prisoner Swap Mounts," *Daily Mail*, June 10, 2014 (http://www.dailymail.co.uk/news/article-2653672/Now-White-House-says-Hagel-final-call-Bergdahl-criticism-Obama-prisoner-swap-mounts.html).

5. Morrissey, Ed, "Hillary on Taliban 5: These Five Guys Are Not a Threat to the United States," *Hot Air*, June 11, 2014 (http://hotair.com/archives/2014/06/11/hillary-on-taliban-5-these-five-guys-are-not-a-threat-to-the-united-states/).

6. Tumulty, Karen, "Bergdahl Release Arrangement Could Threaten the Safety of Americans, Republicans Say," *Washington Post*, May 31, 2014 (http://www.washingtonpost.com/politics/bergdahl-release-arrangement-could-threaten-the-safety-of-americans-republicans-say/2014/05/31/35e47a2a-e8ff-11e3-afc6-a1dd9407abcf_story.html).

7. Weaver, Matthew, "Isis declares caliphate in Iraq and Syria," *The Guardian*, June 30, 2014 (http://www.theguardian.com/world/middle-east-live/2014/jun/30/isis-declares-caliphate-in-iraq-and-syria-live-updates).

8. Chulov, Martin, "Iran sends troops into Iraq to aid fight against ISIS militants," *The Guardian*, June 14, 2014 (http://www.theguardian.com/world/2014/jun/14/iran-iraq-isis-fight-militants-nouri-maliki).

9. "Escort Services for Unaccompanied Alien Children," FedBizOpps .gov, January 29, 2014 (https://www.fbo.gov/index?s=opportunity&mode= form&id=c6d7c0050b912fbc917a46d6709d38bd&tab=core&tabmode=list&=).

10. "An Orchestrated Immigration Wave at the Texas Border? Not So Paranoid to Think So," *Investor's Business Daily*, June 13, 2014 (http://news .investors.com/ibd-editorials/061314-704725-texas-border-immigration -wave-may-well-be-orchestrated.htm).

11. Howell, Kellan, "Border Agent Laments Gang Members Enter- ing U.S.: 'Why Are We Letting Him in Here?'" *Washington Times*, June 14, 2014 (http://www.washingtontimes.com/news/2014/jun/14/border-agents -lament-mexican-gang-members-entering/).

12. "Rampant Sex at Illegal Alien Child Shelters," Pat Dollard, June 10, 2014 (http://patdollard.com/2014/06/rampant-sex-at-illegal-alien-child -shelters/).

13. Dinan, Stephen, "Border Patrol Agents Forced to Change Diapers, Heat Baby Formula for Surge of Illegal Immigrant Children," Fox Nation, June 15, 2014 (http://nation.foxnews.com/2014/06/15/border-patrol-agents -forced-change-diapers-heat-baby-formula-surge-illegal-immigrant).

14. "Savage: Media 'Hiding' Illegal-Alien Disease Threat," *World Net Daily*, July 3, 2014 (http://www.wnd.com/2014/07/savage-media-hiding-illegal -alien-disease-threat/).

15. Starnes, Todd, "Medical staff warned: Keep your mouths shut about illegal immigrants or face arrest," FoxNews.com, July 2, 2013 (http://www .foxnews.com/opinion/2014/07/02/medical-staff-warned-keep-quiet-about -illegal-immigrants-or-face-arrest/).

16. Lee, Tony, "Jan Brewer: MS-13 Gang Members Could Be Cross- ing Border with Children," *Breitbart*, June 13, 2014 (http://www.breitbart .com/Big-Government/2014/06/13/Jan-Brewer-MS-13-Gang-Members -Could-Be-Crossing-Border-with-Children).

17. Zoroya, Gregg, "100,000 Veterans Face Long Waits to See VA Doctors," *USA Today*, June 10, 2014 (http://www.usatoday.com/story/news/ nation/2014/06/09/va-waiting-lists-phoenix-shinseki-gibson/10224797/).

18. Dinan, Stephen, "Tip of the Iceberg: Senator Coburn Says VA Scan- dal Goes Deeper Than Wait Lists," *Washington Times*, June 14, 2014 (http:// www.washingtontimes.com/news/2014/jun/14/sen-tom-coburn-says-va -scandal-goes-deeper-wait-li/).

19. Quoted in Jasper, William F., "Last Man Standing: Nevada Ranch Family in Fedgov Face-off," *New American*, April 11, 2014

(http://www.thenewamerican.com/usnews/constitution/item/18030-last
-man-standing-nevada-ranch-family-in-fedgov-face-off).

Chapter 2: The Long March

1. "The Majority of Home Purchases Are Now Being Done by Cash Buyers," Dr. Housing Bubble (http://www.doctorhousingbubble.com/cash-buyers-real-estate-all-cash-buyer-percent-of-market/).

2. Katusa, Marin, "The 'Colder War' and the End of the Petrodollar," *Forbes*, May 29, 2014 (http://www.forbes.com/sites/energysource/2014/05/29/the-colder-war-and-the-end-of-the-petrodollar/).

3. Adask, Alfred, "A US BRICS Currency War," *International Forecaster*, April 5, 2014 (http://www.theinternationalforecaster.com/International_Forecaster_Weekly/A_US_BRICS_Currency_War).

4. Melloy, John, "Inflation Actually Near 10% Using Older Measure," CNBC, April 12, 2011 (http://www.cnbc.com/id/42551209).

5. "How the NSA Is Tracking People Right Now," *Washington Post*, http://apps.washingtonpost.com/g/page/world/how-the-nsa-is-tracking-people-right-now/634/.

6. "Most online accounts investigated by NSA belong to ordinary Internet users, report claims," FoxNews.com, July 6, 2014 (http://www.foxnews.com/politics/2014/07/06/most-online-accounts-investigated-by-nsa-belong-to-ordinary-internet-users/).

7. Hicks, Josh, "Issa Report: IRS Applied 'Systematic Scrutiny' Only to Conservative Groups," *Washington Post*, April 7, 2014 (http://www.washingtonpost.com/blogs/federal-eye/wp/2014/04/07/issa-report-irs-applied-systematic-scrutiny-only-to-conservative-groups/),

8. Dickson, Sam, "Shattering the Icon of Abraham Lincoln," Institute for Historical Review (http://www.ihr.org/jhr/v07/v07p319_Dickson.html).

Chapter 3: The War on Our Borders, Language, and Culture

1. Churchwell, Logan, "Illegal Immigrants Released into Texas to Ease Over-Crowding of Detention Centers," *Breitbart*, March 26, 2014 (http://www.breitbart.com/Breitbart-Texas/2014/03/26/Illegal-Aliens-Released-to-Curb-Over-Crowding-of-Texas-Detention-Centers).

2. O'Keefe, Makenzie, "Man Rescued During September Floods Looks to Sue Rescuers," CBS Denver, March 4, 2014 (http://denver.cbslocal.com/2014/03/04/man-rescued-during-september-floods-looks-to-sue-rescuers/).

3. "Illegal Alien May Sue Firefighters Who Rescued Him from Flood Waters," Local 12 WKRC Cincinnati, http://www.local12.com/news/features/around-the-web/stories/illegal-alien-may-sue-firefighters-who-rescued-him-from-flood-waters-wkrc.shtml#.U6A7f3aGeM8.

4. Spagat, Elliot, "Migrants Seek to Enter US in San Diego Protest," *Yahoo! News*, March 10, 2014 (http://news.yahoo.com/migrants-seek-enter-us-san-diego-protest-210712048.html).

5. Dinan, Stephen, "Deportations Come Mostly from Border, DHS Chief Says," *Washington Times*, March 12, 2014 (http://www.washingtontimes.com/news/2014/mar/12/deportations-come-mostly-from-border-dhs-chief-say/).

6. "ICE Texas Field Offices Remove More Than 800 Sex Offenders So Far This Year: More Than 2,000 Removed Every Year in Past 3 Years," ICE.gov, press release, March 13, 2014 (http://www.ice.gov/news/releases/1403/140313dallas.htm).

7. Ibanez, Camila, "Full Families Challenge U.S.-Mexico Border with Mass Reentry," Waging Nonviolence, March 10, 2014 (http://wagingnonviolence.org/2014/03/full-families-challenge-u-s-mexico-border-mass-reentry/).

8. "The Dream Act by Executive Order Draws in New Wave of Illegal Immigrants," *Investor's Business Daily*, December 26, 2013 (http://news.investors.com/ibd-editorials/122613-684285-dream-act-acts-as-a-magnet-for-more-illegal-immigration.htm?p=full).

9. "U.S. Frees 36,007 Illegal Aliens with Serious Criminal Convictions," *Judicial Watch*, May 13, 2014 (http://www.judicialwatch.org/blog/2014/05/u-s-frees-36007-illegal-aliens-serious-criminal-convictions/).

10. Adams, Becket, "Obama Promises Hispanics: Your Obamacare Signup Info Will Not Be Used to Track Down Family Members Who Are Here Illegally," *Blaze*, March 18, 2014 (http://www.theblaze.com/stories/2014/03/18/obama-promises-hispanics-your-obamacare-signup-info-will-not-be-used-to-track-down-family-members-who-are-here-illegally/).

11. Starr, Penny, "DHS Secretary on Illegal Aliens: 'They're Here, and They're Not Going Away,'" CNSNews.com, February 7, 2014 (http://www.cnsnews.com/news/article/penny-starr/dhs-secretary-illegal-aliens-they-re-here-and-they-re-not-going-away).

12. Starr, Penny, "Homeland Security Secretary: Illegals Have 'Earned Right to be Citizens," CNSNews.com, January 24, 2014 (http://www.cnsnews.com/news/article/penny-starr/homeland-security-secretary-illegals-have-earned-right-be-citizens).

13. May, Caroline, "Jeh Johnson: DHS Already Preparing to Implement Immigration Reform," *Daily Caller*, February 7, 2014 (http://

dailycaller.com/2014/02/07/jeh-johnson-dhs-already-preparing-to
-implement-immigration-reform/).

14. Lee, Tony, "Report: Obama Admin Slashing Fines for Businesses Caught Hiring Illegals," *Breitbart*, February 26, 2014 (http://www.breitbart .com/Big-Government/2014/02/26/Report-Obama-Admin-Slashing-Fines -for-Businesses-Caught-Hiring-Illegals).

15. Carroll, Conn, "Democrats Choose Immigrant Fraudsters over Veterans and Unemployed," *Townhall.com*, January 10, 2014 (http://townhall.com/ tipsheet/conncarroll/2014/01/10/democrats-choose-immigrant-fraudsters -over-veterans-and-unemployed-n1776910).

16. "Freeing Workers from the Insurance Trap," *New York Times*, February 4, 2014 (http://www.nytimes.com/2014/02/05/opinion/freeing -workers-from-the-insurance-trap.html).

17. Cefaratti, Todd, "Ex-CBO Chief: Obamacare Subsidies Create a Disincentive for Working Just Like Welfare," *TPNN*, February 20, 2014 (http:// www.tpnn.com/2014/02/20/ex-cbo-chief-obamacare-subsidies-creates-a -disincentive-for-working-just-like-welfare/).

18. Buchanan, Patrick J., "End of the Line for the Welfare State?" CNSNews.com, February 11, 2014 (http://cnsnews.com/commentary/ patrick-j-buchanan/end-line-welfare-state).

19. Taylor, Kristinn, "Black Labor Force Participation Rate Under Obama Hits Rock Bottom—Lowest Level Ever Recorded," *Gateway Pundit*, January 13, 2014 (http://www.thegatewaypundit.com/2014/01/black-labor -force-participation-rate-under-obama-hits-rock-bottom-lowest-level -ever-recorded/).

20. Martel, Frances, "Charter School Parents, Opponents Sue NYC Mayor Bill de Blasio," *Breitbart*, March 10, 2014 (http://www.breitbart.com/ Big-Government/2014/03/10/Charter-School-Parents-Opponents-Both -Sue-Bill-De-Blasio).

21. Watson, Paul Joseph, "The War on Men: 10 Ways Masculinity is Under Attack," Infowars.com, February 19, 2014 (http://www.infowars.com/ the-war-on-men-10-ways-masculinity-is-under-attack/).

22. MacIntosh, Jeane, "Obama Wants Marines to Wear 'Girly' Hats," *New York Post*, October 23, 2013 (http://nypost.com/2013/10/23/obama -wants-marines-to-wear-girly-hats/).

23. Maloof, F. Michael, "Top Generals: Obama Is 'Purging the Military,'" *WND*, October 31, 2013 (http://www.wnd.com/2013/10/top-generals -obama-is-purging-the-military/).

24. Quoted in Starnes, Todd, "Pentagon Training Manual: White Males Have Unfair Advantages," Fox News, October 31, 2013 (http://www

.foxnews.com/opinion/2013/10/31/pentagon-training-manual-white-males-have-unfair-advantages/).

25. Starr, Penny, "DOD Reviewing Its 'Equal Opportunity' Training—After Anti-Christian Materials Exposed," CNSNews.com, January 7, 2014 (http://cnsnews.com/news/article/penny-starr/dod-reviewing-its-equal-opportunity-training-after-anti-christian-materials).

26. Starr, Penny, "DOD to Continue Using Liberal Southern Poverty Law Center as Training Resource," CNSNews.com, February 24, 2014 (http://cnsnews.com/news/article/penny-starr/dod-continue-using-liberal-southern-poverty-law-center-training-resource).

27. Bedard, Paul, "'Shocked' Anti-Defamation League Slaps FBI 'Diss' on Hate Crimes," *Washington Examiner*, March 26, 2014 (http://washingtonexaminer.com/shocked-anti-defamation-league-slaps-fbi-diss-on-hate-crimes/article/2546305).

28. Klukowski, Ken, "Air Force: Christians' Religious Speech Not Legally Protected Right," *Breitbart*, March 16, 2014 (http://www.breitbart.com/Big-Peace/2014/03/16/Air-Force-Christians-Religious-Speech-Not-Legally-Protected-Right).

29. Lowry, Rich, "The Strange Hate for 'Lone Survivor,'" *New York Post*, January 21, 2014 (http://nypost.com/2014/01/21/the-strange-hate-for-lone-survivor/).

30. Reilly, Ryan J., "DOJ Plans to Recognize More Rights for Same-Sex Couples," *Huffington Post*, February 8, 2014 (http://www.huffingtonpost.com/2014/02/08/eric-holder-gay-marriage-doj-policy_n_4752270.html?ncid=webmail30).

31. Hollingsworth, Barbara, "Planned Parenthood Produces Video Promoting Bondage and Sadomasochism to Teens," *CNSNews.com*, February 26, 2014 (http://cnsnews.com/news/article/barbara-hollingsworth/planned-parenthood-produces-video-promoting-bondage-and).

32. Jilani, Zaid, "How Working in Washington Taught Me We're All a Little Like RT America," *Expanded Thoughts* (blog), tumblr.com March 6, 2014 (http://zaidjilani.tumblr.com/post/78770477756/how-working-in-washington-taught-me-were-all-a-little).

33. Drake, Meghan, "Survey: U.S. Press Freedom Plunges Under Obama to 46th in World, After Romania," *Washington Times*, February 11, 2014 (http://www.washingtontimes.com/news/2014/feb/11/press-freedom-suffers-under-obama-global-survey-fi/).

34. Assenheim, Marilyn, "FCC's Mignon Clyburn Don't Need No Stinkin' Votes to Implement Unconstitutionality," *Girls Just Wanna Have Guns*, February 22, 2014 (http://girlsjustwannahaveguns.com/2014/02/fccs-mignon-clyburn-dont-need-stinkin-votes-implement-unconstitutionality/).

35. Halpin, John, et al., "The Structural Imbalance of Political Talk Radio," Center for American Progress, June 20, 2007 (http://ameri canprogress.org/issues/media/report/2007/06/20/3087/the-structural -imbalance-of-political-talk-radio/); quoted in Carroll, Conn, "FCC 'Survey' Straight from Podesta's Fairness Doctrine Playbook," *Townhall.com*, February 24, 2014 (http://townhall.com/tipsheet/conncarroll/2014/02/24/ fcc-survey-straight-from-podestas-fairness-doctrine-playbook-n1799837).

36. "Report: Islamists' Slaughter of Syrian Christians Ignored by Obama, Major Media," WorldTribune.com, November 26, 2013 (http://www .worldtribune.com/2013/11/26/report-islamis-slaughter-of-syrian-christians -ignored-by-obama-liberal-media/).

37. Lynch, Sarah, "Egypt's Christians Under Attack Since Morsi's Ouster," *USA Today*, August 15, 2013 (http://www.usatoday.com/story/news/ world/2013/08/15/egypt-coptic-church-islamists/2640419/).

38. Marlin, George J., "Cuomo to Catholics: You're Not Welcome in NY," *Catholic Thing*, January 19, 2014 (http://www.thecatholicthing.org/ columns/2014/cuomo-to-catholics-youre-not-welcome-in-ny.html).

39. Bigelow, William, "Pope Francis Attacks Capitalism, Calls for State Control," *Breitbart*, November 27, 2013 (http://www.breitbart.com/ Big-Peace/2013/11/27/Pope-Francis-Attacks-Capitalism-Calls-for-State -Control).

40. Diaz, Mario, "Diaz: What Obamacare Means to Little Sisters of the Poor," *Washington Times*, October 10, 2013 (http://www.washingtontimes .com/news/2013/oct/10/diaz-what-obamacare-means-to-little-sisters-of -the/?page=all).

41. Hollingsworth, Barbara, "Gallup: Only 5% of Religious Americans Are Non-Christians," CNSNews.com, December 30, 2013 (http://cnsnews.com/ news/article/barbara-hollingsworth/gallup-only-5-religious-americans-are -non-christians).

42. Gray, Lisa, "Principal Who Told Kids Not to Speak Spanish Will Lose Job," *Houston Chronicle*, March 18, 2014 (http://www.chron.com/ news/houston-texas/houston/article/Principal-who-told-kids-not-to-speak -Spanish-will-5327528.php).

Chapter 4: The War on the U.S. Military

1. Flatten, Mark, "House GOP Leaders Want Probe of Veterans Affairs' Purging of Medical Test Orders," *Washington Examiner*, March 4, 2014 (http://washingtonexaminer.com/house-gop-leaders-want-probe -of-veterans-affairs-purging-of-medical-test-orders/article/2545004).

2. Malkin, Michelle, "How America Treats Illegal Aliens vs. Veterans," Creators.com, May 23, 2014 (http://www.creators.com/conservative/michelle-malkin/how-america-treats-illegal-aliens-vs-veterans.html).

3. Longman, Phillip, "The Best Care Anywhere," *Washington Monthly*, January–February 2005 (http://www.washingtonmonthly.com/features/2005/0501.longman.html).

4. Kouri, Jim, "Obama General Destroys Career of Army Officer to Appease Muslims," *Conservative Action Alerts*, October 9, 2012 (http://www.conservativeactionalerts.com/2012/10/obama-general-destroys-career-of-army-officer-to-appease-muslims/).

5. Gordon, J. D., "Gordon: Purging America's Military," *Washington Times*, November 12, 2013 (http://www.washingtontimes.com/news/2013/nov/12/gordon-transforming-the-us-military/).

6. Ricks, Thomas E., "The Obama administration's inexplicable mishandling of Marine Gen. James Mattis," *Best Defense* (blog), *Foreign Policy*, January 18, 2013 (http://ricks.foreignpolicy.com/posts/2013/01/18/the_obama_administration_s_inexplicable_mishandling_of_marine_gen_james_mattis).

7. "The Best From 'Mad Dog Mattis,'" *Washington Free Beacon*, March 18, 2013 (http://freebeacon.com/national-security/the-best-from-mad-dog-mattis/).

8. Halper, Daniel, "Obama Fires Top General Without Even a Phone Call," *Weekly Standard*, January 25, 2013 (http://www.weeklystandard.com/blogs/obama-fires-top-general-without-even-phone-call_697744.html).

9. Fisher, Max, "Amazing Details from the Drunken Moscow Bender That Got an Air Force General Fired," *WorldViews* (blog), *Washington Post*, December 19, 2013 (http://www.washingtonpost.com/blogs/worldviews/wp/2013/12/19/amazing-details-from-the-drunken-moscow-bender-that-got-an-air-force-general-fired/).

10. "US Nuclear Commander Tim Giardina Fired amid Gambling Investigation," *Guardian*, October 9, 2013 (http://www.theguardian.com/world/2013/oct/09/us-nuclear-commander-tim-giardina-fired-amid-gambling-investigation).

11. Ibid.

12. Kredo, Adam, "Obama to Kill Tomahawk, Hellfire Missile Programs," *Washington Free Beacon*, March 24, 2014 (http://freebeacon.com/national-security/obama-to-kill-tomahawk-hellfire-missile-programs/).

13. Greenfield, Daniel, "Obama's War on American Generals," *FrontPage Magazine*, February 19, 2013 (http://frontpagemag.com/2013/dgreenfield/obamas-war-on-american-generals/).

14. Ibid.

15. "Obama Relieves McChrystal over Critical Remarks, Names Petraeus as Replacement," Fox News, June 23, 2010 (http://www.foxnews.com/politics/2010/06/23/mcchrystal-afghanistan-fate/).

16. Hastings, Michael, "The Runaway General," *Rolling Stone*, June 22, 2010 (http://www.rollingstone.com/politics/news/the-runaway-general-20100622).

17. Brooks, Rosa, "Obama vs. the Generals," *Politico Magazine*, November 2013 (http://www.politico.com/magazine/story/2013/11/obama-vs-the-generals-99379.html?ml=m_ms).

18. "Report: First Western Eyewitness in Benghazi to Go Public Gives Account of Attack, Warning Signs," Fox News, October 28, 2013 (http://www.foxnews.com/politics/2013/10/28/report-first-western-eyewitness-in-benghazi-to-go-public-gives-account-attack/).

19. Gaffney, Frank J., Jr., "Gaffney: The Real Reason Behind Benghazigate," *Washington Times*, October 22, 2012 (http://www.washingtontimes.com/news/2012/oct/22/the-real-reason-behind-benghazigate/).

20. Tapper, Jake, "Exclusive: Dozens of CIA Operatives on the Ground During Benghazi Attack," *The Lead with Jake Tapper* (blog), CNN, August 7, 2013 (http://thelead.blogs.cnn.com/2013/08/01/exclusive-dozens-of-cia-operatives-on-the-ground-during-benghazi-attack/).

21. "Valerie Jarrett Gave Benghazi Stand-Down Order," *Investor's Business Daily*, August 7, 2013 (http://news.investors.com/ibd-editorials/080713-666729-jarrett-gave-benghazi-stand-down-order.htm).

22. Drover, Frank, "'Rogue' U.S. General Arrested for Activating Special Forces Teams; Ignoring Libya Stand-Down Order," *Daily Sheeple*, October 28, 2012 (http://www.thedailysheeple.com/rogue-u-s-general-arrested-for-activating-special-forces-teams-ignoring-libya-stand-down-order_102012); Robbins, James S., "TRR: Is a General Losing His Job over Benghazi?" *The Robbins Report* (blog), *Washington Times*, October 28, 2012 (http://www.washingtontimes.com/blog/robbins-report/2012/oct/28/general-losing-his-job-over-benghazi/).

23. Williams, J. B., "Benghazi: Where Are Gen. Ham and Adm. Gaouette?" *NewsWithViews*, May 16, 2013 (http://www.newswithviews.com/JBWilliams/williams247.htm).

24. "Happening Now: General Ham Testifying in a Closed Hearing to the House Armed Services Committee," *RedFlag News*, June 26, 2013 (http://www.redflagnews.com/headlines/major-developing-story-june-26th-general-carter-ham-to-testify-about-benghazi).

25. Chivers, C. J., and Thom Shanker, "Admiral at Center of Inquiry Is Censured by Navy," *New York Times*, March 26, 2013 (http://www.nytimes.com/2013/03/27/us/rear-admiral-charles-m-gaouette-is-disciplined-by-navy.html?_r=0).

26. Herridge, Catherine, "Exclusive: Benghazi Hero Fought Alongside Fallen SEALs, Still Recovering at Walter Reed," Fox News, July 25, 2013 (http://www.foxnews.com/politics/2013/07/25/exclusive-benghazi-hero -wounded-in-action-identified-recovering-at-walter-reed/).

27. Hoft, Jim, "Looking Back on Benghazi: US Hero Waited 20 Hours on Rooftop with Shredded Leg While Obama Went Campaigning," *Gateway Pundit*, January 16, 2014 (http://www.thegatewaypundit.com/2014/ 01/looking-back-on-benghazi-us-hero-waited-20-hours-on-rooftop-with -shredded-leg-while-obama-went-campaigning/).

28. Muñoz, Carlos, "Report: CIA using polygraph tests to ensure Benghazi operations stay secret," *Hill*, August 1, 2013 (http://thehill.com/ blogs/defcon-hill/operations/315157-report-dozens-of-cia-operatives-in -benghazi-at-time-of-consulate-attack-).

29. Johnson, Bridget, "New Benghazi Report Finds 'Severely Degraded' Readiness and a Pentagon Struggling to Catch Up," *PJ Media*, February 11, 2014 (http://pjmedia.com/tatler/2014/02/11/new-benghazi-report-finds -severely-degraded-readiness-and-a-pentagon-struggling-to-catch-up/).

30. Lopez, Claire M., "CIA Files from Benghazi: Now in the Hands of Al Qaeda?" *Pundicity*, February 13, 2014 (http://lopez.pundicity.com/ 14415/benghazi-cia-files).

31. Dareini, Ali Akbar, "Iran's Guard Says It Has Multiple Warhead Missiles," *Big Story*, AP, March 5, 2014 (http://bigstory.ap.org/article/iran -says-guard-has-multiple-warhead-missiles).

32. Newman, Marissa, "Iranian general: Obama's Threats are 'the Joke of the Year,'" *Times of Israel*, March 4, 2014 (http://www.timesofisrael.com/ iranian-general-obamas-threats-are-the-joke-of-the-year/).

33. Ibid.

34. De Luce, Dan, "Pentagon Plans to Shrink US Army to Pre-WWII Level," *Yahoo! News UK and Ireland*, February 25, 2014 (https://uk.news .yahoo.com/pentagon-proposes-shrink-us-army-pre-wwii-level-183915139 .html#mroS8Rb).

35. Wong, Kristina, "Pentagon Budget Slashes Benefits," *Hill*, February 24, 2014 (http://thehill.com/blogs/defcon-hill/budget-appropriations/ 199050-hagel-unveils-basics-of-2015-defense-budget-request).

36. Bedard, Paul, "Expert: Iran Ships a Dry Run for Later Nuclear/ EMP Attack; Humiliate Obama," *Washington Examiner*, February 14, 2014 (http://washingtonexaminer.com/expert-iran-ships-a-dry-run-for-later -nuclearemp-attack-humiliate-obama/article/2544041).

37. Kahlili, Reza, "Iranian Commander: We Have Targets Within America," *Daily Caller*, February 1, 2014 (http://dailycaller.com/2014/02/ 01/iranian-commander-we-have-targets-within-america/).

38. Klein, Aaron, "Iran Proposes Joint Naval Exercise with Russia. Show of Strength as Interim Nuclear Deal Takes Effect," *KleinOnline*, February 14, 2014 (http://kleinonline.wnd.com/2014/02/14/iran-proposes -joint-naval-exercise-with-russia-meant-to-check-u-s-warships-in-region/).

39. Gertz, Bill, "High Speed Threat," *Washington Free Beacon*, January 31, 2014 (http://freebeacon.com/national-security/high-speed-threat/).

40. "Iran Sends Warships to US Maritime Borders," Infowars.com, February 8, 2014 (http://www.infowars.com/iran-sends-warships-to-us -maritime-borders/).

41. Zion, Ilan Ben, "Iranian TV airs simulated bombing of Tel Aviv, US aircraft carrier," *Times of Israel*, February 8, 2014 (http://www.timesofisrael .com/iranian-tv-airs-simulated-bombing-of-tel-aviv/).

42. Buchanan, Patrick J., "Staying Out of Other People's Wars," *CNSNews.com*, February 7, 2014 (http://www.cnsnews.com/commentary/ patrick-j-buchanan/staying-out-other-peoples-wars).

43. "Obama's Army Only 85% Ready to Fight," *Investor's Business Daily*, January 31, 2014 (http://news.investors.com/ibd-editorials/013114-688529 -army-combat-readiness-at-85-percent.htm).

44. Wong, Kristina, "Two Navy Admirals Suspended amid Mush-rooming Bribery, Prostitution Scandal," *Washington Times*, November 10, 2013 (http://www.washingtontimes.com/news/2013/nov/10/two-navy -admirals-suspended-as-military-cracks-dow/).

45. Associated Press, "Marines Delay Female Fitness Plan After Half Fail Pull-Up Test," Fox News, January 2, 2014 (http://www.foxnews.com/ politics/2014/01/02/marines-delay-female-fitness-plan-after-half-fail -pullup-test/).

46. Taylor, Guy, and Rowan Scarborough, "Ominous warning: Admiral concedes U.S. losing dominance to China," *Washington Times*, January 16, 2014 (http://www.washingtontimes.com/news/2014/jan/16/us -military-dominance-pacific-decline-says-top-adm/).

47. Higbie, Carl, "Navy SEALs Ordered to Remove 'Don't Tread on Me' Navy Jack from Uniforms," *Daily Caller*, November 1, 2013 (http://dai lycaller.com/2013/11/01/navy-seals-ordered-to-remove-dont-tread-on-me -navy-jack-from-uniforms/). This article includes the e-mail quoted in the text.

Chapter 5: The War on the Middle Class

1. "Baltimore's People of the Woods: Inside the Hidden Homeless Camps Made of Milk Crates, Wooden Doors and Tarps on the Outskirts of Town," *MailOnline*, February 21, 2014 (http://www.dailymail.co.uk/

news/article-2564858/Baltimores-people-woods-Inside-hidden-homeless
-camps-milk-crates-wooden-doors-tarps-outskirts-town.html).

2. "Constitution of the United States," The Charters of Freedom, National Archives (http://www.archives.gov/exhibits/charters/constitution_transcript.html).

3. Dr. Econ, "Is the Federal Reserve a Privately Owned Corporation?" Federal Reserve Bank of San Francisco, September 2003 (http://www.frbsf.org/education/publications/doctor-econ/2003/september/private-public-corporation).

4. Meyer, Ali, "Bernanke Leaves Fed with Record Balance Sheet of $4,102,138,000,000," *CNSNews.com*, January 31, 2014 (http://www.cnsnews.com/news/article/ali-meyer/bernanke-leaves-fed-record-balance-sheet-4102138000000).

5. Kurtzleben, Danielle, "National Debt Interest Payments Dwarf Other Government Spending," *U.S. News and World Report*, November 19, 2012 (http://www.usnews.com/news/articles/2012/11/19/how-the-nations-interest-spending-stacks-up).

6. Chantrill, Christopher, "Government Revenue in the US," usgovernmentrevenue.com (http://www.usgovernmentrevenue.com/fed_revenue_2012US).

7. Lokey, Colin, "Policy Failure: ZIRP, Bubbles, and How the Fed Has Cost Savers 9 Trillion in 11 Years," *Seeking Alpha*, October 11, 2012 (http://seekingalpha.com/article/918041-policy-failure-zirp-bubbles-and-how-the-fed-has-cost-savers-9-trillion-in-11-years).

8. Roberts, Paul Craig, "The Money Changers Serenade: A New Plot Hatches," Infowars.com, December 1, 2013 (http://www.infowars.com/the-money-changers-serenade-a-new-plot-hatches/).

9. Roberts, Paul Craig, "The Money Changers Serenade: A New Bankers' Plot to Steal Your Deposits," *Global Research*, November 22, 2013 (http://www.globalresearch.ca/the-money-changers-serenade-a-new-bankers-plot-to-steal-your-deposits/5359018).

10. Roberts, Paul Craig, "Defeated by the Taliban, Washington Decides to Take on Russia and China," Infowars.com, December 5, 2013 (http://www.infowars.com/defeated-by-the-taliban-washington-decides-to-take-on-russia-and-china/).

11. Huszar, Andrew, "Andrew Huszar: Confessions of a Quantitative Easer," *Wall Street Journal*, November 11, 2013 (http://online.wsj.com/news/articles/SB10001424052702303763804579183680751473884); quoted in Roberts, "The Money Changers Serenade: A New Plot Hatches."

12. Kelly, "Gold Wars Synopsis," *Gold Wars*, November 21, 2013 (http://gold-wars.com/book/gold-wars-synopsis/).

13. Quinn, James, "Obama Promises US Taxpayer Will Never Again Foot Bill for Banks," *Telegraph* (UK), July 21, 2010 (http://www.tele graph.co.uk/finance/newsbysector/banksandfinance/7903365/Obama -promises-US-taxpayer-will-never-again-foot-bill-for-banks.html).

14. Levine, Matt, "EU Is Shocked That Banks Colluded on LIBOR," *Bloomberg View*, December 4, 2013 (http://www.bloomberg.com/news/ 2013-12-04/eu-is-shocked-that-banks-colluded-on-libor.html).

15. The Doc, "Jim Rickards Explains How Gold Will Reach $7,000/ oz at the Sovereign Man Event in Chile," *Silver Doctors*, May 9, 2013 (http://www.silverdoctors.com/jim-rickards-explains-how-gold-will-reach -7000oz-at-the-sovereign-man-event-in-chile/).

16. Rhyne, Denise, "Naked Silver Shorting," You Should Buy Gold .com, December 2011 (http://www.youshouldbuygold.com/2011/12/naked -silver-shorting/).

17. Ross, Alice K., Nick Mathiason, and Will Fitzgibbon, "Robot Wars: How High Frequency Trading Changed Global Markets," The Bureau of Investigative Journalism, September 16, 2012 (http://www.thebureau investigates.com/2012/09/16/robot-wars-how-high-frequency-trading -changed-global-markets/).

18. "The Impact of the September 2008 Economic Collapse," The Pew Charitable Trusts, April 28, 2010 (http://www.pewtrusts.org/en/ research-and-analysis/reports/2010/04/28/the-impact-of-the-september -2008-economic-collapse).

19. Boyer, Dave, "That's Rich: Poverty Level Under Obama Breaks 50-Year Record," *Washington Times*, January 7, 2014 (http://www.washingtontimes.com/ news/2014/jan/7/obamas-rhetoric-on-fighting-poverty-doesnt-match-h/).

20. Taylor, Kristinn, "Black Labor Force Participation Rate Under Obama Hits Rock Bottom—Lowest Level Ever Recorded," *Gateway Pundit*, January 13, 2014 (http://www.thegatewaypundit.com/2014/01/black-labor -force-participation-rate-under-obama-hits-rock-bottom-lowest-level-ever -recorded/).

21. Jones, Imara, "The Crisis in Black and Brown Youth Unemploy- ment," *Colorlines*, January 15, 2014 (http://colorlines.com/archives/2014/01/ youth_unemployment.html).

22. U.S. Department of Labor, Bureau of Labor Statistics, "Economic News Release," August 20, 2013 (http://www.bls.gov/news.release/youth .nr0.htm).

23. Durden, Tyler, "People Not in Labor Force Soar to Record 91.8 Million; Participation Rate Plunges to 1978 Levels," *Zero Hedge*, January 10, 2014 (http://www.zerohedge.com/news/2014-01-10/people-not-labor -force-soar-record-918-million-participation-rate-plunges-1978-level).

24. Will, George F., "For Liberals, Gestures Mean More Than Market Reality," *Investor's Business Daily*, January 10, 2014 (http://news.investors.com/ibd-editorials-perspective/011014-686045-gesture-liberalism-dismisses-the-need-for-consumer-choice.htm?p=full).

25. Jones, Susan, "Biden: 'Single Women with Children in a Dead-End Job' Can Quit Because of Obamacare," CNSNews.com, February 26, 2014 (http://cnsnews.com/news/article/susan-jones/biden-single-women-children-dead-end-job-can-quit-because-obamacare).

26. "Hurting the 0.3%," *Wall Street Journal*, February 18, 2014 (http://online.wsj.com/news/articles/SB1000142405270230349140457939126009141 9176).

27. Congressional Budget Office, "Labor Market Effects of the Affordable Care Act: Updated Estimates," appendix to *The Budget and Economic Outlook: 2014 to 2024*, February 2014 (http://www.cbo.gov/sites/default/files/cbofiles/attachments/45010-breakout-AppendixC.pdf).

28. Boyer, Dave, "Obama: 'Whenever I Can Take Steps Without Legislation,' I Will," *Washington Times*, February 8, 2014 (http://www.washingtontimes.com/news/2014/feb/8/obama-whenever-i-can-take-steps-without-legislatio/).

29. Plumer, Brad, "Why Are 47 Million Americans on Food Stamps? It's the Recession—Mostly," *Washington Post*, September 23, 2013 (http://www.washingtonpost.com/blogs/wonkblog/wp/2013/09/23/why-are-47-million-americans-on-food-stamps-its-the-recession-mostly/).

30. "Judicial Watch Uncovers USDA Records Sponsoring U.S. Food Stamp Program for Illegal Aliens," *Judicial Watch*, April 26, 2013 (http://www.judicialwatch.org/press-room/press-releases/judicial-watch-uncovers-usda-records-sponsoring-u-s-food-stamp-program-for-illegal-aliens/).

31. Snyder, Michael, "The More Illegal Immigrants That Go on Food Stamps the More Money JP Morgan Makes," *The Economic Collapse*, April 28, 2013 (http://theeconomiccollapseblog.com/archives/the-more-illegal-immigrantsthat-go-on-food-stamps-the-more-money-jp-morgan-makes).

32. "Economics and the Civil War," *History Central* (http://www.historycentral.com/CivilWar/AMERICA/Economics.html).

33. Turchin, Peter, "Blame Rich, Overeducated Elites As Our Society Frays," *Bloomberg View*, November 20, 2013 (http://www.bloomberg.com/news/2013-11-20/blame-rich-overeducated-elites-as-our-society-frays.html).

34. Durden, Tyler, "The World's 2170 Billionaires Control $33 Trillion in Net Worth, Double the US GDP," *Zero Hedge*, November 23, 2013 (http://www.zerohedge.com/news/2013-11-23/worlds-2170-billionaires-control-33-trillion-net-worth-double-us-gdp).

35. Schwartz, Nelson D., "The Middle Class Is Steadily Eroding. Just Ask the Business World." *New York Times*, February 2, 2014 (http://www.nytimes.com/2014/02/03/business/the-middle-class-is-steadily-eroding-just-ask-the-business-world.html?action=click&contentCollection=Opinion&module=MostEmailed&version=Full&region=Marginalia&src=me&pgtype=article&_r=0).

36. Katz, Ian, "China's Treasury Holdings Climb to Record in Government Data," *Bloomberg News*, January 15, 2014 (http://www.bloomberg.com/news/2014-01-15/china-s-treasury-holdings-rose-to-record-in-november-data-show.html).

37. "PBOC Says No Longer in China's Interest to Increase Reserves," *Bloomberg News*, November 20, 2013 (http://www.bloomberg.com/news/2013-11-20/pboc-says-no-longer-in-china-s-favor-to-boost-record-reserves.html).

38. Miller, Terry, "America's Dwindling Economic Freedom," *Wall Street Journal*, January 13, 2014 (http://online.wsj.com/news/articles/SB10001424052702303848104579308811265028066?mg=reno64-wsj&url=http%3A%2F%2Fonline.wsj.com%2Farticle%2FSB1000142405270230384810457930881126502806.html).

39. Goad, Benjamin, "Government Report Finds Regulations Have Spiked Under Obama," *Hill*, May 15, 2013 (http://thehill.com/regulation/administration/299617-government-report-shows-spike-in-regulations-under-obama).

40. Kudlow, Lawrence, "Obama Doesn't Understand the Power of the Free Market," *Investor's Business Daily*, December 6, 2013 (http://news.investors.com/ibd-editorials-on-the-right/120613-682112-challenge-of-our-time-is-to-boost-economic-growth.htm).

41. Quoted in Gapper, John, "Capitalism: In search of balance," *Financial Times*, December 23, 2013, (http://www.ft.com/intl/cms/s/0/4a0b8168-6bc0-11e3-a216-00144feabdc0.html).

42. "Rerum Novarum: Encyclical of Pope Leo XIII On Capital and Labor," *The Holy See*, http://www.vatican.va/holy_father/leo_xiii/encyclicals/documents/hf_l-xiii_enc_15051891_rerum-novarum_en.html.

43. Shedlock, Mike, "Bottom 5 States in Fiscal Condition: New Jersey, Connecticut, Illinois, Massachussetts, California," Mish's Global Economic Trend Analysis, January 19, 2014 (http://globaleconomicanalysis.blogspot.com/2014/01/bottom-5-states-in-fiscal-condition-new.html).

44. Bedard, Paul, "Wall Street Adviser: Actual Unemployment Is 37.2%, 'Misery Index' Worst in 40 Years," *Washington Examiner*, January 21, 2014 (http://washingtonexaminer.com/wall-street-advisor-actual-unemployment-is-37.2-misery-index-worst-in-40-years/article/2542604).

45. "Stagflation, Anyone?" *Investor's Business Daily*, February 18, 2014 (http://news.investors.com/ibd-editorials/021814-690354-are-we-entering-another-stagflation-era.htm).

Chapter 6: The War on American Medicine

1. Goodman, John, "Popular Medicare Drug Plans Are Under Assault," *Forbes*, February 25, 2014 (http://www.forbes.com/sites/johngoodman/2014/02/25/popular-medicare-drug-plans-are-under-assault/).

2. Herrick, Devon M., "ObamaCare Weakens Medicare Drug Program That Works," *Investor's Business Daily*, February 24, 2014 (http://news.investors.com/ibd-editorials-perspective/022414-691012-obamacare-would-encourage-higher-prices-for-drugs-under-medicare.htm).

3. Rousselle, Christine, "Vermont Democrats Labeling State's Single-Payer Health Plan a Failure," Townhall.com, March 18, 2014 (http://townhall.com/tipsheet/christinerousselle/2014/03/18/vermont-democrats-labeling-states-singlepayer-health-plan-a-failure-n1810856).

4. Bajak, Frank, "Doctors Say Venezuela's Health Care in Collapse," *Big Story*, AP, November 6, 2013 (http://bigstory.ap.org/article/doctors-say-venezuelas-health-care-collapse).

5. Hall, Wynton, "Obamacare Skyrockets Cancer Patient's Meds to $14,000," *Breitbart*, February 24, 2014 (http://www.breitbart.com/Big-Government/2014/02/24/Obamacare-Skyrockets-Cancer-Patient-s-Meds-to-14-000-for-8-Week-Supply).

6. Hall, Wynton, "Democrats Declare War Against Obamacare Cancer Patients," *Breitbart*, February 24, 2014 (http://www.breitbart.com/Big-Government/2014/02/24/Democrats-Declare-War-Against-Obamacare-Cancer-Patients).

7. Bajak, "Doctors Say Venezuela's Health Care in Collapse."

8. Hurtubise, Sarah, "Fourth Georgia Hospital Closes Due to Obamacare Payment Cuts," *Daily Caller*, February 18, 2014 (http://dailycaller.com/2014/02/18/fourth-georgia-hospital-closes-due-to-obamacare-payment-cuts/).

9. Gupta, Girish, "Venezuelan Military Seizes Major Retain Chain," *USA Today*, November 9, 2013 (http://www.usatoday.com/story/news/world/2013/11/09/venezuela-seizes-stores/3486581/).

10. Klein, Philip, "Obamacare Official: 'Let's Just Make Sure It's Not a Third-World Experience,'" *Washington Examiner*, March 22, 2013 (http://washingtonexaminer.com/obamacare-official-lets-just-make-sure-its-not-a-third-world-experience/article/2525132).

11. Rabin, Roni Caryn, "Doctors Are Concerned About Pay Scales Under Health Care Law," *McClatchy DC*, November 20, 2013 (http://www.mcclatchydc.com/2013/11/20/209165/doctors-are-concerned-about-pay.html).

12. "New Health Plans Sold Through Exchanges Not Accepted At Some Prestigious NYC Hospitals," *Washington Post*, November 20, 2013 (this article is no longer available online).

13. Alonso-Zaldivar, Ricardo, "Concerns About Cancer Centers Under Health Law," *Yahoo! News*, March 18, 2014 (http://news.yahoo.com/concerns-cancer-centers-under-health-law-201055387--politics.html;_ylt=AwrBEiGoqShT13AAnEfQtDMD).

14. "Nation's Elite Cancer Hospitals Off-Limits Under Obamacare," *New York Post*, March 19, 2014 (http://nypost.com/2014/03/19/nations-elite-cancer-hospitals-off-limits-under-obamacare/).

15. McCaughey, Betsy, "How ObamaCare Slaps the Sick," *New York Post*, March 4, 2014 (http://nypost.com/2014/03/04/how-obamacare-slaps-the-sick/).

16. Reuters, "UnitedHealth Drops Thousands of Doctors from Insurance Plans: *WSJ*," *Yahoo! News*, November 15, 2013 (http://news.yahoo.com/unitedhealth-drops-thousands-doctors-insurance-plans-wsj-030014903--finance.html).

17. Klein, Aaron, "Chavez-Linked Group Crafted 'Keep Your Health Plan,'" *WND*, November 14, 2013 (http://www.wnd.com/2013/11/hugo-chavez-linked-group-crafted-you-can-keep-your-plan/).

18. McCarthy, Andrew C., "Obamacare's Unconstitutional Origins," *National Review Online*, October 5, 2013 (http://www.nationalreview.com/article/360460/obamacares-unconstitutional-origins-andrew-c-mccarthy).

19. Savage, Michael, *Trickle Up Poverty* (New York: William Morrow, 2010), pp. 52–55.

20. "Obamacare Architect: Genetic 'Lottery Winners' Have Been Paying an 'Artificially Low Price,'" *Real Clear Politics*, November 13, 2013 (http://www.realclearpolitics.com/video/2013/11/13/obamacare_architect_genetic_lottery_winners_have_been_paying_an_artificially_low_price.html).

21. Brewster, Tom, "How the NSA, GCHQ, and Crooks Can Hack Mobile Apps," *Wired.co.uk*, January 30, 2014 (http://www.wired.co.uk/news/archive/2014-01/30/how-the-nsa-gchq-and-crooks-can-hack-mobile-apps/viewgallery/305411).

22. Robbins, James S., "Move Over NSA, Here Comes the Obamacare Big Brother Database," *Rare*, July 20, 2013 (http://rare.us/story/move-over-nsa-here-comes-the-obamacare-big-brother-database/).

23. Melchior, Jillian Kay, "Convicted Terrorist Worked as Obamacare Navigator in Illinois," *National Review Online*, February 26, 2014 (http://www.nationalreview.com/article/372065/convicted-terrorist-worked-obamacare-navigator-illinois-jillian-kay-melchior).

24. Fund, John, "The Truth About Navigators," *National Review Online*, November 11, 2013 (http://www.nationalreview.com/article/363699/truth-about-navigators-john-fund).

25. Lehman, Chris, "Oregon Lawmakers Grill Director of Health Insurance Exchange," *NW News Network*, January 15, 2014 (http://nwnewsnetwork.org/post/oregon-lawmakers-grill-director-health-insurance-exchange).

26. Jones, Susan, "Obama Changes Affordable Care Act Requirements by Himself," CNSNews.com, November 14, 2013 (http://www.cnsnews.com/news/article/susan-jones/obama-changes-affordable-care-act-requirements-himself).

27. Hunter, Melanie, "Hidden Code on Obamacare Website: 'No Reasonable Expectation of Privacy,'" CNSNews.com, October 24, 2013 (http://cnsnews.com/news/article/melanie-hunter/hidden-code-obamacare-website-no-reasonable-expectation-privacy).

28. Gehrke, Joel, "Obamacare Launch Spawns 700+ Cyber-Squatters Capitalizing on Healthcare.gov, State Exchanges," *Washington Examiner*, October 23, 2013 (http://washingtonexaminer.com/obamacare-launch-spawns-700-cyber-squatters-capitalizing-on-healthcare.gov-state-exchanges/article/2537691).

29. "Healthcare.gov Doesn't Protect Personal Information of Obamacare Applicants," *RT*, October 30, 2013 (http://rt.com/usa/care-act-privacy-site-976/).

30. Astrue, Michael, "Why the President Will Euthanize Health Care.gov in 2014," *Weekly Standard*, November 12, 2013 (http://www.weeklystandard.com/blogs/why-president-will-euthanize-healthcaregov-2014_766929.html).

31. Scheiner, Eric, "Security Expert Claims to Gain Info on 70-K ObamaCare Records in 4 Minutes," CNSNews.com, January 21, 2014 (http://www.cnsnews.com/mrctv-blog/eric-scheiner/security-expert-claims-gain-info-70-k-obamacare-records-4-minutes).

32. Finkle, Jim, and Joseph Menn, "Exclusive: FBI Warns of U.S. Government Breaches by Anonymous Hackers," Reuters, November 15, 2013 (http://www.reuters.com/article/2013/11/15/us-usa-security-anonymous-fbi-idUSBRE9AE17C20131115).

33. Gertz, Bill, "The Belarusian Connection," *Washington Free Beacon*, February 3, 2014 (http://freebeacon.com/national-security/the-belarusian-connection/).

34. Morgan, David, "Up to 40 Percent of Obamacare Website Hasn't Been Built Yet: Official," *Huffington Post*, November 20, 2013 (http://www.huff ingtonpost.com/2013/11/20/obamacare-website-40-percent_n_4309270 .html?ncid=webmail20).

35. Cardenas, Al, "Obamacare Unravels," *U.S. News and World Report*, February 18, 2014 (http://www.usnews.com/opinion/blogs/al -cardenas/2014/02/18/6-principles-for-an-alternative-to-obamacare).

36. Bedard, Paul, "Duke University: 44% of U.S. Firms Consider Cutting Health Care to Current Workers," *Washington Examiner*, February 5, 2014 (http://washingtonexaminer.com/duke-university-44-u.s.-firms -consider-cutting-health-care-to-current-workers/article/2543506).

37. McCaughey, Betsy, "Obama Affordable Care Act Hurts Twice As Many As It Helps," *Investor's Business Daily*, January 7, 2014 (http://news .investors.com/ibd-editorials-on-the-right/010714-685543-obamacare -hurts-twice-as-many-as-it-helps.htm?p=full).

38. "C.G.I. Conseillers En Gestion Et Informatique," *Industry Canada*, June 19, 2013 (http://www.ic.gc.ca/app/ccc/srch/nvgt.do?lang=eng&prtl=1 &sbPrtl=&estblmntNo=234567031749&profile=cmpltPrfl&profileId=501& app=sold).

39. Pollock, Richard, "Feds Reviewed Only One Bid for Obamacare Website Design," *Washington Examiner*, October 13, 2013 (http://washing tonexaminer.com/article/2537194).

40. Pollock, Richard, "Canadian Officials Fired IT Firm Behind Troubled Obamacare Website," *Washington Examiner*, October 10, 2013 (http://washingtonexaminer.com/canadian-officials-fired-it-firm-behind -troubled-obamacare-website/article/2537101).

41. "Michelle Obama and CGI Federal," FactCheck.org, December 10, 2013 (http://www.factcheck.org/2013/12/michelle-obama-and-cgi -federal/).

42. "How to Bid on Government Contracts," *WikiHow* (http://www .wikihow.com/Bid-on-Government-Contracts).

43. Melchior, Jillian Kay, "Colorado Health-Exchange Director Indicted for Fraud, Theft," The Corner, *National Review Online*, February 13, 2014 (http://www.nationalreview.com/corner/371043/colorado-health -exchange-director-indicted-fraud-theft-jillian-kay-melchior).

44. Associated Press, "Plea Deal Made in Low-Income Housing Embezzlement," *Washington Times*, June 17, 2014 (http://www.washingtontimes.com/ news/2014/jun/17/former-director-reaches-plea-agreement-in-theft/).

45. Terhune, Chad, "Obamacare Enrollees Hit Snags at Doctors' Offices," *Los Angeles Times*, February 4, 2014 (http://www.latimes.com/busi ness/la-fi-obamacare-patients-20140205,0,5417742.story#axzz2sRcUPkFx).

46. Schweizer, Peter, "At Least One Group of Americans Loves ObamaCare," Fox News, November 12, 2013 (http://www.foxnews.com/opinion/2013/11/12/at-least-one-group-americans-loves-obamacare/).

47. Miller, S. A., "Obama Donor's Firm Hired to Fix Web Mess It Created," *New York Post*, November 1, 2013 (http://nypost.com/2013/11/01/obama-donors-firm-hired-to-fix-web-mess-it-helped-make/).

48. Schweizer, "At Least One Group of Americans Loves ObamaCare."

49. "Full Transcript: President Obama's Nov. 14 News Conference on the Affordable Care Act," *Washington Post*, November 14, 2013 (http://www.washingtonpost.com/politics/transcript-president-obamas-nov-14-statement-on-health-care/2013/11/14/6233e352-4d48-11e3-ac54-aa84301ced81_story.html).

50. Viebeck, Elise, "O-Care Premiums to Skyrocket," *Hill*, March 19, 2014 (http://thehill.com/blogs/healthwatch/health-reform-implementation/201136-obamacare-premiums-are-about-to-skyrocket).

51. Angle, Jim, "ObamaCare Patients with Serious Pre-Existing Diseases Could Face Expensive Drug Costs," Fox News, February 16, 2014 (http://www.foxnews.com/politics/2014/02/16/obamacare-patients-with-serious-pre-existing-diseases-could-face-expensive-drug/).

52. Berry, Susan, "Cost of Generic Drugs Soaring Due to Increased Demand from Obamacare," *Breitbart*, February 1, 2014 (http://www.breitbart.com/Big-Government/2014/01/31/Why-Are-Costs-For-Generic-Medications-Soaring).

53. Levey, Noam N., "Critics Call Obama Funding Plan for Health Insurer Losses a 'Bailout,'" *Los Angeles Times*, May 21, 2014 (http://www.latimes.com/nation/la-na-insurance-bailout-20140521-story.html#page=1).

Chapter 7: The War on Civil Rights

1. Caldwell, Patrick, "The GOP's Filibuster Freak-Out: 13 Dramatic Reactions from Senate Republicans," *Mother Jones*, November 21, 2013 (http://www.motherjones.com/politics/2013/11/senate-republican-filibuster-nuclear-option-freakout).

2. Levin, Carl, "Senate Floor Statement on Proposed 'Nuclear Option,'" U.S. Senate, November 21, 2013 (http://www.levin.senate.gov/newsroom/speeches/speech/senate-floor-statement-on-proposed-nuclear-option).

3. Brekke, Dan, and David Marks, "In Wake of Arrest, Sen. Leland Yee Quits Secretary of State's Race," *News Fix* (blog), KQED News, March 27, 2014 (http://blogs.kqed.org/newsfix/2014/03/26/reports-state-senator-leland-yee-under-arrest-for-corruption).

4. Hrabe, John, "FBI Says Anti-Gun Lawmaker Arranged Weapons Deal with Muslim Rebels," CalNewsroom.com, March 27, 2014 (http://www.calnewsroom.com/2014/03/27/fbi-anti-gun-lawmaker-arranged-weapons-deal-with-muslim-rebels/).

5. The Infinite, "Dispelling the Myth—One Billion Hollow Point Bullets for Target Practice?" *Planet Infowars*, April 8, 2013 (http://planet.infowars.com/resistance/dispelling-the-myth-one-billion-hollow-point-bullets-for-target-practice).

6. Hoft, Jim, "Obama DHS Purchases 2,700 Light-Armored Tanks to Go with Their 1.6 Billion Bullet Stockpile," *Gateway Pundit*, March 3, 2013 (http://www.thegatewaypundit.com/2013/03/obama-dhs-purchases-2700-light-armored-tanks-to-go-with-their-1-6-billion-bullet-stockpile/).

7. Watson, Steve, "Big Sis Refuses to Answer Congress on Bullet Purchases," Infowars.com, March 21, 2013 (http://www.infowars.com/big-sis-refuses-to-answer-congress-on-ammo-purchases/).

8. Watson, Paul Joseph, "Homeland Security to Purchase 141,000 Rounds of Sniper Ammo," Infowars.com, February 11, 2014 (http://www.infowars.com/homeland-security-to-purchase-141000-rounds-of-sniper-ammo/).

9. Hathaway, Jesse, "Ohio National Guard Training Envisions Right-Wing Terrorism," *Media Trackers*, February 10, 2014 (http://mediatrackers.org/ohio/2014/02/10/ohio-national-guard-training-envisions-right-wing-terrorism).

10. Watson, Paul Joseph, "U.S. Army Builds 'Fake City' in Virginia to Practice Military Occupation," Infowars.com, February 14, 2014 (http://www.infowars.com/u-s-army-builds-fake-city-in-virginia-to-practice-military-occupation/).

11. "Judicial Watch Uncovers USDA Records Sponsoring U.S. Food Stamp Program for Illegal Aliens," *Judicial Watch*, April 25, 2013 (http://www.judicialwatch.org/press-room/press-releases/judicial-watch-uncovers-usda-records-sponsoring-u-s-food-stamp-program-for-illegal-aliens/).

12. Yoo, John, "Obamacare Debacle Much Worse for Constitution, Presidency Than Katrina Was for Bush," American Enterprise Institute, November 21, 2013 (http://www.aei.org/article/politics-and-public-opinion/obamacare-debacle-much-worse-for-constitution-presidency-than-katrina-was-for-bush/).

13. Shapiro, Ilya, "President Obama's Top 10 Constitutional Violations of 2013," *Forbes*, December 23, 2013 (http://www.forbes.com/sites/realspin/2013/12/23/president-obamas-top-10-constitutional-violations-of-2013/).

14. Ibid.

15. Pavlich, Katie, "Former Virginia Governor Bob McDonnell and Wife Maureen Indicted on Federal Corruption Charges," Townhall.com, January 21, 2014 (http://townhall.com/tipsheet/katiepavlich/2014/01/21/former -virginia-governor-bob-mcdonnell-and-wife-maureen-indicted-on-federal -corruption-charges-n1782534).

16. Gehrke, Joel, "Attorney General Eric Holder Can't Explain Constitutional Basis for Obama's Executive Orders," *Washington Examiner*, January 29, 2014 (http://washingtonexaminer.com/attorney-general-eric -holder-cant-explain-constitutional-basis-for-obamas-executive-orders/ article/2543100).

17. Hunter, Melanie, "'I Don't Know Anything...' Holder Denies Knowing IRS Investigator Was Obama Contributor," CNSNews.com, January 30, 2014 (http://cnsnews.com/news/article/melanie-hunter/i-dont -know-anything-holder-denies-knowing-irs-investigator-was-obama).

18. Ibid.

19. "Lawmakers: IRS Knew for Months of 'Lost' Lerner Emails, More Documents Missing," Fox News, June 17, 2014 (http://www.foxnews.com/ politics/2014/06/17/lawmakers-irs-knew-for-months-lost-lerner-emails -more-documents-missing/).

20. Lee, Tony, "True the Vote Founder Catherine Engelbrecht on IRS: 'I Was Targeted Because of My Political Beliefs,'" *Breitbart*, February 6, 2014 (http://www.breitbart.com/Big-Government/2014/02/06/True -the-Vote-Founder-on-IRS-I-Was-Targeted-Because-of-My-Political -Beliefs).

21. Dreilinger, Danielle, "Recovery School District will be country's first all-charter district in September 2014," *New Orleans Times-Picayune*, December 19, 2013 (http://www.nola.com/education/index.ssf/2013/12/ recovery_school_district_will_3.html).

22. Associated Press, "DOJ Tries to Stop School-Choice for Poor Children in Failing Louisiana Public Schools," CNSNews.com, August 24, 2013 (http://cnsnews.com/news/article/doj-tries-stop-school -choice-poor-children-failing-louisiana-public-schools).

23. Hinderaker, John, "Eric Holder Sues to Block Louisiana School Choice," *Powerline*, August 25, 2013 (http://www.powerlineblog.com/ archives/2013/08/eric-holder-sues-to-block-louisiana-school-choice.php).

24. Williams, Timothy, "Execution Case Dropped Against Abu-Jamal," *New York Times*, December 7, 2011 (http://www.nytimes.com/2011/12/08/ us/execution-case-dropped-against-convicted-cop-killer.html?_r=0).

25. Pavlich, Katie, "Democrats Block Widow of Murdered Police Officer from Testifying Against Obama DOJ Nominee Debo Adeg-

bile," Townhall.com, February 6, 2014 (http://townhall.com/tipsheet/katiepavlich/2014/02/06/democrats-block-widow-of-murdered-police-officer-to-testify-at-obama-nominee-confirmation-vote-n1790390).

26. Lowery, Wesley, "How Mumia Abu-Jamal Doomed Debo Adegbile in the Senate," *The Fix* (blog), *Washington Post*, March 5, 2014 (http://www.washingtonpost.com/blogs/the-fix/wp/2014/03/05/how-mumia-abu-jamal-doomed-dego-adegbile/).

27. Ibid.

28. "CBS 2 Exclusive: De Blasio's Caravan Caught Speeding, Violating Traffic Laws," CBS New York, February 20, 2014 (http://newyork.cbslocal.com/2014/02/20/cbs-2-exclusive-mayor-de-blasios-caravan-caught-speeding-violating-traffic-laws/).

29. Wilde, Robert, "NYC Mayor Bill de Blasio Imposes Charter School 'Moratorium,'" *Breitbart*, February 7, 2014 (http://www.breitbart.com/Big-Government/2014/02/07/NYC-Mayor-De-Blasio-Takes-Away-School-Choice-from-Families).

30. Schram, Jamie, Yoav Gonen, and Jeane MacIntosh, "DeBlasio's Buddy Sprung from Jail After Mayor Calls NYPD," *New York Post*, February 11, 2014 (http://nypost.com/2014/02/11/bill-de-blasio-called-cops-to-spare-pastor-pal-from-jail/).

31. Mindich, David T. Z., "Lincoln's Surveillance State," *New York Times*, July 5, 2013 (http://www.nytimes.com/2013/07/06/opinion/lincolns-surveillance-state.html?_r=0).

32. Nelson, Steven, "Mikulski Says Cellphone 'Kill Switch' Fears Baseless, 'Conspiratorial,'" *U.S. News and World Report*, February 21, 2014 (http://www.usnews.com/news/articles/2014/02/21/mikulski-says-cellphone-kill-switch-fears-baseless-conspiratorial).

33. "Obama Uses Government to Harass, Intimidate Foes," *Investor's Business Daily*, January 24, 2014 (http://news.investors.com/ibd-editorials/012414-687585-lawless-use-of-executive-branch-for-political-purposes.htm).

34. "Obama's IRS 'Confusion,'" *Wall Street Journal*, February 7, 2014 (http://online.wsj.com/news/articles/SB100014240527023041812045793651 61576171176?mod=WSJ_Opinion_LEADTop).

35. Klein, Edward, "Who is Valerie Jarrett?" *Daily Caller*, May 22, 2012 (http://dailycaller.com/2012/05/22/who-is-valerie-jarrett/).

36. Newby, Joe, "Report says Valerie Jarrett gave the order to stand down in Benghazi," Examiner.com, August 8, 2013 (http://www.examiner.com/article/report-says-valerie-jarrett-gave-the-order-to-stand-down-benghazi).

37. Russell, George, "John Podesta, Key Player in Administration's Regulation Drive, Also Helped UN Develop Radical New Global Agenda," Fox News, February 13, 2014 (http://www.foxnews.com/world/2014/02/13/john-podesta-key-player-in-administrations-regulation-drive-has-also-helped-un/).

38. "Obama on Executive Actions: 'I've Got a Pen and I've Got a Phone,'" CBS DC, January 14, 2014 (http://washington.cbslocal.com/2014/01/14/obama-on-executive-actions-ive-got-a-pen-and-ive-got-a-phone/).

39. "Rep. Weber: Obama Is a Socialistic Dictator," Infowars.com, January 28, 2014 (http://www.infowars.com/rep-weber-obama-is-a-socialistic-dictator/).

40. Cruz, Ted, "Ted Cruz: The Imperial Presidency of Barack Obama," Wall Street Journal, January 28, 2014 (http://online.wsj.com/news/articles/SB10001424052702304632204579338793559838308).

41. "Congressman: We Can Defeat Amnesty, Executive Orders," WND, January 31, 2014 (http://www.wnd.com/2014/01/congressman-we-can-defeat-amnesty-executive-orders/).

42. Berger, Judson, "Administration Eases Restrictions on Asylum Seekers with Loose Terror Ties," Fox News, February 6, 2014 (http://www.foxnews.com/politics/2014/02/06/administration-eases-restrictions-on-asylum-seekers-with-loose-terror-ties/).

43. Greenfield, Daniel, "'Activist' for Anti-Israel Group with Ties to Obama Exposed as Terrorist," FrontPage Magazine, October 25, 2013 (http://www.frontpagemag.com/2013/dgreenfield/activist-for-anti-israel-group-with-ties-to-obama-exposed-as-terrorist/).

44. "Turley: Obama's 'Become the Very Danger the Constitution Was Designed to Avoid,'" RealClearPolitics, December 4, 2013 (http://www.realclearpolitics.com/video/2013/12/04/turley_obamas_become_the_very_danger_the_constitution_was_designed_to_avoid.html).

45. Feldmann, Linda, "Is Barack Obama an Imperial President?" Christian Science Monitor, January 26, 2014 (http://www.csmonitor.com/USA/Politics/2014/0126/Is-Barack-Obama-an-imperial-president).

46. Strong, Jonathan, "The I-Word," National Review Online, December 5, 2013 (http://nationalreview.com/article/365566/i-word-jonathan-strong).

Chapter 8: The War on Science

1. Durden, Tyler, "Ship Sent to Rescue Global Warming Researchers in Antarctic, Gets Trapped in Antarctic," Zero Hedge, January 3, 2014 (http://www.zerohedge.com/news/2014-01-03/ship-sent-rescue-global-warming-researchers-trapped-antarctic-gets-trapped-antarctic).

2. "Kerry Urges US Envoys to Make Climate Change a Priority," *Yahoo! News*, March 8, 2014 (this article is no longer available online).

3. Jones, Susan, "Podesta: Obama's 'Warmed Up' to Executive Action; Will Use It for 'Climate Change and Energy Transformation Agenda,'" *CNSNews.com*, January 28, 2014 (http://www.cnsnews.com/news/article/susan-jones/podesta-obamas-warmed-executive-action-will-use-it-climate-change-and).

4. Bell, Larry, "Podesta appointment means government by fiat on climate, environment issues," *Cfact*, January 10, 2014 (http://www.cfact.org/2014/01/10/podesta-appointment-means-government-by-fiat-on-climate-environment-issues/).

5. "IPCC Official: 'Climate Policy Is Redistributing the World's Wealth,'" *USMessageBoard*, November 19, 2010 (http://www.usmessageboard.com/economy/142699-we-redistribute-world-s-wealth-by-climate-policy.html).

6. Bastasch, Michael, "Epic Fail: UN Climate Talks Fall Apart As 132 Countries Storm Out," *Daily Caller*, November 20, 2013 (http://dailycaller.com/2013/11/20/epic-fail-un-climate-talks-fall-apart-as-132-countries-storm-out/).

7. "Smog in China Prompts Authorities to Display Sun on Giant Screens," *Telegraph* (UK), January 17, 2014 (this article is no longer available online).

8. Bastasch, Michael, "UN Climate Chief: Communism Is Best to Fight Global Warming," *Daily Caller*, January 15, 2014 (http://dailycaller.com/2014/01/15/un-climate-chief-communism-is-best-to-fight-global-warming/).

9. "Greenpeace Co-Founder: No Scientific Proof Humans Are Dominant Cause of Warming Climate," Fox News, February 26, 2014 (http://www.foxnews.com/science/2014/02/26/greenpeace-co-founder-no-scientific-proof-humans-are-dominant-cause-warming/).

10. Bastasch, Michael, "Greenpeace Co-Founder: No Scientific Evidence of Man-Made Global Warming," Infowars.com, February 26, 2014 (http://www.infowars.com/greenpeace-co-founder-no-scientific-evidence-of-man-made-global-warming/).

11. "University of East Anglia Emails: The Most Contentious Quotes," *Telegraph* (UK), November 23, 2009 (http://www.telegraph.co.uk/earth/environment/globalwarming/6636563/University-of-East-Anglia-emails-the-most-contentious-quotes.html).

12. "Media, Surprisingly, Ask to See Climate Scientist's Emails," *Investor's Business Daily*, March 18, 2014 (http://news.investors.com/ibd-editorials/031814-693773-media-demand-to-read-hockey-stick-creator-michael-mann-emails.htm).

13. Watson, Steve, "Professor Calls for Climate Change 'Deniers' to Be Imprisoned," Infowars.com, March 17, 2014 (http://www.infowars.com/college-professor-calls-for-climate-change-deniers-to-be-imprisoned/).

14. Torcello, Lawrence, "Is Misinformation About the Climate Criminally Negligent?" *Conversation* (UK), March 13, 2014 (https://theconversation.com/is-misinformation-about-the-climate-criminally-negligent-23111).

15. Bawden, Tom, "Official prophecy of doom: Global warming will cause widespread conflict, displace millions of people and devastate the global economy," *Independent* (UK), March 18, 2014 (http://www.independent.co.uk/environment/climate-change/official-prophecy-of-doom-global-warming-will-cause-widespread-conflict-displace-millions-of-people-and-devastate-the-global-economy-9198171.html).

16. Martinson, Erica, "EPA's Fake Spy John Beale Gets 32 Months in Prison," *Politico*, December 18, 2013 (http://www.politico.com/story/2013/12/epa-john-beale-fake-spy-cia-prison-101289.html).

17. "Ex-EPA Official Told Lawmakers of Project to 'Modify the DNA' of Capitalism," Fox News, January 22, 2014 (http://www.foxnews.com/politics/2014/01/22/ex-epa-official-told-lawmakers-project-to-modify-dna-capitalism/).

18. Hollingsworth, Barbara, "Five Months Later, EPA Still Hasn't Complied with Congressional Subpoena," CNSNews.com, January 24, 2014 (http://cnsnews.com/news/article/barbara-hollingsworth/five-months-later-epa-still-hasn-t-complied-congressional).

19. Houston, Terrence, "Supreme Court: Justices Weigh EPA Greenhouse Gas Regulatory Power," *Ecological Society of America*, February 28, 2014 (http://www.esa.org/esablog/ecology-in-policy/esa-policy-news-february-28-2014-supreme-court-hears-epa-challenge-potus-links-ca-drought-to-climate-change/).

20. Bastasch, Michael, "Supreme Court Hears Arguments on Obama's Global Warming Agenda," *Daily Caller*, February 24, 2014 (http://dailycaller.com/2014/02/24/supreme-court-hears-arguments-on-obamas-global-warming-agenda/).

21. Barron-Lopez, Laura, "Supreme Court Weighs EPA Authority to Regulate Greenhouse Gases," *Hill*, February 23, 2014 (http://thehill.com/blogs/e2-wire/e2-wire/198962-supreme-court-weighs-epa-authority-to-regulate-greenhouse-gases).

22. Roberts, John, "'Secret Dealing'? Emails Show Cozy Relationship Between EPA, Environmental Groups," Fox News, January 22, 2014 (http://www.foxnews.com/politics/2014/01/22/emails-show-cozy-relationship-between-epa-environmental-groups-on-keystone-coal/).

23. Ibid.

24. Markay, Lachlan, "Democrats Who Oppose Keystone XL Pipeline Own Shares in Competing Companies," *Washington Free Beacon*, February 12, 2014 (http://freebeacon.com/issues/democrats-who-oppose-keystone-xl-pipeline-own-shares-in-competing-companies/).

25. Savage, Michael, *Trickle Down Tyranny* (New York: William Morrow, 2012), p. 13.

26. Munro, Neil, "Obama Wants Ukraine to 'De-Escalate,' Focuses on Campaigning for Democrats," *Daily Caller*, March 4, 2014 (http://dailycaller.com/2014/03/04/obama-wants-ukraine-to-deesclate-focuses-on-campaigning-for-democrats/).

27. Martinson, Erica, "Uttered in 2008, Still Haunting Obama in 2012," *Politico*, April 5, 2012 (http://www.politico.com/news/stories/0412/74892.html).

28. King, Bob, "Steven Chu's Europe Gas Quote Haunts President Obama," *Politico*, February 21, 2012 (http://www.politico.com/news/stories/0212/73138.html).

29. "Solar," Institute for Energy Research (http://www.instituteforenergyresearch.org/energy-overview/solar/).

30. Wilde, Robert, "Obama to Give Wind Farms 30-Year Pass on Eagle Deaths," *Breitbart*, December 6, 2013 (http://www.breitbart.com/Big-Government/2013/12/05/Obama-to-Sign-Rule-Allowing-Death-of-Eagles).

31. Noon, Marita, "Death by Renewables," *Cfact*, December 16, 2013 (https://www.cfact.org/2013/12/16/death-by-renewables/).

32. Bell, Larry, "Greenpower Gridlock: Why Renewable Energy Is No Alternative," *Cfact*, December 16, 2013 (https://www.cfact.org/2013/12/16/green-power-gridlock-why-renewable-energy-is-no-alternative/).

33. Jeffrey, Terence P., "Electricity Price Index Soars to New Record at Start of 2014; U.S. Electricity Production Declining," CNSNews.com, February 21, 2014 (http://cnsnews.com/news/article/terence-p-jeffrey/electricity-price-index-soars-new-record-start-2014-us-electricity).

34. Cooper-White, Macrina, "Sun Scientists Debate Whether Solar Lull Could Trigger Another 'Little Ice Age,'" *Huffington Post*, January 24, 2014 (http://www.huffingtonpost.com/2014/01/24/solar-lull-little-ice-age-sun-scientists_n_4645248.html).

35. Hotz, Robert Lee, "Strange Doings on the Sun," *Wall Street Journal*, November 10, 2013 (http://online.wsj.com/news/articles/SB10001424052702304672404579183940409194498).

36. Santini, Jean-Louis, "Calm Solar Cycle Prompts Questions About Impact on Earth," Phys.org, November 24, 2013 (http://phys.org/news/2013-11-calm-solar-prompts-impact-earth.html).

37. Morano, Marc, "Nearly 1000 Record Low Temperatures Set As Another Round of Arctic Air Forecast To Deep Freeze The U.S.," *Climate Depot*, November 29, 2013 (http://www.climatedepot.com/2013/11/29/nearly-1000-record-low-temperatures-set-as-another-round-of-arctic-air-forecast-to-deep-freeze-the-u-s/).

38. Bastasch, Michael, "Global Warming? Satellite Data Shows Arctic Sea Ice Coverage Up 50 Percent!" *Daily Caller*, December 16, 2013 (http://dailycaller.com/2013/12/16/global-warming-satellite-data-shows-arctic-sea-ice-coverage-up-50-percent/).

39. Goddard, Steven, "2013 Will Finish One of the Ten Coldest Years in US History, with the Largest Drop in Temperature," *Real Science*, December 20, 2013 (http://stevengoddard.wordpress.com/2013/12/20/2013-one-of-the-ten-coldest-years-in-us-history-with-the-largest-drop-in-temperature/).

40. Ciandella, Mike, "Frozen Out: 98% of Stories Ignore That Ice-Bound Ship Was on Global Warming Mission," *NewsBusters*, January 2, 2014 (http://newsbusters.org/blogs/mike-ciandella/2014/01/02/frozen-out-98-stories-ignore-ice-bound-ship-was-global-warming-missi).

41. Wilde, Robert, "Study: Volcanic Eruptions Cooling Planet Earth," *Bretibart*, February 25, 2014 (http://www.breitbart.com/Big-Government/2014/02/25/Study-Volcanic-Eruptions-Cooling-Planet-Earth).

42. "Fire And Ice—Volcanoes, Not CO_2, Melt West Antarctic," *Investor's Business Daily*, December 10, 2013 (http://news.investors.com/ibd-editorials/121013-682455-active-volcanoes-melting-west-antarctic-ice.htm?p=full).

43. Cooper, Barry, "Climate-Change Scare Becomes 'Thermal Theatre,'" *Calgary Herald*, October 2, 2013 (http://www2.canada.com/calgaryherald/news/theeditorialpage/story.html?id=31055bb3-8c7c-46e6-bb62-3200a48694f3).

44. Pollak, Joel B., "2014 Is Global Warming's Worst Year Ever," *Breitbart*, February 19, 2014 (http://www.breitbart.com/Big-Peace/2014/02/19/2014-is-Global-Warming-s-Worst-Year-Ever).

45. Hartnett-White, Kathleen, and Vance Ginn, "The Texas Hockey Stick: Charting the Lone Star Oil Boom," *Investor's Business Daily*, December 6, 2013 (http://news.investors.com/ibd-editorials-viewpoint/120613-682109-texas-oil-production-up-141-percent-over-january-2009.htm?p=full).

46. Murdock, Deroy, "America's Greenest Energy Source," *New York Post*, December 4, 2013 (http://nypost.com/2013/12/04/americas-greenest-energy-source/).

47. Fumento, Michael, "Global-Warming 'Proof' Is Evaporating," *New York Post*, December 5, 2013 (http://nypost.com/2013/12/05/global-warming-proof-is-evaporating/).

48. Boyer, Dave, "Obama Orders Government to Prepare for Impact of Global Warming," *Washington Times*, November 1, 2013 (http://www.washingtontimes.com/news/2013/nov/1/obama-orders-government-prep-global-warming/).

49. Brown, Travis H., "Fracking Fuels an Economic Boom in North Dakota," *Forbes*, January 29, 2014 (http://www.forbes.com/sites/travis brown/2014/01/29/fracking-fuels-an-economic-boom-in-north-dakota/).

Chapter 9: The War on Our Schools

1. Armario, Christine, "'Wake-Up Call': U.S. Students Trail Global Leaders," NBCNews.com, December 7, 2010 (http://www.nbcnews.com/id/40544897/ns/us_news-life/t/wake-up-call-us-students-trail-global-leaders/#.U52Pv3aGeM8).

2. Ibid.

3. Arkin, Daniel, "US Teens Lag in Global Education Rankings as Asian Countries Rise to the Top," NBCNews.com, December 3, 2013 (http://usnews.nbcnews.com/_news/2013/12/03/21733705-us-teens-lag-in-global-education-rankings-as-asian-countries-rise-to-the-top).

4. "National Assessment of Adult Literacy (NAAL)," Institute of Education Sciences, National Center for Education Statistics (http://nces.ed.gov/naal/lit_history.asp).

5. Wilson, Ann, "Outcome Based Education—Questions Demanding Answers," *Say No to Psychiatry!* (http://www.sntp.net/education/OBE_1.htm).

6. Ibid.

7. Inglee, Jenny, "If High School Seniors Can't Read Their Diplomas, Should They Be Allowed to Graduate?" *TakePart*, January 23, 2013 (http://www.takepart.com/article/2013/01/23/graduation-rates-are-all-time-high-not-so-fast).

8. U.S. Department of Education, National Institute of Literacy, "Illiteracy Statistics," April 28, 2013; available at *Statistic Brain* (http://www.statisticbrain.com/number-of-american-adults-who-cant-read/).

9. "How Many People Go to College Every Year?" *How to E-D-U* (http://howtoedu.org/college-facts/how-many-people-go-to-college-every-year/).

10. "One-third of students need remedial college math, reading," *USA Today*, May 11, 2010 (http://usatoday30.usatoday.com/news/education/2010-05-11-remedial-college_N.htm).

11. Jones, Susan, "Custom Writing Service Says Students 'No Longer Have to Face the Burden of Academic Coursework,'" CNSNews.com, January 20, 2014 (http://cnsnews.com/news/article/susan-jones/custom-writing-service-says-students-no-longer-have-face-burden-academic).

12. Simon, Ruth, and Michael Corkery, "Push to Gauge Bang for Buck from College Gains Steam," *Wall Street Journal*, February 11, 2013 (http://online.wsj.com/article/SB10001424127887324880504578298162378392502.html?mod=ITP_pageone_0).

13. Geiger, Roger, and Donald E. Heller, "Financial Trends in Higher Education: The United States," *CSHE Working Paper #6*, College of Education, Penn State, January 2011(http://www.ed.psu.edu/cshe/working-papers/wp-6/view).

14. Diamond, Laura, and James Salzer, "Campus Jobs Rise in Recession," *Atlanta Journal-Constitution*, July 15, 2012 (http://www.ajc.com/news/news/local/campus-jobs-rise-in-recession/nQXGB/); Geiger and Heller, "Financial Trends in Higher Education: The United States."

15. Joyner, James, "Administrative Bloat at America's Colleges and Universities," *Outside the Beltway*, December 30, 2012 (http://www.outsidethebeltway.com/administrative-bloat-at-americas-colleges-and-universities/).

16. Dirks, Arthur L., "Organization of Knowledge: The Emergence of Academic Specialty in America," *Bridgewater State University* (http://webhost.bridgew.edu/adirks/ald/papers/orgknow.htm).

17. Snyder, Michael, "20 Completely Ridiculous College Courses Being Offered at U.S. Universities," *The Economic Collapse*, June 5, 2013 (http://theeconomiccollapseblog.com/archives/20-completely-ridiculous-college-courses-being-offered-at-u-s-universities).

18. MacDonald, Heather, "The Humanities Have Forgotten Their Humanity," *Wall Street Journal*, January 3, 2014 (http://online.wsj.com/news/articles/SB10001424052702304858104579264321265378790).

19. Hassett, Kevin, "Commencement Speakers: Conservatives Need Not Apply," *Los Angeles Times*, May 19, 2013 (http://articles.latimes.com/2013/may/19/opinion/la-oe-hassett-colleges-muzzle-conservatives-20130519).

20. Ryman, Anne, "Profs: Kindle No Threat to College Textbooks," *Arizona Republic*, July 6, 2010 (http://www.azcentral.com/business/articles/2010/07/06/20100706amazon-kindle-school-textbooks.html).

21. Weisbaum, Herb, "Cost of College Textbooks Out of Control, Group Says," *USA Today*, February 2, 2014 (http://www.usatoday.com/story/money/personalfinance/2014/02/02/cnbc-college-textbooks-expensive/5038807/).

22. "University of Massachusetts Seeks to End Racial Self-Segregation in Campus Housing," *JBHE Weekly Bulletin*, March 23, 2006 (http://www.jbhe.com/latest/index032306_p.html).

23. "Student Loan Debt Exceeds One Trillion Dollars," *NPR*, April 24, 2012 (http://www.npr.org/2012/04/24/151305380/student-loan-debt-exceeds-one-trillion-dollars).

24. Snyder, Michael, "15 Signs That You Better Get Prepared for the Obama Recession of 2013," *The Economic Collapse*, January 31, 2013 (http://theeconomiccollapseblog.com/archives/15-signs-that-you-better -get-prepared-for-the-obama-recession-of-2013).

25. "Read the Standards," Common Core State Standards Initiative (http://www.corestandards.org/read-the-standards).

26. Hope, Merrill, "Orwellian 'Newspeak' Coming to Common Core Classrooms Everywhere," *Breitbart*, February 23, 2014 (http://www.breit bart.com/Breitbart-Texas/2014/02/23/The-Common-Language-of-the -Common-Core).

27. Moore, Terrence O., *The Story-Killers* (CreateSpace, 2013); quoted in Berry, Susan, "Hillsdale Professor Dr. Terrence Moore: Common Core 'Superficial, Biased, Embarrassingly Dumb,'" *Breitbart*, January 19, 2014 (http://www.breitbart.com/Big-Government/2014/01/18/Hillsdale -College-Professor-Terrence-Moore-Common-Core-Superficial-Biased -Embarrassingly-Dumb).

28. "Louisiana Voucher Assault, Round 2," *Wall Street Journal*, December 1, 2013 (http://online.wsj.com/news/articles/SB10001424052702304791 704579210202920302792?mod=WSJ_Opinion_AboveLEFTTop).

29. Phillip, Abby D., "How Eric Holder Responded to Bobby Jindal's CPAC Segregationist Swipe," ABC News, May 7, 2014 (http://abcnews.go .com/blogs/politics/2014/03/how-eric-holder-responded-to-bobby-jindals -cpac-segregationist-swipe/).

30. "Holder: Pre-School Teachers Now Racist, Too," *Investor's Business Daily*, March 24, 2014 (http://news.investors.com/ibd-editorials/ 032414-694424-education-secretary-attorney-general-accuse-preschool -teachers-of-racism.htm).

31. Sperry, Paul, "'Obama Makes Up His Own Rules,'" *New York Post*, February 15, 2014 (http://nypost.com/2014/02/15/barack-obama -makes-up-his-own-rules/).

32. Berry, Susan, "Common Core Roots Lie in Ties Between Barack Obama, Bill Ayers," *Breitbart*, December 5, 2013 (http://www.breitbart .com/Big-Government/2013/12/04/Roots-of-Common-Core-Lie-In -Association-Between-Barack-Obama-And-Bill-Ayers).

33. Tucker, Jill, "Tiny Marin County District Clings to Struggling School," *SFGate*, April 5, 2014 (http://www.sfgate.com/education/ article/Tiny-Marin-County-district-clings-to-struggling-5378122.php# page-1).

Chapter 10: The War on Our Allies

1. "Israel, Saudi Arabia Agree Iran Shouldn't Be Appeased," *Investor's Business Daily*, November 18, 2013 (http://news.investors.com/ibd -editorials/111813-679665-rumored-iran-deal-brings-israel-and-saudi -together.htm).

2. Richter, Paul, "New Iran Agreement Includes Secret Side Deal, Tehran Official Says," *Los Angeles Times*, January 13, 2014 (http://www.latimes .com/world/worldnow/la-fg-wn-iran-nuclear-side-deal-20140113,0,4116168 .story#axzz2qO0LPYw1).

3. Kredo, Adam, "Iran: 'We Will in No Way, Never, Dismantle' Nuclear Infrastructure," *Washington Free Beacon*, January 13, 2014 (http://freebeacon.com/national-security/iran-we-will-in-no-way-never -dismantle-nuclear-infrastructure/).

4. Halper, Daniel, "Iran's Rouhani: 'World Powers Surrendered to Iranian Nation's Will,'" *Weekly Standard*, January 14, 2014 (http://www .weeklystandard.com/blogs/irans-rouhani-world-powers-surrendered -iranian-nations-will_774616.html#).

5. "Iranian General: US Pursuing Diplomacy Because They Cannot Defeat Us Militarily," *Truth Revolt*, January 14, 2014 (http://www.truth revolt.org/news/iranian-general-us-pursuing-diplomacy-because-they -cannot-defeat-us-militarily).

6. Kahlili, Reza, "Iran's Supreme Leader: Jihad Will Continue Until America Is No More," *Daily Caller*, May 25, 2014 (http://dailycaller .com/2014/05/25/irans-supreme-leader-jihad-will-continue-until-america -is-no-more/).

7. Weizman, Steve, "Netanyahu Takes Iran Nuclear Campaign to Kremlin," *Ma'an News Agency*, November 19, 2013 (http://www.maannews .net/eng/ViewDetails.aspx?ID=649149).

8. Fund, John, "Obama's Valerie Jarrett: Often Whispered About, But Never Challenged," *The Corner, National Review Online*, October 25, 2013 (http://www.nationalreview.com/corner/362203/obamas-valerie-jarrett -often-whispered-about-never-challenged-john-fund).

9. Capizola, Janeen, "The Unspoken WH Rule: Don't Cross Valerie Jarrett," *BizPac Review*, October 28, 2013 (http://www.bizpacreview .com/2013/10/28/the-unspoken-wh-rule-dont-cross-valerie-jarrett-86103).

10. West, Diana, "Why Won't the Media Cover Huma Abedin's Ties to the Global Jihad Movement?" Townhall.com, July 26, 2013 (http:// townhall.com/columnists/dianawest/2013/07/26/why-wont-the-media-cover -huma-abedins-ties-to-the-global-jihad-movement-n1649288/page/full).

11. McCarthy, Andrew C., "Huma Abedin's Muslim Brotherhood Ties," *National Review Online*, July 25, 2012 (http://www.national review.com/articles/312211/huma-abedin-s-muslim-brotherhood-ties -andrew-c-mccarthy).

12. Issacharoff, Avi, "The Current Israel-US rift Was Only a Matter of Time," *Times of Israel*, November 15, 2013 (http://www.timesofisrael .com/the-current-israel-us-rift-was-only-a-matter-of-time/).

13. Butters, Andrew Lee, "Is Egypt's Parliament Finally Ready for Prime Time?" *Time*, January 31, 2011 (http://www.time.com/time/world/ article/0,8599,2045444,00.html).

14. Cunningham, Erin, "Egypt's Military-Backed Government Declares Muslim Brotherhood a Terrorist Organization," *Washington Post*, December 25, 2013 (http://www.washingtonpost.com/world/middle _east/egypts-military-backed-government-declares-muslim-brother hood-a-terrorist-organization/2013/12/25/7cf075ca-6da0-11e3-aecc-85cb 037b7236_story.html).

15. Kirkpatrick, David D., "Saudis Put Terrorist Label on Muslim Brotherhood," *New York Times*, March 7, 2014 (http://www.nytimes .com/2014/03/08/world/middleeast/saudis-put-terrorist-label-on-muslim -brotherhood.html?_r=0).

16. Daly, Corbett, "Clinton on Qaddafi: 'We came, we saw, he died,'" CBS News, October 20, 2011 (http://www.cbsnews.com/news/clinton -on-qaddafi-we-came-we-saw-he-died/).

17. Coughlin, Con, "US Government Shutdown: Barack Obama Is Presiding over the End of America's Superpower Status," *Telegraph* (UK), October 1, 2013 (http://blogs.telegraph.co.uk/news/concoughlin/100238900/ us-government-shutdown-barack-obama-is-presiding-over-the-end-of -americas-superpower-status/).

18. Hoft, Jim, "Kerry Announces $75 Million Boost in Palestinian Aid Hours After Terrorist Murders Israeli Soldier on Bus," *Gateway Pundit*, November 14, 2013 (http://www.thegatewaypundit.com/2013/11/kerry -announces-75-million-boost-in-aid-to-palestinians-hours-after-terrorist -murders-israeli-soldier-on-bus/).

19. Edelson, Larry, "You Need to Take Action Now as World Conflicts Ramp Up," *Money and Markets*, January 20, 2014 (http://www.mon eyandmarkets.com/you-need-to-take-action-now-as-world-conflicts -ramp-up-57601).

20. Ahlert, Arnold, "Obama's Ongoing Betrayal of America's Sacrifices in Iraq," *Canada Free Press*, October 16, 2013 (http://canadafreepress .com/index.php/article/58587).

21. Raheem, Kareem, "Car Bomb Attacks Across Iraq Kill At Least 39," Reuters, December 8, 2013 (http://www.reuters.com/article/2013/12/08/us-iraq-violence-idUSBRE9B703920131208).

22. Vick, Karl, and Aryn Baker, "Extremists in Iraq Continue March Toward Baghdad," *Time*, June 11, 2014 (http://time.com/2859454/iraq-tikrit-isis-baghdad-mosul/).

23. "Israel Media: Obama Blocked Sale of 'David's Sling' to Poland," WorldTribune.com, May 23, 2014 (http://www.worldtribune.com/2014/05/23/obama-blocks-sale-israeli-bmd-system-poland/).

24. Yu, Miles, "Inside China: Nuclear Submarines Capable of Widespread Attack on U.S.," *Washington Times*, October 31, 2013 (http://www.washingtontimes.com/news/2013/oct/31/inside-china-nuclear-submarines-capable-of-widespr/).

25. Watson, Paul Joseph, "China Set to Seize South China Sea Island by Force," Infowars.com, January 13, 2014 (http://www.infowars.com/china-set-to-seize-south-china-sea-island-by-force/).

26. Daniels, Kit, "Japan Prepares for War with China," Infowars.com, February 18, 2014 (http://www.infowars.com/japan-prepares-for-war-with-china/).

27. Heller, Jeffrey, and Elizabeth Pineau, "France Assures Israel It Will Stand Firm on Iran Deal," Reuters, November 17, 2013 (http://www.reuters.com/article/2013/11/17/us-iran-nuclear-idUSBRE9AG0DP20131117).

28. Schofield, Matthew, "News Report Charges U.S. with Conducting Illegal Operations from German Soil," *McClatchy DC*, November 15, 2013 (http://www.mcclatchydc.com/2013/11/15/208731/news-report-charges-us-with-conducting.html).

29. Urban, Mark, "Saudi Nuclear Weapons 'on Order' from Pakistan," BBC News, November 6, 2013 (http://www.bbc.co.uk/news/world-middle-east-24823846).

30. Gertz, Bill, "Pentagon Concerned by China's New High-Speed Missile," *Washington Free Beacon*, January 28, 2014 (http://freebeacon.com/national-security/pentagon-concerned-by-chinas-new-high-speed-missile/).

31. Hines, Nico, "Senior UK Defense Advisor: Obama Is Clueless About 'What He Wants to Do in the World,'" *Daily Beast*, January 15, 2014 (http://www.thedailybeast.com/articles/2014/01/15/senior-uk-defense-advisor-obama-is-clueless-about-what-he-wants-to-do-in-the-world.html).

32. "NSA Spying Did Not Result in a Single Foiled Terrorist Plot," *Washington's Blog*, October 15, 2013 (http://www.washingtonsblog.com/2013/10/nsa-spying-did-not-result-in-one-stopped-terrorist-plot-and-the-government-actually-did-spy-on-the-bad-guys-before-911.html).

33. Askar, Jamshid Ghazi, "'Must-Read' Magazine Article Draws Scrutiny to NSA's Information-Gathering on Americans," *Deseret News*, May 17, 2011 (http://www.deseretnews.com/article/700136099/Must-read -magazine-article-draws-scrutiny-to-NSAs-information-gathering-on -Americans.html?pg=all).

34. Pipes, Daniel, and Sharon Chadha, "CAIR: Islamists Fooling the Establishment," *Middle East Quarterly*, Spring 2006 (http://www.meforum .org/916/cair-islamists-fooling-the-establishment).

35. Jackson, Victoria, "Muslim Brotherhood Infiltrates Top Gov. Positions," *Patriot Update*, December 5, 2011 (http://patriotupdate.com/ articles/muslim-brotherhood-infiltrates-top-gov-positions/).

36. Elibary, Mohamed, tweet, Twitter.com, October 31, 2013 (https:// twitter.com/MohamedElibiary/status/395921435471777792).

37. Lucas, Fred, "How the White House Responded When We Asked Them Why a Muslim Brotherhood Lobbyist Met with Obama and Biden," *Blaze*, February 6, 2014 (http://www.theblaze.com/stories/2014/02/06/ why-did-a-muslim-brotherhood-lobbyist-meet-with-obama-and-biden -the-white-house-tells-theblaze-to-ask/).

38. "Muslim Brotherhood Infiltrates Obama Administration," *Investor's Business Daily*, December 5, 2013 (http://news.investors.com/ibd -editorials/120513-681914-radical-islamist-officials-find-home-in-white -house.htm?p=full).

39. Watson, Paul Joseph, "DHS Gave Muslim Brotherhood VIP Treatment, No TSA Pat Downs," Infowars.com, January 20, 2014 (http:// www.infowars.com/dhs-gave-muslim-brotherhood-vip-treatment-no-tsa -pat-downs/).

40. Heller, Aron, "In New Row, Israel at Odds with US over Visas," *Big Story*, AP, March 28, 2014 (http://www.bigstory.ap.org/article/new -row-israel-odds-us-over-visas).

41. "Judicial Watch: Benghazi Documents Point to White House on Misleading Talking Points," *Judicial Watch*, April 29, 2014 (http://www .judicialwatch.org/press-room/press-releases/judicial-watch-benghazi -documents-point-white-house-misleading-talking-points/).

42. Associated Press, "Netanyahu: Boycott Attempts Won't Hurt Israel," Townhall.com, February 2, 2014 (http://townhall.com/news/ politics-elections/2014/02/02/israeli-minister-slams-kerrys-boycott- warning-n1788448).

43. Benson, Guy, "Oh My: Kerry Concedes WH Syria Policy Is in Total Shambles," Townhall.com, February 3, 2014 (http://townhall.com/ tipsheet/guybenson/2014/02/03/crumble-kerry-private-admits-whs-syria -policy-is-in-shambles-n1788909).

44. Chiacu, Doina, "Syria a U.S. Homeland Security Threat: DHS Chief," Reuters, February 7, 2014 (http://www.reuters.com/article/2014/02/07/us-usa-security-homeland-idUSBREA161PM20140207).

45. Pruden, Wesley, "Pruden: The Deadly Price of Presidential Weakness," *Washington Times*, November 28, 2013 (http://www.washingtontimes.com/news/2013/nov/28/pruden-the-price-of-presidential-weakness/).

46. Wenzel, Robert, "An Important Second Listen to the 'F——k the EU' Ukraine Recording," *Economic Policy Journal*, March 3, 2014 (http://www.economicpolicyjournal.com/2014/03/an-important-second-listen-to-f-k-eu.html).

47. McAdams, Daniel, "McCain: 'It's Tragic' There's No U.S. Military Option in Ukraine," *Prison Planet*, March 9, 2014 (http://www.prisonplanet.com/mccain-its-tragic-theres-no-u-s-military-option-in-ukraine.html).

48. Cohen, Stephen F., "Neo-Cold Warriors," *Nation*, September 30, 2013 (http://www.thenation.com/article/176416/neo-cold-warriors#).

49. Rose, Thomas, "One Week After Russia's Crimean Invasion, US Imposes Travel Sanctions…Against Israelis," *Breitbart*, March 9, 2014 (http://www.breitbart.com/Breitbart-London/2014/03/08/One-Week-After-Russia-s-Crimean-Invasion-US-Imposes-Travel-Sanctions-Against-Israelis).

50. Shakhtar, F. C., "Rinat Akhmetov and Vitali Klitschko Met at Donbass Arena," *FC Shakhtar Donetsk*, March 9, 2014 (http://shakhtar.com/en/news/30803).

51. De Luce, Dan, "Pentagon Plans To Shrink US Army to Pre-WWII Level," *Yahoo! News UK and Ireland*, February 25, 2014 (https://uk.news.yahoo.com/pentagon-proposes-shrink-us-army-pre-wwii-level-183915139.html#mroS8Rb).

52. Voice of Russia, "China Announces Rise of 12.2 Per Cent in Annual Military Budget," GlobalSecurity.org, March 5, 2014 (http://www.globalsecurity.org/wmd/library/news/china/2014/china-140305-vor01.htm?_m=3n.002a.1053.om0ao017mo.yox).

53. Klein, Aaron, "Soros Heavily Invested In Ukraine Crisis," *WND*, March 4, 2014 (http://www.wnd.com/2014/03/soros-heavily-invested-in-ukraine-crisis/).

54. Kaminski, Matthew, "Prince Alwaleed bin Talal: An Ally Frets About American Retreat," *Wall Street Journal*, November 22, 2013 (http://online.wsj.com/news/articles/SB10001424052702304337404579211742820387758?mod=WSJ_Opinion_LEADTop).

Chapter 11: The Savage Truth: Stopping the Coming Civil War

1. "Law Prof: Obama Power Grab Threatens to Make President 'Government unto Himself,'" Fox News, February 27, 2014 (http://www.foxnews.com/opinion/2014/02/27/law-prof-obama-grab-threatens-to-make-president-government-unto-himself/).

2. Howley, Patrick, "Justice Department Won't Release Names of Lawyers Responsible for More Than 650 Ethical Violations," *Daily Caller*, March 17, 2014 (http://dailycaller.com/2014/03/17/justice-department-wont-release-names-of-lawyers-responsible-for-more-than-650-ethical-violations/).

3. Gehrke, Joel, "Obama Threatens Vetoes of Bills Requiring Him to Follow the Law," *Washington Examiner*, March 12, 2014 (http://washingtonexaminer.com/obama-threatens-vetoes-of-bills-requiring-him-to-follow-the-law/article/2545545).

4. Seitz-Wald, Alex, "The Tea Party: We Are the 22 Percent," *National Journal*, September 26, 2013 (http://www.nationaljournal.com/politics/the-tea-party-we-are-the-22-percent-20130926).

5. Jones, Jeffrey M., "Record-High 42% of Americans Identify as Independents," *Gallup Politics*, January 8, 2014 (http://www.gallup.com/poll/166763/record-high-americans-identify-independents.aspx).

Index